JAPAN'S
Political System

SECOND EDITION

JAPAN'S
Political System

ROBERT E. WARD
Stanford University

Prentice-Hall, Inc., Englewood Cliffs, New Jersey 07632

Library of Congress Cataloging in Publication Data

WARD, ROBERT EDWARD.
    Japan's political system.

    (Comparative Asian governments series)
    Includes bibliographies and index.
    1. Japan—Politics and government. 2. Japan—
Politics and government—1945–   I. Title.
JQ1615.1978.W3   1978   320.9'52'04   77-21600
ISBN   0-13-509588-3

COMPARATIVE ASIAN GOVERNMENTS SERIES

Editor
ROBERT E. WARD

© 1978, 1967 by Prentice-Hall, Inc.
Englewood Cliffs, New Jersey 07632

10 9 8 7 6 5 4 3 2

Printed in the United States of America

PRENTICE-HALL INTERNATIONAL, INC., *London*
PRENTICE-HALL OF AUSTRALIA PTY. LIMITED, *Sydney*
PRENTICE-HALL OF CANADA, LTD., *Toronto*
PRENTICE-HALL OF INDIA PRIVATE LIMITED, *New Delhi*
PRENTICE-HALL OF JAPAN, INC., *Tokyo*
PRENTICE-HALL OF SOUTHEAST ASIA PTE. LTD., *Singapore*
WHITEHALL BOOKS LIMITED, *Wellington, New Zealand*

CONTENTS

PREFACE

This series is based on the proposition that it is no longer valid or profitable to study comparative politics within an essentially North American– and European–centered frame of reference. Although admittedly more familiar, more comprehensible, and—in the past, at least—closer and more important to us, the political histories, ideologies, and institutions of these areas constitute only a small (though vital) fragment of the political universe with which the student of contemporary political systems must be concerned. The political history of the twentieth century is in large part the history of the reemergence of non-European areas and states to positions of independence and prominence on the world scene. We can ignore this fact only at our peril.

Asia, Latin America, and Africa together account for approximately 62 percent of the land area and 73 percent of the population of the earth. Today, four factors combine to give new meaning and importance to these figures. First, the age of imperialism and colonialism—at least in the classic sense of these terms—has largely been liquidated. Thus non-Western states —often themselves recent graduates from colonial status—are obtaining a degree of political independence and freedom of decision and maneuver that is, in a collective sense, unique in their recent histories.

Second, this development is both impelled and accompanied by what is often referred to as "a revolution of rising expectations." Great masses of people in the underdeveloped areas are being exposed to the highly revolutionary concept that meaningful types of economic, political, and social change are possible in their countries and that these carry with them the promise of a better life for themselves and their children. They are becoming actively dissatisfied with the products and performance of their traditional societies and are demanding some measure of modernization. These demands coincide with a period when the skills and technologies necessary to support such modernization are for the first time becoming widely available. Thus, most of the governments of these non-Western states—some eagerly, others with trepidation and reluctance—are being committed to more or less systematic, long-term efforts to modernize at least segments of their societies. Gradually, therefore, the technological and power gap that has long separated West from non-West is beginning to narrow, and the material circumstances of the two areas are becoming less disparate.

Third, both of the previously mentioned developments are taking place at a time when modern communications and weaponry have made all of us uneasy neighbors in a world still characterized by rivalry and strife. While the much heralded détente of the early 1970s in the United States' relations with the Soviet Union and the People's Republic of China has resulted in an appreciable relaxation of the extreme tensions that marked the height of the cold war period, it would be fatuous to assume on this account that a new era of peace and amity among the superpowers has dawned. Although somewhat diminished, a menacing degree of tension still exists in global terms; the People's Republic of China continues to isolate itself from the more meaningful types of international interaction; relations between communist and noncommunist states are still limited, tentative, and suspicious; and bitter rivalries and antagonisms continue to characterize an uncomfortable proportion of both current and prospective international relations. In such circumstances, the political and military weakness of most of these non-Western states is no longer so controlling a factor. First, this weakness is not a fixed condition; some of these states, such as China, have become formidable powers in their own right. Second, the very existence of widespread international tensions endows these states with an importance and with possibilities of maneuver that they might otherwise lack. No matter how remote their location or "underdeveloped" their circumstances, the territory, resources, skills, and allegiances of each of these states are of significant value. From this complex of factors is emerging a world that—even in the conduct of its hostilities—is characterized by new degrees and dimensions of unity and interdependence.

Finally, the energy crisis of 1973–74 was precipitated by the joint action of the Arab states by drastically and selectively limiting their oil exports to the United States and Western Europe in an attempt to isolate Israel from its sources of overseas support and assistance, and it has brought about a new and unprecedented situation with respect to access to some critical raw materials. In the past, the active development and marketing of such basic resources as oil, bauxite, or copper located in developing societies have usually been primarily controlled by large American or European firms. The oil crisis, however, demonstrated to the governments of many resource rich but economically underdeveloped countries the feasibility both of much greater local participation in and control over the exploitation of their resources and of dramatically increasing the profits to be realized through their sale abroad by means of price-fixing agreements among the producing countries. This development, too, has served to increase markedly the importance and influence of some non-Western states in their relations with the Western world.

It is essential that the discipline of comparative politics keep abreast of such developments and expand its frames of reference and concern to include the political systems of these emergent non-Western areas. Such a resolution is easy to make but hard to put into practice. The governments involved are so numerous, their political heritages and institutions so complex and diverse, and the materials and skills relevant to their study and analysis so scattered, uneven in quality, and difficult to use that—for introductory purposes, anyway—it is necessary to be highly selective. The present volume focuses only on the political system of Japan; other books in this series deal in comparable terms with the People's Republic of China, India, Southeast Asia, and the Near and Middle East. All were designed in accordance with certain shared views about the nature of modern political systems and the manner in which these may most meaningfully be compared. Defining a political system and the factors that are relevant to the comparison of political systems clarifies the nature of these shared views. This involves the identification of those qualities and problems that are treated for Japan and for the political systems under consideration in other volumes of the series.

A political system is a mechanism for the identification and posing of problems and for the making and administering of decisions in the realm of public affairs, an area that is variously defined by different societies. The official machinery by which these problems and decisions are legally identified, posed, made, and administered is called government. Government provides both an official, authoritative mechanism for the identification and posing of problems and the making and administering of decisions and a means of formalizing and bestowing legitimacy on the products of this process. In practice, it does more than this; by providing a context and an apparatus for the making of official decisions, it also comes to influence the types of problems that are posed and decisions that are taken.

Government—in the sense of society's legislative, executive, judicial, and bureaucratic machinery—is not, however, the sole concern of students of comparative politics. It is only a part of the whole political system that includes, in addition to government, such informal or unofficial factors as (1) the society's historical heritage and geographic and resource endowments, its social and economic organization, its ideologies and value systems, and its political culture and style; and (2) its party, interest, and leadership structure. Government, plus these two categories of related and mutually affective factors, thus constitutes the political system of a society.

The first step in the analysis of a given political system is to ascertain those aspects of a society's historical, geographical, social, economic, and ideological heritage and endowment that are significantly related to its political decision-making system. This provides both a picture of the working environment of a system's politics and an inventory of the basic problems, resources, attitudes, groups, political alignments, and styles of action that relate to its political decision making. For this reason, such factors are referred to in the following chapters as "the foundations of politics."

In practice it is not easy to agree, for a given society, on just which of its many characteristics are of present and primary political importance—that is, "foundational"—and which are of only historical or secondary importance. They are not necessarily the same from country to country, nor are they constant for different stages in the history of a single society. Their satisfactory identification and evaluation in any given case is itself a matter that calls for considerable study and sophistication and about which judgments differ. It should be emphasized that these "foundations of politics," although they are here distinguished from one another, categorized, and treated separately, in fact constitute a unified, national, interrelated, and interactive complex. Their separation here for expository purposes should not lead one to forget this fact.

The interaction between these foundational aspects of a political system and the governmental organs of that system constitute "the dynamics of politics." Social, economic, political, and ideological claims and supports rising from these foundational aspects of a system are constantly being presented to officials and organs of government with the demand that they be converted into public policy. Political parties, interest or pressure groups, and political leaders play the role of conveyor belts between the makers of such claims and the organs of government that make official decisions and establish public policy. They thus serve as active or dynamic agents within a political system, sifting and choosing among the claims that demand action, formulating these in viable terms, gathering support, and presenting the results in the form of demands for political action. These dynamic factors of politics—political parties, interest or pressure groups, and political leaders—thus bridge the intrasystem gap between the political foundations and the formal decision-making organs of government.

The third major component of political systems is government, which is the formal and legitimacy-conferring machinery for the identification and posing of problems and the making and administering of decisions in the realm of public affairs. More specifically, it is the legislative, executive, judicial, and administrative or bureaucratic machinery of state, and the constitutional and legal framework within which these operate. Although distinctive functions and organs of these sorts are usually identifiable in most nonprimitive societies, it should not be assumed that they are neatly and individually institutionalized along the lines indicated by these traditional categories or that they actually perform the functions indicated. Legislative and executive functions, for example, are often combined, and modern legislatures seldom legislate in the complete, classical sense of that term. It should also be noted that for authoritarian systems such as the Soviet Union or the People's Republic of China, it is largely meaningless to attempt to distinguish between the governmental roles and powers of the Communist Party and the formal apparatus of state.

In studying any system, we are interested in both the input and the output aspects of its mechanism. Consequently, for a given political system we are interested not only in the previously described "input" process by which it poses, makes, and administers its decisions but also in the nature, quality, and effectiveness of the decisions taken—that is, in the efficiency and performance characteristics of political systems as well as in their mechanics. The "output," or efficiency, of a political system can be gauged by its capacity to survive and by its ability to make decisions that are widely accepted. Assessment of the former is relatively simple. The latter, in a democratic system, can usually be determined by the response that its decisions elicit from social groups, interest groups, and other associations. In an authoritarian system, the test is similar, though the nature of the groups concerned and the manner of ascertaining their responses are different.

An efficient political system maintains a balance between stability and change. Change is an inevitable consequence of the competing political claims that arise among groups as a result of shifting technical, social, and economic conditions and of the demands that such groups press as they struggle to gain positions of influence and power. Efficiency, therefore, is a function of governmental response to such groups and demands. To be efficient, however, such a response must take place within a context of stable and generally accepted political institutions. Otherwise, emerging groups attempt to gain power by revolutionary means that have disruptive effects upon the entire system. From this point of view, there is no guarantee that a democratic political system is more efficient than an authoritarian one.

In the chapters that follow, this question of governmental efficiency is discussed primarily in terms of two aspects of governmental performance. The author is concerned first with matters of relatively short-term performance. How does the Japanese government define its appropriate spheres of political concern and activity? How does it allocate attention, funds, and resources among these spheres of concern? Beyond such relatively specific and short-term issues, however, certain long-term performance characteristics of political systems are also important. How efficiently has Japan coped with the larger problems of political development and modernization? What forms of political organization and action—democratic, authoritarian, or variants of these—has it found most appropriate to its needs? In whose behalf is the system operating? These are the underlying and enduring problems of all political systems in our time. Their import and urgency vary within a particular system as well as from system to system, but some combination of these problems is critical for all societies. Together, they provide major themes for all the volumes of this series.

So much, then, for the manner in which we visualize our task. A political system has been defined as a mechanism for the identification and posing of problems and the making and administering of decisions in the realm of public affairs. Certain broad categories of analysis for such systems have been established: political foundations, political dynamics, the formal decision-making organs of government on the input side of the process, and governmental efficiency and performance, both short-run and long-run, on the output side. In the chapters that follow, these categories are applied in such a way as to illuminate the functioning and performance of the Japanese political system.

ROBERT E. WARD

JAPAN'S
Political System

Chapter *1*

INTRODUCTION

One hundred years ago, Japan was a little-known kingdom just emerging from a period of self-imposed national isolation that had lasted for almost two and one-half centuries. Its territory was restricted to the four main islands of Hokkaido, Honshu, Shikoku, and Kyushu. Its population numbered slightly more than thirty million, some 90 percent of whom were peasants living in the countryside and working their small farms with tools and techniques differing little from those their ancestors had utilized for the preceding millennium. The national economy, though changing, was still semifeudal in character, while the total impression conveyed by the society has been described by one authority as roughly comparable, in Western terms, to early Tudor times—that is, to the England of more than four hundred years ago.

Politically, the country was theoretically an empire ruled by an emperor who claimed direct descent, through an unbroken line of illustrious predecessors, from Amaterasu-omikami, the goddess of the sun. In fact, the emperors had long been carefully cloistered in the Imperial City of Kyoto, ritually remote from all meaningful contact with the crude world of politics. Since 1603, Japan had actually been governed by a delicately balanced system, often described as "centralized feudalism," in which prime authority rested with a Shogun, the head of the great House of Tokugawa, who ruled from his family's historic capital of Edo (modern Tokyo).

Politics, like social organization, was carefully stratified along hereditary class lines, and only a small elite was privileged to participate in the making

1

or administering of political decisions. Pre-Restoration Japan was, in short, a species of traditional Asian society, being predominantly rural, agrarian, immobile, stratified, authoritarian, and oligarchic in its primary socio-political characteristics. From the Western viewpoint, it was strange and exotic to a degree perhaps most vividly portrayed in the period's favorite art form, the wood-block prints known as *ukiyoe,* which captured so faithfully the style, temper, and appearance of the "floating world" of late Tokugawa times.

Just over a century from the Restoration of 1868 that overthrew Tokugawa rule, there is an almost miraculously different Japan. During this period, the isolated kingdom had become a great empire that briefly dominated the whole of Eastern Asia, only to lose all its territorial gains in the catastrophic defeat of 1945. Its population, according to the 1975 census, increased to upwards of one hundred eleven million, a more than threefold increase within a single century, and the great majority of the people dwelt in cities rather than in the country. From small beginnings sprang a modern industrial and commercial economy. It is now the third most advanced and productive in the world and is fast overtaking the Soviet Union in terms of gross national product, thus lagging decisively behind only the United States.

Massive changes in social organization had also taken place. The rigid system of class stratification had been abolished; free, public, and universal education had become the norm; social and economic mobility and opportunities had been greatly enhanced and expanded; equality before the law had been established; and the national standards of living, well-being, and security soared to levels hitherto unknown in either Japan or Asia. Politically, the emperor remained in Tokyo—rather than in Kyoto—but still as a symbol rather than a ruler. The Shogun and the old nobility had disappeared and been replaced by a popularly elected National Diet, or Parliament, which operated through a responsible Cabinet. Universal adult suffrage had become the rule, and both national and local government were elective and representative. Public affairs were administered by a large, specialized, and professional bureaucracy, and public decision-making systems were predominantly secular, rational, and scientific. Thus change has overtaken Japan at a dizzying rate. When Westerners today visit Tokyo, Osaka, or Kobe for the first time and view the familiar sights of big city life, they are often inclined to wonder if this can indeed be "the Orient."

It is not necessary to seek far or delve deep, however, to discover the historic continuities that underlie and, to a large extent, channel the forces of change in modern Japan. Surrounding the Western-appearing cities, for example, lie the fields and villages of Japan, where social, economic, and political changes have been accepted more slowly and in more piecemeal fashion. It is an exaggeration to claim that in reality there are two Japans —urban and modern (or Western) on the one hand, rural and traditional on the other. The facts do not lend themselves to such neat categorizations. However, the old Japan survives in a variety of contexts, both rural and urban. The family and the work group are still the basic units of social organization. Discipline, loyalty, diligence, and frugality continue to be highly esteemed virtues. The imprint of the past is readily discernible in patterns of social thought, decision making, and individual and group conduct. These characteristics are doubtless attenuating, but they are still present and influential on a significant scale. Such basic continuities, although less obvious than the changes, are of fundamental importance to any understanding of the overall course and circumstances of Japan's recent development.

Japan's experience in solving, on the whole successfully, the myriad national, group, and individual problems that beset its attempts to modernize is a subject of vital interest for students of the modern world. In terms of the most meaningful indexes of modernization, Japan stands far in advance of the rest of Asia. It represents what might be termed Asia's sole exemplar of a "mature" society. Most of the other states of non–Soviet Asia—led by Israel, China, India, and Turkey—have only recently begun to perceive and deal systematically and independently with problems and programs that are sixty to ninety years old in Japan. Although the circumstances of these more recent attempts at modernization differ in significant respects from those confronting Japan in the latter part of the nineteenth century, such differences should not be permitted to obscure the important degrees of similarity that exist throughout Asia in such spheres as social and economic organization, internal power relationships, status vis-à-vis the West, national aspirations, and selection of national goals and the means to their achievement. Because of such shared factors, Japan's experience somewhat foreshadows the experiences and problems of more recently modernizing Asian states and affords useful insights into such general phenomena as modernization, industrialization, authoritarianism, imperialism, and democratization. Indeed, it may be a particularly important exemplar of political modernization. In these times, when we are occasionally told that the political future of Asia may depend on the outcome of a competition between the Chinese and the Indian paths to modernization, it should not be forgotten that there is also a Japanese path that has led the Japanese to considerably more advanced national circumstances than are enjoyed by either the Chinese or the Indians.

Another and more immediate reason why Japan today looms so large in our eyes is the fact that Japan's defeat in 1945 and the communist victory in China in 1949 fundamentally altered the power situation in Eastern Asia and in the world. In 1949–50, the United States expanded its Containment Policy to include Eastern Asia with a view to "containing," that is, preventing, any further expansion of communist power in that area. Prior to 1945, imperial Japan effectively checked Soviet Russian influence and ambitions in Eastern Asia, while a weak and divided China, although generally favorable to the United States, was a negligible power on the international scene. The principal effect of the Allied victory in August 1945 was to eliminate Japan as a force in Eastern Asia and thereby to enhance greatly the power of the Soviet Union in the entire Sino-Japanese area.

With Mao Tse-tung's victory in the Chinese civil war and the rapid consummation of the Sino-Soviet Alliance in February 1950, communist influence and strength increased tremendously throughout all Asia, and the United States felt that its position was reciprocally weakened. Since no friendly power was capable of checking communist ambitions in Eastern Asia, the United States decided to fill the resultant gap. Yet it could not do so effectively without local cooperation. It needed bases in Asia near the frontiers of Sino-Russian power and Asian friends and allies to make this policy effective. To some extent, these needs were met through the Southeast Asia Treaty Organization (SEATO); through various relationships and arrangements with the Philippine Republic, South Vietnam, the Chinese Nationalist Government on Taiwan; and the South Korean Republic, and through the establishment of a postwar base on Okinawa. All these, although of individual and collective value, still left the United States in a relatively weak position in—or, rather, off the coast of—Eastern Asia. The advent of growing differences and hostility between the People's Republic of China and the Soviet Union after 1959 did not essentially change these circumstances.

Only Japan in the years 1948–50 had the potential of becoming a truly formidable ally in the western Pacific area. A decision to collaborate with a recent and bitter enemy did not come easily, but the apparent danger was growing rapidly. China, a traditional friend and ally, was lost. Only Japan possessed the strategic position, the population, the established economic skills and capacity, the leadership, and the general developmental potential to add sufficient strength in Eastern Asia. Conversely, it was feared that the defection of this Japanese potential to the Chinese or Soviet cause would almost certainly propel communist power to ascendancy throughout Asia. Consequently, since 1948–50 the United States has striven to establish relationships with Japan on as firm and friendly a basis as possible, even after the informal demise of the Containment Policy in the early 1970s.

From a defeated and occupied enemy, Japan thus rose in a brief six-year period to become the United States' most important and valued ally in Asia. In terms of global strategy, its position in Asia somewhat resembles that of West Germany in Europe. Like West Germany, Japan's economy and productive capacity are one of the Western Alliance's greatest assets. Again, if Germany may be regarded as the western anchor of a chain of Allied military alliances and bases, Japan may be considered the eastern anchor of this somewhat discontinuous and dubious chain of "positions of strength." Against this background, the question of Japan's willingness to continue as the United States' principal military base and diplomatic associate in Asia had assumed international prominence. This and related questions about alternative international arrangements that Japan might come to prefer have today become major issues in United States foreign policy and world affairs in general. Japan, therefore, occupies a truly critical position in world politics as well as in Asian politics.

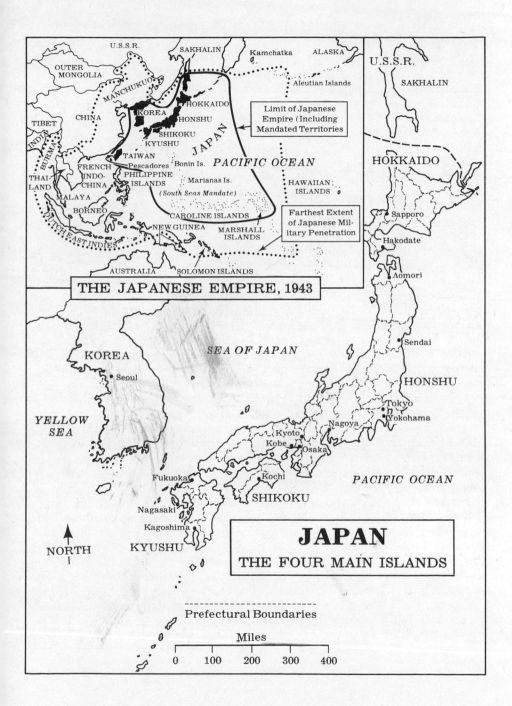

THE JAPANESE EMPIRE, 1943

U.S.S.R.

OUTER MONGOLIA

SAKHALIN

Kamchatka

ALASKA

MANCHUKUO

Aleutian Islands

CHINA

KOREA

HOKKAIDO

HONSHU

Limit of Japanese Empire (Including Mandated Territories

TIBET

SHIKOKU

KYUSHU

JAPAN

PACIFIC OCEAN

INDIA

BURMA

TAIWAN

Pescadores

Bonin Is.

THAILAND

FRENCH INDO-CHINA

PHILIPPINE ISLANDS

Marianas Is.

(South Seas Mandate)

HAWAIIAN ISLANDS

MALAYA

Farthest Extent of Japanese Military Penetration

BORNEO

DUTCH EAST INDIES

CAROLINE ISLANDS

NEW GUINEA

MARSHALL ISLANDS

AUSTRALIA

SOLOMON ISLANDS

U.S.S.R.

SAKHALIN

HOKKAIDO

Sapporo

Hakodate

Aomori

Sendai

KOREA

SEA OF JAPAN

HONSHU

Seoul

Tokyo

Yokohama

YELLOW SEA

Nagoya

Kyoto

Kobe

Osaka

Fukuoka

Kochi

PACIFIC OCEAN

Nagasaki

SHIKOKU

Kagoshima

NORTH

KYUSHU

JAPAN
THE FOUR MAIN ISLANDS

- - - - - - - - - - - - - - - - - - - -
Prefectural Boundaries

Miles

0   100   200   300   400

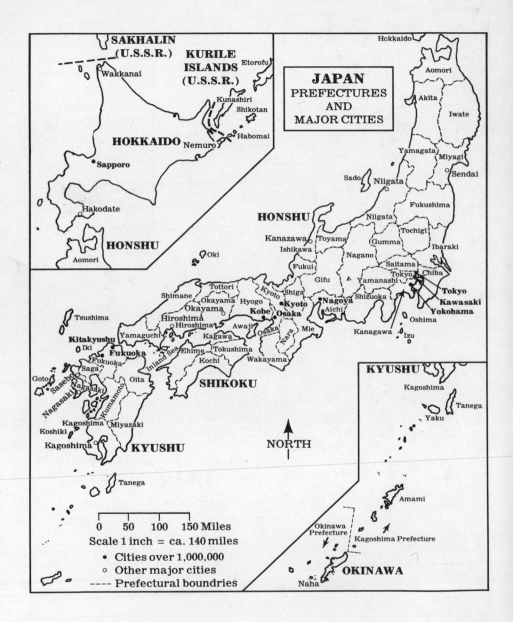

JAPAN
PREFECTURES
AND
MAJOR CITIES

SAKHALIN (U.S.S.R.)

KURILE ISLANDS (U.S.S.R.)

Wakkanai
Etorofu
Kunashiri
Shikotan
HOKKAIDO Nemuro
Habomai
Sapporo
Hakodate
HONSHU
Aomori

Hokkaido

Aomori

Akita

Iwate

Yamagata
Miyagi
Sendai

Sado
Niigata

HONSHU

Niigata

Fukushima

Kanazawa
Toyama
Gumma
Tochigi

Ishikawa
Nagano
Ibaraki

Fukui
Saitama

Gifu
Tokyo
Chiba

Yamanashi

Oki

Tottori
Kyoto
Shiga
Shizuoka
Tokyo

Shimane
Nagoya
Kawasaki

Okayama
Hyogo
Aichi
Yokohama

Kyoto

Tottori
Okayama
Kobe
Osaka

Hiroshima
Kanagawa

Tsushima
Hiroshima
Awaji
Izu

Oshima

Kitakyushu
Yamaguchi
Kagawa
Osaka
Nara
Mie

Iki
Ehime
Tokushima

Fukuoka
Inland Sea
Kochi
Wakayama

Fukuoka
Saga

Goto
Sasebo
Oita
SHIKOKU

Nagasaki
Kumamoto

Nagasaki
Miyazaki

Koshiki
Kagoshima

Kagoshima
KYUSHU

KYUSHU

Kagoshima

Taneg a

Yaku

Tanega

Amami

NORTH

Okinawa
Prefecture

Kagoshima Prefecture

0   50   100   150 Miles

Scale 1 inch = ca. 140 miles

• Cities over 1,000,000

○ Other major cities

---- Prefectural boundries

Naha
OKINAWA

Chapter 2

The Foundations of Politics
HISTORY

A country's political system is a product of its total culture. Its politics does not develop separately from the geographic, social, economic, ideological, scientific, or historical elements of that culture but interacts with all of them as both cause and effect. In studying the Japanese political system, therefore, its nonpolitical determinants, or "the foundations of politics," should be examined first. These factors constitute the larger framework called "Japanese culture," in which politics is only one element. In the chapters that follow, the historical, ecological, social, and ideological foundations of the Japanese political system are briefly investigated. The reader is asked to bear in mind, however, that these are artificial divisions and that Japanese society, like any society, is actually a seamless web.

The modern period in Japanese political history dates from the series of events in 1867–68 known as the "Meiji Restoration." At that time, the Emperor Meiji assumed formal power over the state, an act that marked the end of the long rule of the Tokugawa Shogunate (1603–1867). Prior to 1867, the Imperial House had long since abdicated any pretense to actual authority. With very few exceptions, the emperors of Japan have lacked any appreciable political power since roughly the ninth century A.D. During this long period, Japan was governed by a variety of aristocratic and feudal systems that, since the latter part of the twelfth century, have normally been controlled by warrior groups. Japan, for much of this time, actually lacked any effective central authority. In 1603, however, after a series of fierce civil

TABLE 2-1

BRIEF CHRONOLOGY OF MODERN JAPANESE POLITICAL HISTORY

Date	Event
1603	Beginning of Tokugawa Period
1867	End of Tokugawa Period
1867–68	Meiji Restoration and beginning of Meiji Period
1889–90	Promulgation and enforcement of the Meiji Constitution
1894–95	Sino-Japanese War
1904–05	Russo-Japanese War
1912	End of Meiji Period and beginning of Taisho Period
1924–32	Period of greatest strength and achievement by prewar Japanese political parties
1926	End of Taisho Period and beginning of Showa Period
1931	Outbreak of the Manchurian Incident
1932–45	Period of growing military ascendancy and ultranationalism in Japanese politics
1936	Military Revolt in Tokyo (26 Feb.)
1937	Outbreak of the China Incident
1941	Outbreak of general warfare in the Pacific (7 Dec.)
1945	War in the Pacific ends (15 Aug.)
	Japan's formal surrender (2 Sept.)
1945–52	Allied Occupation of Japan (2 Sept. 1945–28 Apr. 1952)
1946	Promulgation of the new Japanese Constitution (3 Nov.)
1947	Enforcement of the new Japanese Constitution (3 May)
	Beginning of the cold war between U.S. and Soviet Union
1950	North Korean invasion of South Korea (25 June)
1951	Treaty of Peace between the U.S. and a majority of the Allied Powers and Japan (8 Sept.)
	Security Treaty between the U.S. and Japan (8 Sept.); revised in 1960
1952	Allied Occupation ends and Japan regains its sovereign and independent status (28 Apr.)
1955	Formation of Japan Socialist Party and Liberal Democratic Party
1956	Japan admitted to United Nations; normalization of Japanese relations with Soviet Union
1960	Revision of Security Treaty with U.S.
1965	Normalization of Japan's relations with Republic of Korea (South Korea)
1968–69	Period of intense student demonstrations
1971	Period of the "Nixon shocks" and devaluation of the yen
1972	Normalization of Japan's relations with the People's Republic of China and derecognition of the Republic of China (Taiwan); return of Okinawa to Japan by the U.S.
1974	President Ford's official visit to Japan
1975	Japanese emperor's official visit to the U.S.
1976	Japan ratifies Nuclear Non-Proliferation Treaty

wars, Tokugawa Ieyasu[1] established the ascendancy of his house and imposed on Japan a much greater measure of national government and control (see table 2–1). By modern standards, it was far from being a centralized government; some three-fourths of the national territory and considerable political power were still held by more than two hundred fifty feudal lords known as *daimyo*. However, it did constitute the most effective and durable national political system Japan had ever known. It is from the breakdown of this system that the modern Japanese polity proceeds.

[1]Throughout this book, personal names are given in Japanese fashion, that is, with last names appearing first.

The Restoration

The events of 1867–68 did not in themselves constitute a revolution, although their long-term consequences were in the deepest sense revolutionary. There was no sustained civil war or insurrection, no massive shift in the basis of political power, no reign of terror, and no sudden emergence of a new political or social elite. Still, it was far more than a mere palace revolution. Most of the leaders of the Restoration Movement were members of the privileged military or samurai class, operating with the approval and sometimes the active support of their particular feudal lords and a section of the imperial court nobility. A majority of them came from four of the most remote and powerful fiefs in Tokugawa Japan: Satsuma and Hizen in Kyushu, Choshu in the extreme southwestern section of Honshu, and Tosa in southern Shikoku. They represented primarily these fiefs, not the contemporary samurai class or the anti-Tokugawa elements of the aristocracy as a whole, much less the population of Japan.

The motives of those who opposed the Tokugawa were many and varied. Historic clan enmities against the Tokugawa mingled with the dissatisfactions of the samurai over their deteriorating economic and social status. These feelings were reinforced after 1854 by the threat to Japan's security posed by the consequences of the Perry Treaty, which opened the country to foreign commerce and, it was feared, to Western imperialistic exploitations as well. Much of the blame was attributed, often unjustly, to the Tokugawa Shogunate.

The rebels hoped to legitimize their ambitions by restoring to the Imperial House its rightful position and power, which had long been denied it by the House of Tokugawa and its shogunal predecessors. Their program was, therefore, called the Restoration Movement, and its immediate goals were well symbolized by the slogan *Sonno joi* ("Revere the Emperor; expel the barbarians"). Behind such slogans there lay, of course, a variety of more deep-seated and "historic" causes: the widely disruptive effects of the introduction of a monetary system into the old rice-based economy of Tokugawa Japan; the increasing stresses stemming from the commercialization and industrialization of the economy; the very rigidity of the Tokugawa system in the face of cumulative challenges; growing dissatisfaction with the existing class system and relationships; the spread of urbanization and the resulting growth of new social and economic problems; and the development in the Japanese of a sense of nationalism. All these disruptive forces merged in 1867–68 to catalyze the successful movement to overthrow Tokugawa power and produce the "Meiji Restoration," named after the regnal title of the fifteen-year-old boy who then ascended the throne.

Modern Japanese political history may be said to date from this series of events. The Restoration did not mean, however, that the Meiji emperor was actually "restored" to the powers claimed by his eighth-century ancestors, who were vested by right of divine descent with absolute power over the state. The leaders of the Restoration never seriously considered such a step. In fact, their conception of the imperial position in government probably did not become definite until the last half of the 1880s, when it was finally embodied in the Constitution of 1889. What did come of the Restoration, however, was the establishment of a new oligarchy, originally military in nature and regional in its political loyalties, with the Satsuma and Choshu clans as primary powers and the Tosa and Hizen fiefs as secondary ones. This new ruling group gradually solidified its control within Japan and launched the country on its difficult and perilous path to modernization. The new oligarchy was led by a truly remarkable group of men: Kido, Saigo, Inoue, Okubo, Iwakura, Ito, Yamagata, Matsukata, and Okuma—a veritable flowering of leadership such as occasionally appears at critical junctures in a nation's history. Although in no sense "democrats," they were able to transcend limitations of background and education and to comprehend the need for a strong and industrialized Japan. Their vision, ability, and strength contributed much to the creation of a new Japan.

The Pre-Constitutional Period, 1868–89

The twenty-two years that divided the Restoration from the promulgation of the Meiji Constitution in 1889 were years of consolidation and experimentation. The first concern of the new oligarchy was for its own security. Its domestic enemies were many and powerful, and they were not finally overcome until the government's new conscript army put down the great Satsuma Rebellion of 1877. It also continued to fear economic and political intervention by the imperialistic powers of the West. For years, the Meiji oligarchy was preoccupied with plans to strengthen and modernize the country to prevent such intervention. Fear of the West spurred the development of Japanese nationalism and greatly affected the outlook and policies of the new Japan.

Old institutions were uprooted and new ones were introduced at an unsettling rate. The traditional four-class system of samurai, peasant, artisan, and merchant, along with the rights and privileges of the samurai and the Tokugawa fiefs, were abolished, as was the old land-tenure system; in their place came mass public education, conscription, equality before the law, railroads, modern industrial plants, technology, a merchant marine, and a modern army and navy. Politically, the period was marked by experimentation with various forms of government, with no particular one winning out. A professional bureaucracy was established to cope with the expanding needs of the state. A small number of educated Japanese gained their first insight into the political philosophies and systems of the West. Some, led by the Meiji oligarchs, preferred the authoritarian strain in Western thought, perhaps best exemplified at the time by the Prussian state and the dominant Austro-Prussian school of constitutional law. These seemed to the oligarchs to be both more congenial to their native tradition and better suited to the urgent needs of the Japanese state for strong leadership and unchallenged national unity.

Other political leaders, mostly from the ranks of the political dissidents, preferred some version of the liberal tradition in Western thought and studied closely the writings of Mill, Bentham, Locke, Montesquieu, Rousseau, and many others. Members of the "liberal" group organized the first political parties in Japan during the 1870s and, to contest the continued dominance of the oligarchs from Satsuma and Choshu, launched demands for limited suffrage, more representative government, and a national parliament. This was a seminal period in Japanese political history; although characterized by change and experimentation, it gave birth to both the authoritarian and the liberal traditions that have since constituted the two main streams in Japan's political development. Many of the issues, personalities, and styles of political competition that were to dominate the Japanese political scene for decades clearly emerged during these twenty-two years prior to 1889.

The Meiji Constitution, 1889–90

The years 1889 and 1890 were years of decision in Japanese history, a political watershed marked by the adoption of the Meiji Constitution, which was promulgated in 1889 and enforced in 1890. This remarkable document served as the legal basis of government in Japan for fifty-five years, until Japan's defeat and occupation in 1945. It was formally superseded by the present Constitution, which was adopted in 1947. In the Meiji Constitution, the oligarchs incorporated their view that a permanent and modern system of government was needed for effective domestic control and international security. No resuscitated form of the shogunate under Satsuma and Choshu auspices was practicable, although it was considered.

The Constitution also reflected the natural desire of the oligarchs to perpetuate their own authority and that of their selected successors. They justified this provision on the grounds that Japan needed the decisive leadership that only they could supply. Finally, the Constitution adopted those minimal concessions to the doctrine of representative government that its framers judged necessary to placate international public opinion and mounting domestic political opposition. Although scarcely ideal as a foundation for a liberal political system, at least by present-day standards, it should not be forgotten that the Meiji Constitution and governmental system were not notably illiberal in terms of prevailing European practice in 1890. They did mark a major departure from earlier Japanese political institutions and processes.

The Constitution was secretly drafted and ratified and on 11 February 1889, the two thousand five hundred and forty-ninth anniversary of the legendary founding of the Japanese state, it was publicly presented to the Japanese people as a token of the imperial benevolence. The system of government thus established rested on a theory of the state, referred to by the Japanese as *kokutai*. This meant that the Japanese state was intelligible only in terms of its imperial institution and that, for both theoretical and legal purposes, the emperor, as the successor of an unbroken line of divinely descended ancestors, embodied the Japanese state. The reigning emperor, therefore, was the sole ultimate repository of all state powers—executive, administrative, legislative, and judicial. To this authority was added the spiritual authority that derived from his position as a lineal descendant of the sun goddess. He was thus the central figure in the nation's major cult —if not religion—State Shinto. In theory, then, the Meiji Constitution resulted in a system of government that was centralized to a degree unprecedented among the major states of the modern world.

In practice, however, the situation was quite different. Only Meiji, of the three emperors who reigned under this Constitution, normally played a significant political role. The personal intervention of the emperor that brought about the acceptance of the Allied terms and Japan's surrender in 1945 was, as far as we know, almost unprecedented. The actual power of the sovereign, therefore, was normally not too different from that of most of his pre-Restoration forebears. He lent legitimacy and an aura of sanctity to the political decisions of his ministers and advisers and simply authenticated their policies through ritualized acts. One should not, however, conclude that the emperor had no real political significance. To the contrary, since 1868 he has been of basic importance. He provides the Japanese with their sense of historical continuity and serves as their symbol of national identification and as the moral basis and justification for the existence and powers of government. These prerequisites for a stable system of national government did not effectively exist in pre-Restoration Japan, and it is a credit to the Meiji oligarchy's brilliance and leadership that they were able so effectively to use the symbol of the emperor as a means of unifying the country and building a modern political system.

Power under the Meiji Constitution did not, therefore, reside with the emperor. In practice, his authority was delegated to a complex array of offices and officials. These delegations were seldom precise or clear-cut, and the resultant system of authority and responsibility was a maze of overlap, duplication, obscurity, and rivalry. Reduced to simplest terms, however, the following were the main elements of the government. The emperor's executive and administrative authority was divided into military and nonmilitary components. The military component was apportioned to the general staffs of the Army and Navy for command and operational functions and to ministers of the Army and of the Navy for administrative functions. Military responsibility was further confused by the establishment of several other military boards and offices with vague and sometimes overlapping functions. The emperor's nonmilitary authority was delegated largely to a prime minister and Cabinet composed of ministers of state who were in theory responsible to the emperor.

The national military and civilian authorities were supreme. Local governments had no significant autonomous authority but functioned under centralized ministerial control. Legislative authority was divided, residing in part in a bicameral legislature and in part in the Cabinet, which could in emergencies rule by executive order and decree. The emperor's judicial authority was assigned to a dual system of courts, judicial and administrative, and was subject to extensive supervision by the Ministry of Justice. The entire government was staffed by professional military and civilian personnel, technically responsible to the emperor, who were distinctly elitist in training and spirit. In addition, a large staff ministered to the Imperial House and the emperor himself. This staff often seems to have had a voice in major political decisions.

Even from this brief description, it is apparent that the Meiji Constitution was not intended to establish a democratic political system in Japan. It was frankly conceived by its framers as a means of perpetuating the type of authoritarian rule with which they were personally identified, and this it did with great success for many years. Still, for reasons indicated earlier, it did make certain minimal concessions to popular rights and representative government. These proved to be of greater importance than their drafters anticipated, because they provided the legal and institutional foundations for the subsequent development of political liberalism in Japan.

Among the most important democratic concessions contained in the Constitution were significant grants of civil rights. Although shrewdly hedged about with protective clauses, they did assure Japanese subjects much greater freedom of speech, publication, association, and religious belief than they had ever enjoyed. The most important concession of all, however, was the national parliament, or Diet, in particular its lower House of Representatives. This house was a popularly elected body intended to represent the people of Japan. It was given qualified powers, shared equally with a conservative, aristocratic, and appointive House of Peers, to initiate legislation, pass laws, query ministers of state, levy taxes, and approve the national budget. Through persistent and clever exploitation of these powers, the leaders of Japan's political parties were able, over a period of thirty-odd years, to liberalize appreciably the political institutions inherited from the Meiji oligarchs. This process of liberalization, however, was slow, difficult, and piecemeal, and after a brief period of modest ascendancy between 1918 and 1932, it succumbed to the resurgent forces of Japanese authoritarianism.

A prime reason for this failure was the strong authoritarian and antipopular bias systematically built into Japan's basic political institutions by a Constitution that encouraged an elaborate imperial myth and created a powerful but irresponsible cabinet system of government, an equally irresponsible and ultimately more powerful military apparatus, an able but elitist bureaucracy, and no really effective means of coordinating or controlling these disparate elements. The Meiji Constitution provided Japan with a satisfactory and markedly effective government for many years, but it proved fatally inadequate to meet the national needs during the turbulent 1930s and 1940s.

Post-Constitutional Developments, 1890–1932

The time period within which one chooses to analyze a segment of history can greatly affect one's emphasis and conclusions. For example, examining only the forty-two-year period of Japanese political history from the enactment of the Meiji Constitution in 1890 to April 1932, the month before the assassination of Prime Minister

Inukai, it could reasonably be concluded that Japan's political system was slowly "evolving" along relatively liberal and democratic lines. To be sure, such a judgment would have to lean heavily on the developments of the last eight of these forty-two years and to skirt with caution a number of embarrassing questions posed by the actual quality of "party government" in post-1924 Japan and by the direction and implications of the nation's foreign policies. Such a case, however, could still be made and often has been. Considered in a larger historical perspective, though, it is more accurate to say that Japanese political history during these years was largely a product of two major streams of domestic development: one authoritarian, and the other parliamentary and at least protoliberal. Throughout most of the period, authoritarianism was actually in the ascendancy, and it was to remain so until Japan's defeat in 1945.

Political power was shared during these years among the following major contestants: (1) the Meiji oligarchs and their direct successors in top civilian positions; (2) an increasingly distinct and professionalized group of military leaders; (3) the higher ranks of the civil bureaucracy; (4) leaders of the larger and more important conservative political parties; (5) a big business group usually known as the *zaibatsu;* and (6) an hereditary peerage, many of whom held high posts in the Imperial Court, in the Privy Council, or in the House of Peers. This classification is somewhat arbitrary in view of the many shifts in political roles and allegiances that took place throughout the period, but it does afford a rough framework for analyzing the major developments of the time.

The Meiji oligarchy was, to begin with, largely of samurai background and martial tradition. In the early days, it provided both the civil and military leadership in Japan, and there was little differentiation between the two. It was split along clan rather than functional lines, and such lines were of some importance until as late as the 1920s. During the 1890s, however, the civilian and military wings of this group began to develop along increasingly distinct paths. This was due partially to a natural process of specialization in a rapidly modernizing society and partially to the Meiji Constitution, which distinguished sharply between civil and military leadership. By 1900, two separate successor groups to the original Meiji leadership had appeared: one primarily civilian, the other military. Although they often disagreed, the gap that separated them on most major issues was usually neither wide nor continuous, and they generally cooperated more than they competed. With time, the connections of both groups with the original Meiji oligarchy declined in importance and, with the deaths of such elder statesmen as Yamagata and Matsukata in the early 1920s, disappeared almost completely. Thereafter, it became difficult to distinguish second- and third-generation leaders in these groups from the professional bureaucracy.

The social background of Japan's bureaucracy, like that of the Meiji oligarchy, was predominantly samurai and martial. This segment of the population both needed employment as a result of the abolition of its former class status and possessed the educational and administrative skills essential to a modern bureaucracy. As the need for trained civil servants grew, however, more recruits were drawn from the general population and educated at the new state and private universities and technical schools, especially at Tokyo Imperial University. A relatively small, cohesive, and professionally trained higher bureaucracy was thus created. Originally closely affiliated with the Meiji oligarchy, in more recent times it has succeeded to much of its political power.

The career leaders of the major political parties constituted a fourth leadership group. Many of the party presidents came from the ranks of the oligarchs, the bureaucracy, and even the military, but below this level was a large number of party professionals. Although these party leaders were ideologically conservative, they were usually at odds with the civil and military oligarchs and, to a lesser degree, with the higher bureaucracy and the peerage over issues of political position and power. From the 1870s on, the parties demanded a larger role in the decision-making process than was allotted them either before or after the Meiji Constitution. In practice, they continuously attempted to place their members in the premiership and in the nonmilitary Cabinet posts and tried in this fashion to force the Cabinet to recognize its responsibility to the party-controlled lower house of the Imperial Diet. Success in this endeavor would have greatly increased their political power.

The *zaibatsu,* a collective term for the great cartels that controlled a major sector of the economy, also figured prominently, if indirectly, in Japan's politics. Their very size and wealth made it inevitable that they would maintain close association with the government. Their political affiliations varied. All had active bureaucratic connections, and they usually cooperated with both the civilian and the military oligarchy. In fact, they regularly provided sinecure posts for government officials upon their retirement from public service. It was not until after World War I that some of the largest *zaibatsu* began to ally themselves closely with the major conservative political parties. Political campaigns and elections were very expensive, especially after the introduction of universal male suffrage in 1925, and the *zaibatsu* contributed large sums to campaign funds, which enabled them to exert a substantial amount of political influence.

For the last group of leaders, the hereditary peerage, the most obvious route to power lay through the upper house of the Imperial Diet, which they could control. The House of Peers, however, did not normally play a very positive role in policy determination. As a legislative body in a cabinet-centered governmental system, it suffered from many of the same disadvantages as did the party-controlled lower house. But certain elements of the peerage were active in two other capacities that were of great political significance. The first was the Privy Council, an appointed body charged with advising the emperor on state affairs, which, from 1890 to the early 1930s, constituted practically a third house of the national legislature. The second agency was the Imperial Household Ministry, which surrounded and served the person of the emperor. The most important of these men was the Lord Privy Seal. Since he and his associates controlled access to the emperor and advised him on Japanese and world problems, these officers possessed considerable political power, especially on such critical occasions as the selection of a new prime minister.

These six principal leadership groups clashed over many issues in the period from 1890 to 1932, but one in particular merits attention. This was the continuing struggle by the political parties for greater political power. The Meiji Constitution had carefully restricted the parties to a minor and largely negative role in the governmental process. As the sole formal political spokesmen for the Japanese people, they felt entitled to a much more important and, ultimately, dominant role in the decision-making process. They were aided in their struggle by the rising educational standards and political expectations of the Japanese people, by the advance in political participation by certain major sectors of the population, and by the general growth of democratic views and practices in other parts of the world.

Within Japan, however, those who would have to give up their power to the parties—particularly the civil and military oligarchies, the bureaucracy, and the peerage—were bitterly opposed to any significant expansion of party power. The party leaders, entrenched in their constitutionally sanctioned, if weak, position in the lower house and purporting to speak for "the people," fought back tenaciously and with gradually increasing success. They were able to demonstrate that the Meiji system of government could not operate smoothly or effectively over any considerable period of time without the positive support of a working majority in the House of Representatives. In the most orthodox of Japanese traditions, the party leaders cleverly exploited a position of seeming weakness and eventually achieved a greater share of political power. By 1924, they were beginning to speak of "true parliamentary government" as having almost been achieved in Japan. In fact, the years from 1924 to 1932 are frequently referred to as a "parliamentary" or "democratic" period in Japanese history and as a happy climax to the long struggle between authoritarian and liberal forces that had been launched even earlier than the Meiji Constitution.

Although the slow emergence of a more broadly based system of government through the rise of political parties was certainly one of the most notable developments of the 1890–1932 period, it would be a serious error to regard it as a triumph of "liberalism." The programs and performance of the parties that achieved a brief victory in the late twenties were not very liberal by either American or Japanese standards. Ideologically, these parties were quite conservative. They were much more interested in achieving and exploiting power than in implementing democratic policies, either domestically or in foreign relations. They produced few outstanding leaders, and by neglecting or outraging major sections of Japanese public opinion, they contributed to the authoritarian resurgence of the thirties. Their accomplishments were few, but any other outcome would have been truly remarkable. By 1924, these parties were only thirty-odd years of age, and they had to operate in a society that had been steeped in authoritarian and antidemocratic traditions for many centuries. In those thirty years, they were embroiled in a constant struggle for survival and petty advantages, with little opportunity to broaden their perspectives or acquire a mature sense of public responsibility. Under such circumstances, their shortcomings scarcely appear surprising. The early history of political parties in the West is not notably different.

The Authoritarian Resurgence, 1932–45

The fourteen-year period from 1932 to 1945 is somewhat embarrassing for those who claim that Japan was gradually evolving into a democratic society. It lasted too long to be shrugged off as merely an episode; it was too dramatic and disastrous in its consequences to be ignored. It marked a reversion to authoritarian and militaristic ways that were certainly far more in the mainstream of Japan's political traditions than were the brief years of "liberalism."

The period began with the assassination of Prime Minister Inukai Tsuyoshi on 15 May 1932. This was merely the most conspicuous of a number of such incidents that represented protests against widespread economic—especially agrarian—distress, the corruption and self-seeking of the party politicians during the years of "parliamentary democracy," and a foreign policy held by many to be insufficiently nationalistic or aggressive. These dissatisfactions were exploited by resurgent forces of Japanese militarism and ultranationalism, who felt threatened by the increasing powers of the political parties and the attendant development of a parliamentary system. The militarists and ultranationalists also believed that these were years of unique opportunity for Japan. With intelligence and courage, they held, Japan could become a world power and create an empire that would ultimately dominate all Eastern Asia. If this opportunity were missed, however, Japan would have to resign itself to a slow process of national attrition, leading inevitably downward to an insecure and second-class status among the powers.

Since the party and civilian leaders of the day showed few signs of being equal to this challenge, both military and civilian ultranationalist groups in the early 1930s plotted to expel the political parties and to replace them by more honest and more aggressive leaders drawn from the ranks of the military or their civilian supporters. The plotters were in disagreement about both ends and means, but through the years they acquired sufficient force and momentum to bring about great changes in Japanese politics. It is perhaps indicative of the real role of the imperial institution in Japanese politics that they initially cloaked their opposition under the guise of working for a "Showa Restoration," in other words, for returning true "political power" to the emperor as in the days of the Meiji Restoration—this despite the fact that the present, or Showa, emperor was apparently opposed quite strongly, although helplessly, to most of what these groups stood for.

During these years, the deterioration of democratic institutions in Japan was steady and rapid—so much so, in fact, that one is inclined to question the extent to which the institutions had really acquired popular support in the preceding period. Domestically, plots and assassinations multiplied, culminating in the famous Young Officers Revolt of 26 February 1936, when some fourteen hundred troops of the First Division seized and held the central districts of Tokyo for three days, while their cohorts attacked seven and assassinated three of the leading statesmen of the day. The principal objects of these attacks—party leaders, big businessmen, and eminent elder statesmen and imperial advisers—tried vainly and ineffectually to salvage what they could from the situation. They sought support from each other, from the emperor and the Imperial Court, and even, as a last resort, from the military themselves—in short, from everyone except the Japanese people. Ultimately they failed, and after 1936, the military once more determined national policies. The other leadership elements—the bureaucracy, *zaibatsu,* nobility, even the party leaders—were not eliminated from the scene. They simply accepted the inevitability of military ascendancy, compromised with the new circumstances, and formed new combinations and working arrangements.

After 1936, Japan is often said to have become a fascist state. Such a judgment, however, is highly dubious when applied to Japan—at least, if one regards Nazi Germany as the prototype of a fascist society. Many similarities existed, of course, between Germany after 1933 and Japan after 1936. Doctrines of racist mythology, national superiority, and divinely sanctioned imperialism were found in both countries. Both planned to expand into neighboring areas. Between 1937 and 1940, Japan, building upon its earlier acquisitions in Manchuria, pressed forward first in North China, then into the remainder of China, and on down into Southeast Asia in an attempt to establish a nebulously defined Greater East Asia Co-Prosperity Sphere under Japanese guidance and control. This route to empire led in fact to Pearl Harbor, to World War II, and finally to defeat and ruin.

Domestically, these were years of growing regimentation and of expanding governmental control over politics, business, and people's lives in general. In these respects, Japan might possibly have been regarded as a fascist state, but it still differed in a number of important ways from European-style fascism. Nothing in Germany or Italy compared with the imperial institution in Japan. Japan had no *Führer,* no *Duce,* in any way comparable to Hitler or Mussolini, and there was nothing in Japan like the Nazi or Fascist parties. Such "national parties" as the Imperial Rule Assistance Association or the Political Society of Japan were relatively negligible in importance. Japan never really succeeded either in establishing a true dictatorship or in organizing its economy or politics along truly totalitarian lines. Japan's experience was thus considerably closer to that of Italy than to that of Germany.

The shattering defeat in 1945 was a stunning blow for Japan, whose modern political history had been composed of little but spectacular successes. The reactions of the Japanese people to this catastrophe varied from class to class and from individual to individual. Some regretted—and perhaps will strive to recapture—the nation's lost status and power; some welcomed the emancipation from the old order and the expanded opportunities offered by their new circumstances; others, probably a majority, were acutely aware that disaster had struck and that this was not unconnected with the rash policies followed by Japan in the thirties. Thus, although the political consequences of the war and defeat are hard to specify precisely, it does seem probable that the experience significantly increased the people's general involvement in and concern about government and politics. In fact, this is perhaps the greatest political change wrought in Japan by the fourteen years of "authoritarian resurgence."

Prior to the intensification of governmental intervention in economic, social, and political activities following 1937, it had still been possible for many Japanese to live lives that were only lightly or intermittently affected by the national government. This included most of the peasantry and a surprising proportion of urban residents as well. Japan's invasion of China in 1937 and World War II brought with them massive conscription, increased taxes, regulation of the labor market and of consumers' expenditures, crop requisitioning, import and export controls, industrial mobilization campaigns, patriotic rallies, and so forth; all these extended the government's activities deeply into the lives of the people. The greater political awareness and new political interests that resulted have in the postwar years provided a more substantial foundation for the ambitious political reforms of the Allied Occupation. Such a process of mass "politicization," of course, is bound to have piecemeal and uneven effects, but strangely enough the most durable political consequence of the years of authoritarianism was probably the very considerable heightening of political consciousness and interest that took place at the lower levels of Japanese society.

The Allied Occupation, 1945–52

At the time of Japan's surrender in August 1945, the nation was confronted with the awesome costs of the war. Combined military and civilian casualties totaled about 1,800,000 dead; civilians alone accounted for 668,000 killed, wounded, or missing. Roughly 25 percent of the national wealth had been destroyed or lost; some 40 percent of the built-up area of the sixty-six major cities subjected to air attacks had been leveled to the ground; about 20 percent of the nation's residential housing and almost 25 percent of all its buildings had been obliterated; 30 percent of its industrial capacity, 80 percent of its shipping, and 47 percent of its thermal power-generating capacity had been destroyed; 46 percent of its prewar territory had been lost, some of it only temporarily, however. Other more intangible costs were harder to calculate: the long-term economic significance of the loss of the empire; the political consequences of being reduced to the status of a second- or third-class power; the effects of being cut off from established trading partners; and the consequences of facing world suspicion and opposition to any revival of Japan's prewar eminence in Eastern Asia. Japan's immediate prospects were ominous and alarming.

Many of the immediate problems were taken out of Japanese hands by the Allied Occupation of the country. The Allies formally ruled Japan from the time of the surrender ceremony aboard the U.S.S. *Missouri*, on 2 September 1945 until 28 April 1952, when the Treaty of Peace signed at San Francisco on 8 September 1951 became effective. Japan was required to surrender unconditionally all its armed forces and to accept the arrangements stipulated in the Potsdam Declaration for the establishment of a military occupation. It was made clear that "the authority of the Emperor and the Japanese Government to rule the state shall be subject to the Supreme Commander for the Allied Powers who will take such steps as he deems proper to effectuate these terms of surrender." At the stroke of a pen, a system of foreign military control was established in Japan that had practically unlimited legal authority to direct all aspects of national life.

In theory the occupation was an Allied responsibility, but in fact it was an almost exclusively American operation that made a few minor gestures in the direction of Allied participation. The occupation leaders chose to exercise their authority indirectly rather than directly. Americans did not themselves take over or replace the existing governmental machinery in Japan. Administration continued in Japanese hands, but it was made subject to American direction and supervision. General Douglas MacArthur was appointed Supreme Commander for the Allied Powers (SCAP), to act as the agent in Japan of the victorious powers in general and of the United States in particular. In September 1945, an episode began that was unique in modern history; a humane, systematic, and prolonged attempt was made by a victorious power, vested with plenary legal authority, to remold along more democratic lines the basic political, social, and economic attitudes, institutions, and behavior patterns of a defeated enemy nation.

The goals and major reform programs of the occupation were not created out of a void during the fall of 1945. They had been under consideration in the Department of State since at least April 1942. By the time of the Japanese offer to surrender in early August 1945, a large number of position papers on the postwar treatment of Japan had been drafted and approved, and by 29 August 1945, a comprehensive statement of the United States' Initial Post-Surrender Policy for Japan had been sent to General MacArthur by the State-War-Navy Coordinating Committee. This document established the United States' basic policies toward Japan in considerable detail and, in elaborated form, became a policy directive to General MacArthur by the Joint Chiefs of Staff. In the simplest possible terms, it set forth the two primary objectives of the occupation:

1. To insure that Japan will not again become a menace to the United States or to the peace and security of the world.
2. To bring about the eventual establishment of a peaceful and responsible government which . . . should conform as closely as may be to principles of democratic self-government but it is not the responsibility of the Allied Powers to impose upon Japan any form of government not supported by the freely expressed will of the people.

In practice, these two goals were commonly called demilitarization and democratization.

It is one thing to set such broad and sweeping goals, quite another to achieve them. Demilitarization was a relatively simple problem. It involved arrangements for the surrender and disarmament of the Japanese armed forces at home and abroad, the destruction or conversion to peaceful uses of Japan's arms-making capacity, the repatriation of Japanese military and civilian personnel from all of Eastern and Southeastern Asia, and the demobilization and return to civilian life of all members of the armed forces. All these tasks were speedily and efficiently performed by the occupation authorities. By the end of 1948, Japan had been completely demilitarized, and more than six million soldiers and civilians had been brought home. In addition, a provision was written into Article 9 of the new Constitution that was subsequently to cause much controversy. It renounced war and even denied the nation the right to threaten or use force as a means of settling international disputes. It also seemed to forbid Japan to maintain land, sea, or air forces or other war potential. Never before in modern history had a great power been so thoroughly demilitarized.

Democratization was a far more subtle and complicated problem. It raised enormously difficult issues: Could democracy be imposed by the orders of a military occupation? What was really meant by "a democratic society"? What aspects of democracy could be successfully transplanted to a society with as different a political tradition and background as Japan? The occupation authorities did not approach these questions with very detailed plans for their accomplishment. Under the pressing needs of the moment, however, an overall strategy gradually took form. Essentially, it was based on the proposition that any democratization program would not long survive the end of the occupation unless sizable and critically placed elements of the Japanese population were convinced of its value. The basic occupation strategy, therefore, was to involve a large section of the Japanese people in supporting and implementing the reform programs. The Japanese interests that benefited from the major programs are listed on the right below:

Reform Program	*Japanese Interest Served*
1. The purge of ultranationalist officials from designated public and private offices	Those who succeeded to the offices thus vacated
2. Expansion of the franchise	All adult Japanese women plus all men from 20 to 25 who had earlier been denied the right to vote
3. The grant to labor of the right to organize and bargain collectively	Japanese labor in general
4. Land reform	About 70 percent of farm households that had been tenants or part owners and part tenants before the war
5. Legal reforms of the traditional family system	Women and the younger generation in general
6. Decentralization of the powers of government	Local and regional interests
7. Educational reforms	The youth of Japan

The intent was, first, to create new interest patterns in Japanese society by granting new rights for which there already existed a substantial national demand and, second, to integrate these new interest patterns into a system of interdependent parts. The hope was that each segment of the population that benefited from a particular reform program would, in its anxiety to protect its particular gain, rally to the defense of the entire system when any portion of it was attacked, lest some revision at any point lead eventually to an assault upon all reforms including their own.

Partially because of this strategy and partially because of a wise recognition of the fact that any viable democratic system must consist of far more than the formal institutions of government, the occupation approached its task on a very broad front. Political prisoners were set free. Politicians and officials who supported ultranationalism or the old regime were purged from office, and more than two hundred thousand individuals were temporarily forbidden to hold public office or certain high managerial positions in private business. The suffrage was expanded to include women as well as men above the age of twenty. New political parties were encouraged. All antidemocratic laws of the old regime were revised. Labor unions were legitimized and encouraged to organize and protect the interests of their rapidly increasing membership. The years of compulsory education were increased from six to nine, and the entire educational system was drastically overhauled, democratized, and decentralized; at the same time, educational opportunities at all levels were greatly expanded. Vast quantities of land were purchased at almost confiscatory prices from absentee, nontilling, and large landowners and made available to tenant farmers for nominal prices. The highly centralized government of prewar times was radically decentralized, and considerable autonomous power was conferred on the prefectures, cities, towns, and villages. The great prewar cartels, known as *zaibatsu*, were deconcentrated, and their holdings were broken up into independent and competing units. New and unprecedented fair trade laws and regulations to protect consumer interests were enacted. Public health standards and practices were modernized and improved. New and far-reaching social welfare and social security legislation was devised and enforced. All these and many more "programs of democratic reform" were launched by the occupation authorities in their broad onslaught on the authoritarian Japanese political tradition.

To anchor these reforms in some durable political form, a new Constitution was adopted on 3 November 1946 (it took effect six months later, on 3 May 1947). This was a most remarkable document. The nature of the political system it established in Japan is described later in some detail. For the present, it suffices to note that (1) it was originally drafted in complete secrecy by Americans on the staff of SCAP's Government Section; (2) the Japanese government was subsequently persuaded to adopt the American draft under circumstances involving some degree of coercion; (3) the spirit and institutions of the new Constitution were unmistakably Anglo-American in nature; (4) the general system of government provided by the Constitution was, technically, among the most democratic in history—for example, considerably more democratic than that provided by the Constitution of the United States; and (5) the expansive civil rights chapter of the Constitution guaranteed procedural and substantive safeguards that provided basic legal protection for many of the occupation's democratic reform programs.

The occupation lasted until 28 April 1952, a total of six years and eight months. Surprisingly, the Japanese were uniformly docile and frequently friendly and cooperative with their conquerors. It was perhaps the friendliest occupation in recent history. It may also prove to have been one of the most effective. Japanese reactions to particular reform programs varied

widely, but the remarkable thing is the extent to which they adopted the
majority of them, made them their own, and have continued, even since the
end of the occupation, to support and abide by them. The occupation's
programs in some spheres, however, such as *zaibatsu* deconcentration, many
aspects of the local autonomy program, and the decentralization of control
over the educational and police systems, have either been abandoned or
seriously qualified. On balance, however, it is the occupation's successful
features, rather than its failures, that stand out. The occupation did bring
important political changes and a notable development of democracy to
Japan. General MacArthur and his staff deserve great credit for their share
in these accomplishments. They served as an essential catalyst at a time
when the Japanese people were in a state of unusual flux and receptivity to
change, when they were defeated, impoverished, uncertain of the future,
desperate for guidance, and lacking in leadership. Once the occupation had
ended, of course, it was primarily up to the Japanese whether they wanted
to sustain these changes.

Japan's political history during these years was powerfully affected by
developments on the international scene and in the United States. Several
factors converged in 1947–48 to produce an important change in the United
States' attitude toward Japan. The first was the sweeping and surprising
success of the occupation during its early days. It seemed to most observers
that the Japanese had sincerely embraced the cause of reform and were
making very promising progress toward a thorough democratization of their
society and government. It was also felt that at least a reasonable degree of
economic security, with some prospects for future improvement, was essential to the continuance of this democratic progress in Japan. For
these reasons and because the occupation was costly to the American tax-
payers, the official attitude in the United States toward the rehabilitation
of the Japanese economy began to shift decisively during the summer
of 1947.

The issue most directly involved was that of reparations. Should Japan be
forced to bear a sizable share of the overall cost of the war through the
payment of international reparations, and if so, to whom and in what form
should they be paid? Although the American occupation leaders agreed in
principle to the justice of such reparations, it proved impossible to obtain
any acceptable international agreement on the scale or method of payment.
Any reparations payments that were made seemed ultimately to take place
at the expense of the United States, since the occupation had to make good
any serious deficits in the Japanese economy in order to maintain viable
economic conditions. It was also impossible to induce Japanese enterprise
to invest in their own economy as long as they feared that the fruits of their
investment could be seized at any time as reparations. In addition, American
official circles were increasingly convinced that Japan was no longer a military threat but was, instead, rapidly becoming a peaceable democratic society. The United States' attitude toward Japan began to shift from being
fundamentally punitive and distrustful to being motivated by the desire to
extend assistance toward the political, the social, and even the economic
rehabilitation of Japan.

Another factor strongly reinforcing this trend was the steady deterioration since the last days of the war of the United States' relations with the Soviet Union. With the United States' decision to provide military and economic aid to Greece in the spring of 1947, the cold war was joined in Europe. At roughly the same time, hope of a negotiated settlement between the Chinese Communists and the Nationalist Government was abandoned, and the civil war in China entered its final stages, presenting the serious threat that a communist victory in China would extend the cold war to Northeastern Asia. Although this event did not actually materialize until the fall of 1949, it affected the United States' view of Japan at a considerably earlier point. If China were lost as an American ally, who could replace it? Obviously Japan was the prime, although embarrassing, choice. By 1949, the United States no longer considered Japan as a recently defeated and still potentially dangerous enemy but as a budding democracy of great promise and an increasingly important, if informal, ally in the cold war.

This shift in attitude directly affected the domestic affairs of Japan. All the basic "reform" programs were conceived and launched in the early stages of the occupation, when most of the formal orders by SCAP to the Japanese government were promulgated. During these years, SCAP exercised stringent and continuous control over Japanese political and governmental activities. However, 1948 marked a turning point in the history of the occupation. After that date, regulatory efforts by the United States steadily slackened, and Japanese initiative and activities increased until, for most domestic purposes, Japan again became practically a sovereign power. This was particularly true after General MacArthur was relieved of his post in April 1951. By the occupation's end in April 1952, Japan had, in fact, long since regained its autonomy in many spheres.

In Retrospect

Looking back over the century of Japan's political history since the Restoration, two major themes emerge to give some measure of continuity to the confusion of events. The first is the long struggle between the authoritarian, although not totalitarian, tradition and the more liberal groups that stood for some form of constitutional and parliamentary government. The particular issues varied with the times and the contestants, but a constant power struggle was waged between the Meiji oligarchs and their successors and opposition elements, who usually advocated causes considered liberal for the day, including a constitution, a parliament, expanded suffrage, and Cabinet responsibility. Until 1945, the authoritarian forces invariably held the advantage, but the opposition was never eliminated, never totally overcome. It displayed an amazing tenacity and capacity to survive; witness the prompt reemergence of liberal groups after 1945. Throughout the prewar years, these groups had won few battles, but they did succeed very gradually in altering the basic terms of political competition to their advantage. They obtained a Constitution, a Parliament, and universal manhood suffrage and, for a brief time in the late 1920s, seemed on the verge of establishing some degree of Cabinet responsibility and a party system that actually worked. Thus the prewar political history of Japan is not one of unrelieved authoritarian ascendancy, particularly if the Japanese record is compared to that of any other Asian state. There was a gradual, if piecemeal, conditioning of the people in at least some of the basic institutions of a democratic society. In 1945, therefore, Japan entered a period of democratic reform with a considerable heritage of useful political experience.

The second major theme running through Japanese political history is the country's attitude toward Western nations. Since 1854, this attitude tended to swing through cycles of hostility and receptivity. Periods characterized by xenophobia and aggressive nationalism regularly alternated with periods of admiration for and imitation of things foreign and Western. Thus relations with the West, and specifically with the United States, opened on a note of hostility with the Perry missions of 1853–54. This continued through the Restoration of 1868, but was gradually replaced in the 1870s and 1880s by a period of emulation of the West that was often carried to ridiculous lengths. The Russo-Japanese War of 1904–05 marked another high point in nativism and nationalism, which in turn gave way after World War I to a period of *demokurashi* (democracy), when Western ways were all the rage in Japan. The pendulum then swung back to the opposite extreme during the ultranationalist and aggressive days of the 1930s and early 1940s, whereas since 1945, Japan has displayed new and exceptionally friendly attitudes toward the West and the United States in particular. In the light of history, how reliable and how durable are these feelings? Signs of a growing disenchantment with the closeness of Japan's ties to and the degree of its dependency upon the United States have been obvious for some years. In view of these and of Japan's history it is difficult not to speculate on at least the possibility of some degree of progressive disengagement by Japan from the American alliance in the years to come.

BIBLIOGRAPHY

The bibliographic suggestions in this and following chapters have no pretensions to completeness. They represent the author's selection of a relatively few books, for the most part readily available, that are suitable for additional class reading or reference in connection with an introductory course on Japanese politics.

General sources

FAIRBANK, JOHN K., ET AL., *East Asia: Tradition and Transformation.* Boston: Houghton Mifflin, 1973, 969 pp.

HALL, JOHN W., *Japan: Prehistory to Modern Times.* New York: Delacorte Press, 1972, 395 pp.

HALL, JOHN W., AND RICHARD K. BEARDSLEY, *Twelve Doors to Japan.* New York: McGraw-Hill, 1965.

REISCHAUER, EDWIN O., *Japan: The Story of a Nation.* New York: Knopf, 1970, 345 pp.

SANSOM, GEORGE, *A History of Japan,* 3 vols. Tokyo: Tuttle, 1974.

SANSOM, GEORGE, *Japan: A Short Cultural History.* New York: Appleton, 1962, 558 pp.

TSUNODA, R., W. T. deBARY, AND D. KEENE. *Sources of the Japanese Tradition.* New York: Columbia University Press, 1958.

TIEDEMANN, ARTHUR, ed., *An Introduction to Japanese Civilization.* New York: Columbia University Press, 1974, 622 pp.

Modern history

AKITA, GEORGE, *Foundation of Constitutional Government in Modern Japan, 1868–1900.* Cambridge, Mass.: Harvard University Press, 1967, 292 pp.

BEASLEY, WILLIAM G., *The Meiji Restoration.* Stanford, Calif.: Stanford University Press, 1972, 512 pp.

BEASLEY, WILLIAM G., *The Modern History of Japan,* rev. ed. London: Weidenfeld and Nicholson, 1973, 358 pp.

BEASLEY, WILLIAM G., ed. *Modern Japan: Aspects of History, Literature, and Society.* London: Allen and Unwin, 1975, 296 pp.

BECKMANN, GEORGE M., *The Making of the Meiji Constitution.* Lawrence, Kan.: University of Kansas Press, 1957.

DUUS, PETER, *The Rise of Modern Japan.* Boston: Houghton Mifflin, 1976, 298 pp.

IKE, NOBUTAKA, *The Beginnings of Political Democracy in Japan.* Baltimore, Md.: Johns Hopkins University Press, 1950.

JANSEN, MARIUS B., *Changing Japanese Attitudes toward Modernization.* Princeton, N.J.: Princeton University Press, 1965, 546 pp.

McLAREN, W. W., *A Political History of Japan During the Meiji Era, 1867–1912.* New York: Russell and Russell, 1965, 380 pp.

NORMAN, E. H., *Origins of the Modern Japanese State.* New York: Pantheon Books, 1975, 497 pp.

SHILLONY, BEN-AMI, *Revolt in Japan: The Young Officers and the February 26,* 1936 Incident. Princeton, N.J.: Princeton University Press, 1973, 264 pp.

SHIVELY, DONALD, ed., *Tradition and Modernization in Japanese Culture.* Princeton, N.J.: Princeton University Press, 1971, 689 pp.

SILBERMAN, BERNARD S., AND H. D. HAROOTUNIAN, eds., *Japan in Crisis: Essays on Taisho Democracy.* Princeton, N.J.: Princeton University Press, 1974, 469 pp.

STORRY, RICHARD, *The Double Patriots.* Boston: Houghton Mifflin, 1957.

WARD, ROBERT E., ed., *Political Development in Modern Japan.* Princeton, N.J.: Princeton University Press, 1968, 637 pp.

WARD, ROBERT E., ed., *Political Modernization in Japan and Turkey.* Princeton, N.J.: Princeton University Press, 1964, 502 pp.

World War II and after

AUSTIN, LEWIS, ed., *Japan: The Paradox of Progress.* New Haven, Conn.: Yale University Press, 1976, 338 pp.

BORG, DOROTHY, AND SHUMPEI OKAMOTO, eds., *Pearl Harbor as History: Japanese-American Relations, 1931–1941.* New York: Columbia University Press, 1973, 801 pp.

BRZEZINSKI, ZBIGNIEW, *The Fragile Blossom: Crisis and Change in Japan.* New York: Harper and Row, 1972, 153 pp.

BUTOW, ROBERT J. C., *Japan's Decision to Surrender.* Stanford, Calif.: Stanford University Press, 1954.

BUTOW, ROBERT J. C., *Tojo and the Coming of the War.* Stanford, Calif.: Stanford University Press, 1961, 584 pp.

DUNN, FREDERICK S., *Peace-Making and the Settlement with Japan.* Princeton, N.J.: Princeton University Press, 1963, 210 pp.

FEIS, HERBERT, *The Atomic Bomb and the End of the War in the Pacific.* Princeton, N.J.: Princeton University Press, 1961, 213 pp.

GIBNEY, FRANK, *Japan: The Fragile Superpower.* Tokyo: Tuttle, 1975, 232 pp.

GUILLAIN, ROBERT, *The Japanese Challenge.* Philadelphia: J. B. Lippincott, 1970, 352 pp.

HALLORAN, RICHARD, *Japan: Images and Realities.* Tokyo: Tuttle, 1976, 281 pp.

IKE, NOBUTAKA, *Japan: The New Superstate.* San Francisco: W. H. Freeman, 1974, 121 pp.

KAWAI, KAZUO, *Japan's American Interlude.* Chicago: University of Chicago Press, 1960.

MARAINI, FOSCO, *Japan: Pattern of Continuity.* Tokyo: Kodansha International, 1971, 240 pp.

MAXON, Y. C., *Control of Japan's Foreign Policy, 1930–1945.* Berkeley, Calif.: University of California Press, 1957.

OPPLER, ALFRED C., *Legal Reform in Occupied Japan: A Participant Looks Back.* Princeton, N.J.: Princeton University Press, 1976, 345 pp.

PACIFIC WAR RESEARCH SOCIETY, *Japan's Longest Day.* Tokyo: Kodansha International, 1968, 240 pp.

REISCHAUER, E. O., *The United States and Japan,* rev. ed. Cambridge, Mass.: Harvard University Press, 1964.

SCAP GOVERNMENT SECTION, *Political Reorientation of Japan,* 2 vols. Washington, D.C.: Government Printing Office, 1950.

TOLAND, JOHN, *The Rising Sun: The Decline and Fall of the Japanese Empire, 1936–1945.* New York: Random House, 1970, 954 pp.

WOHLSTETTER, ROBERTA, *Pearl Harbor: Warning and Decision.* Stanford, Calif.: Stanford University Press, 1962, 426 pp.

Chapter *3*

The Foundations of Politics
ECOLOGY

The ability of political systems to create and control the environment in which they exist is limited. As they inherit a particular political history or social structure, they also inherit a particular set of geographic, economic, and demographic circumstances. These may be alterable, in part at least, by social and scientific planning and controls, but at any given moment in a nation's history, they restrict the range of decisions that a particular political system can realistically make. They thus comprise simultaneously a set of limiting factors of fundamental importance and a set of basic operating resources. Viewed in this light they are among the prime elements that determine the performance of political systems.

Geography

The most obvious geographic facts about present day Japan are that it is small and insular. Its total area is 372,393 square kilometers or 143,781 square miles. This is small compared to the United States (9,519,622 square kilometers or 3,675,547 square miles), the Soviet Union (22,272,200 square kilometers or 8,599,300 square miles), or China (9,561,000 square kilometers or 3,691,500 square miles). It is not small, however, when compared to the United Kingdom (244,004 square kilometers or 94,211 square miles), West Germany (248,534 square kilometers or 95,959 square miles), or France (543,998 square kilometers or 210,039 square miles). In Japan, however, there is an important distinction between the total area of the country and the generally useful or arable land. Only about 16 percent of Japanese territory is arable. In terms of this more meaningful index, Japan suffers a great handicap. The United States has 20 percent arable land; India, 50 percent; the United Kingdom, 30 percent; West Germany, 34 percent; and France, 39 percent. Among the major states, only the People's Republic of China (11 percent arable land) and the Soviet Union (10 percent) may be in less advantageous positions, although the current accuracy of these percentages is somewhat dubious (see appendix 1).

To make matters worse, Japan's national territory has greatly decreased as a result of its defeat in World War II. Japan lost Formosa, the Pescadores Islands, Korea, the Kwantung Leased Territory, and the South Seas Mandated Islands—all of which were formerly a part of the empire (Manchukuo was technically independent). There is little present prospect that southern Sakhalin or the Kuriles will be voluntarily returned by the Soviet Union, although Japan has not yet formally accepted this loss. Until recently Japan had also suffered the loss of administrative control over the Ryukyu (Okinawa) and Ogasawara (Bonin) islands. While acknowledging Japanese "residual sovereignty" over these two island groups, the United States had occupied and administered both—largely for strategic reasons—since the end of World War II. Ogasawara was the first to be returned to Japanese control—on 26 June 1968. Administrative control of the Ryukyus was returned to Japan on 15 May 1972, thus liquidating the last of the warborn territorial problems between Japan and the United States. There continue to be American military bases in both Japan proper and the Ryukyus, however, in accordance with the provisions of the United States–Japan Security Treaties of 1951 and 1960. The only territorial claim resulting from wartime losses that Japan is currently pressing, therefore, is that against the Soviet Union with respect to the southern Kurile Islands.

As a result of the war, Japan lost 311,158 square kilometers, or 46 percent, of its total prewar territory. Japan has since regained 2,489 square kilometers of these losses (Ogasawara and the Ryukyus) for a net loss of 308,669 square kilometers, a figure that still amounts to 45 percent of its prewar holdings. This net loss amounts to about 83 percent of Japan's present territory. Historically, few states have readily accommodated or resigned themselves to territorial losses on such a scale.

The bulk of Japan's present territory is accounted for by the four main islands of Hokkaido, Honshu, Shikoku, and Kyushu. There are also more than 3,300 smaller islands within the national boundaries. Japan is a country of islands and mountains, a fact that has profoundly affected the political character of the country. In the first place, it shapes the political unity of the country. Although Japan is a relatively small state, it is not unified and homogeneous. The islands and the mountains have historically made land communications rather difficult and have produced well-developed patterns of regionality. These regions have traditions and histories of their own and have usually had some sort of political identity as well. In modern political terms, Japan was not really effectively unified until the Restoration (1868), and even today this long history of political decentralization and localism has identifiable political importance and consequences.

Second, the insularity of the country seems to have affected its political history in several significant ways. It has, for example, given Japan a sharply defined national frontier, so unlike the broad and shifting bands of territory that have historically constituted China's frontiers. This has tended to give to the Japanese a sense of group identity, against outsiders at least, and— when joined with the development of a serious foreign and imperialist threat to their collective security, as was the case after Perry had reopened Japan in 1854—has provided fertile ground for the rapid emergence of strong nationalist feelings. Some would go further and claim that this historic isolation from extensive foreign contacts, made possible by Japan's insular condition, also partly accounts for certain narcissistic qualities in Japanese culture, as well as for the alleged inability of the Japanese to view either themselves or their relations with foreign countries objectively. National isolation may also explain the Japanese tendency to alternate between poles of aggressive self-assertion and a sort of collective inferiority complex in its relation to Westerners and Western culture.

Whatever the merits of such speculations about the Japanese national character, it is certainly true that geography has endowed Japan with a degree of national security that is almost unique in the history of the greater states. It is approximately one hundred thirty miles across the Straits of Tsushima to Korea, Japan's closest continental neighbor. It is about four hundred seventy-five miles across the Yellow Sea to the Chinese coast. Japan's safety from invasions from the continent is thus far greater than that of Great Britain, lying twenty-odd miles from the shores of France. Prior to 1945, no one had successfully invaded Japan since the ancestors of the present Japanese race did so in prehistoric times. This fact has had two prime consequences for the Japanese. First, until 1854, it enabled them to turn on and off almost at will the stream of intercourse with the Asian continent or with the rest of the world. It made possible, for example, the effective adoption of a deliberate policy of national seclusion for almost two hundred fifty years prior to 1854. Second, it enabled the Japanese throughout most of their history to concentrate exclusively and almost fiercely on domestic political issues, domestic power struggles, and internecine strife, with little or no concern for the effect this might have on the external safety of the nation. National security carried to this extent is unparalleled among the other great states of modern history. It is hard to specify precisely the consequences of this unique national experience, but the question certainly ought to be posed.

The Economy

In basic resources, Japan is in many respects a poor country. In recent years, it has had to import all its bauxite, natural rubber, phosphate rock, nickel, uranium, cotton, and wool. Also, Japan has to import 99 percent of its crude petroleum and iron ore, 80 percent of its copper, 79 percent of its coking coal, 80 percent of its lead and zinc, and 60 percent of its lumber. Japan suffers similar deficiencies in food, although in the past decade rice imports and all but 1 percent of vegetable imports have been eliminated. Japan continues, however, to import 100 percent of its coffee, 80 percent of its sugar, 96 percent of its soybeans, 92 percent of its wheat, and 82 percent of its barley. On a value basis, Japan's index of self-sufficiency in foods has hovered around 73 percent in recent years. In 1960 it was 90 percent. On a caloric basis, Japan imports about 50 percent of its food supply.

Against this apparent poverty of resources, however, stand Japan's impressive accomplishments in the general field of economic development (see appendixes 2 and 3). In 1974, for example, Japan produced and consumed more energy than any other country in the world except the United States and the Soviet Union. In the production of crude steel and cement, Japan ranked third in the world behind the United States and the Soviet Union (see appendix 3). In the production of merchant shipping, Japan led the world. These achievements are truly remarkable, considering the condition of Japanese industry at the end of the war. As early as 1955, in fact, Japan's official indexes of industrial activity, public utilities, industrial production, and manufacturing had all broken through their prewar and wartime ceilings, and they have since gone on to unprecedented highs. The gross national product has risen from a postwar low of $3.6 billion in 1947 to upwards of $488 billion in 1975.[1] During the same period, the gross national product on a per capita basis rose from $34 to $4,432. Even when adjusted in light of changes in the general price index, this still means that real national per capita income has skyrocketed since 1947. Both production and consumption have risen enormously. As in the case of West Germany, defeat has proven to be a prelude to the greatest spurt of economic development in Japanese history. One is tempted to conclude that, in an economic sense at least, it sometimes pays to lose wars.

These unadorned and sparse statistics and comments do not begin to do justice, however, to what is frequently referred to as the "Japanese economic miracle." There is no very close parallel in recent history to what Japan has accomplished economically during the last three decades. It is not only the fact that this explosion of national energy, skills, and productivity took off from a war-devastated and barely viable economic base but also the further consideration that this is the first instance in which a non-Western society has been able to scale such heights of technological, organizational, and productive achievement. The means of conveying the scale and quality of developments in Japan with any degree of precision are sadly limited. Inadequate though they are, however, the figures in tables 3–1 and 3–2 may illuminate something of the dynamism and accomplishments of the Japanese economy in recent years.

The comparative figures of average annual increases in gross national product set forth in table 3–1 reveal a great deal about the remarkable growth of the Japanese economy in the 1950s and the 1960s. It has been

---

[1]All dollar amounts ($) are United States' dollars.

TABLE 3-1

AVERAGE ANNUAL INCREASES IN GROSS NATIONAL PRODUCT

Country	1950–60	1960–70
Japan	9.1%	11.3%
West Germany	7.9	4.7
France	4.5	5.6
United Kingdom	2.8	2.7
Italy	5.6	5.7
United States	3.2	4.2

Source: Adapted from OECD sources.
Note: Calculated at constant prices.

the most dynamic among the economies of the major developed states with average real growth rates of 9.1 percent per year during the 1950s and 11.3 percent during the 1960s. It has also managed to sustain these remarkable growth rates well beyond what has been possible in other developed economies. The result has been a veritable explosion of national productivity and affluence. By 1974 Japan's gross national product ranked second among the noncommunist states, which is to say third in global terms if the Soviet Union is included (see table 3–2 and appendix 2). In the intervening years, the Japanese economy has been rapidly closing the gap that separates it from the Soviet Union and may well achieve second place in worldwide terms within the next few years. Some of the more optimistic prophets predict that by the end of the century Japan may even surpass the United States in terms of gross national product; this is highly improbable.

Certain important qualifications should be made to such gross overall evaluations of the Japanese economy. Change from relatively fixed to shifting exchange rates among the major international currencies since 1971 has had the effect of drastically inflating the performance of the Japanese economy when valued in United States dollars. (The monetary unit of Japan is the yen [¥].) After many years of exchanging at the rate of ¥360 to $1.00, the exchange rate has fluctuated in more recent years between ¥250 and slightly more than ¥300 to $1.00. This shift in exchange rates makes an enormous difference when translating yen into dollar equivalents. To take an extreme case, if one translates Japan's 1971 nominal gross national product of ¥81 trillion into dollars at the old rate of 360 to 1, it equals about $225 billion, whereas at 300 to 1 it amounts to $270 billion, a difference of $45 billion, or 17 percent, although the yen base remains constant. The cumulative effect of a recent inflation in Japan amounting, for example, to 22.6 percent in wholesale prices and 23 percent in consumer prices in the course of fiscal 1973 (1 April 1973–31 March 1974), must also be considered. Unless one is dealing in constant prices, this, too, artificially increases the size of both the gross national product and the national income.

It should also be noted that the per capita figures for national income in Japan are not nearly as impressive as the figures for gross national product. Japan ranked only sixteenth in this respect in 1972, twelfth in 1973, and seventeenth in 1974. Rankings of this sort are, of course, statistical artifacts

TABLE 3–2

GROSS NATIONAL PRODUCT AND PER CAPITA NATIONAL INCOME FOR SELECTED COUNTRIES

Rank	Country	Base year	Gross national product (in billions of U.S. dollars)	Rank	Country	Base year	Per capita national income (U.S. dollars)
1	United States	1974	$1,397.4	1	Sweden	1974	$6,693
2	Japan	1974	463.4[a]	2	United States	1974	6,030
3	West Germany	1974	412.4	3	West Germany	1974	5,874
4	France	1974	298.0	4	Denmark	1974	5,828
5	United Kingdom	1974	191.2	5	Canada	1974	5,634
6	Italy	1974	149.6	6	Belgium	1974	5,424
7	Canada	1974	142.1	7	Norway	1974	5,222
8	Brazil	1973	76.1	8	France	1974	5,037
9	Argentina	1973	75.5	9	Netherlands	1974	5,034
10	Netherlands	1974	74.3	10	Switzerland	1973	4,697
11	Australia	1974	66.7	11	Australia	1974	4,635
12	Mexico	1974	65.0[b]	12	Finland	1974	4,431
13	India	1973	64.6[b]	13	Iceland	1973	4,313
14	Spain	1973	62.3	14	Austria	1974	4,274
15	Sweden	1974	60.5	15	Luxembourg	1973	4,271
16	Belgium	1974	57.3	16	New Zealand	1973	3,896
17	Switzerland	1974	54.9	17	Japan	1974	3,497[b]

Source: Adapted from International Monetary Fund, *International Financial Statistics*, February 1976.
[a] Figure for Japan based on Prime Minister's Office, Economic Planning Agency data in *Nihon Kokusei Zue*, 1976, p. 87.
[b] Gross Domestic Product

produced by dividing the size of the population into the amount of the national income, and as a consequence, Japan's position on the scale suffers from the size of its population. Underlying the statistic, however, are more meaningful facts about the actual quality of life for the average Japanese; these are discussed at greater length in chapter 11. Briefly, however, the living circumstances of most Japanese do not measure up in many respects to the country's overall affluence.

The issue that really engages everyone's attention, however, is how much longer the economic miracle will last. More specifically, how long can the Japanese gross national product continue to expand at annual rates approximating the 9 and 11 percent averages of the 1950–70 decades? No certain answer is possible, but there is considerable evidence that the period of explosive growth may be drawing to a close, as it did much earlier, for example, in West Germany. The annual real rates of increase in recent Japanese fiscal years (1 April–31 March) have been 5.7 percent in 1971, 11 percent in 1972, 5.4 percent in 1973, and –1.8 percent (negative growth) in 1974. The most authoritative estimates for 1975 are approximately 2.2 percent. The rate of annual increase has definitely slowed, and the basic reasons are clear. The principal ones may be summed up as follows: the revaluation of the yen and its adverse effects on Japanese foreign trade; the drastic inflation—substantially worse than in the other major trading nations—that has afflicted Japan in recent years, although it has dropped substantially since 1975; the consequent and very rapid escalation of wage rates, amounting, for example, to as much as a 32 percent rise for unionized labor in 1974; and a slowing of the rate of increase in productivity per man hour of labor. The quadrupling of the price of imported oil in 1973 (Japan imports 99.7 percent of its oil, which in turn supplies about 80 percent of its total energy consumption) has also added very substantially to Japan's growing economic problems. As a consequence of these and other factors such as a slower rate of technical innovation, it seems probable that the era of Japan's economic miracle is drawing to a close and that the economy will have to adjust to more modest rates of growth comparable to those in other major developed nations of the West. The current estimates usually range between 5 and 6 percent average annual growth between 1977 and 1985.

Beyond these general comments, the contrast between Japan's poor resource endowment and its flourishing industrialized economy immediately suggests the importance of foreign trade to the economy. Most of the raw materials for Japanese industry must come from abroad. They must be imported in large quantities, processed in Japan, and then either consumed at home or exported to foreign markets to obtain the foreign exchange necessary for the purchase of additional raw materials. The Japanese economy is thus like a funnel into which imports are poured, in which manufacturing and processing take place, and out of which flows finished products for domestic consumption and for export.

In recent years, judged in terms of value, Japan's major imports have normally been crude petroleum, machinery, lumber, iron ore, non-ferrous ores, coal, non-ferrous metals, petroleum products, wheat, sugar, and cotton. These account for approximately 68 percent of the total national imports. They come primarily from the United States, Australia, Canada, Iran, Kuwait, Indonesia, South Korea, the Soviet Union, the People's Republic of China, West Germany, and Saudi Arabia. The United States has by far been the most important single supplier of Japan's overseas purchases, providing in 1975, for example, 20 percent of all Japanese imports at a price of almost $12 billion. Japan has for some years been the United States' second best foreign customer, standing behind only Canada. To meet the cost of these imports, Japan's most important exports have been iron and steel, ships, automobiles, radios, metal products, motorcycles, scientific instruments, plastics, and synthetic fabrics. Such items account jointly for approximately 54 percent by value of Japan's total exports. They have been sold primarily to the United States, South Korea, Taiwan, the United Kingdom, West Germany, Australia, Hong Kong, the People's Republic of China, Canada, Singapore, Indonesia, the Soviet Union, and Liberia (whose purchases consist almost entirely of ships). Again, the United States accounts for a top-heavy proportion of this, taking in 1975 20 percent of Japan's total exports at a price of $11.1 billion. This flourishing pattern of imports and exports has in recent years normally resulted in a favorable balance of visible trade for Japan. Its exports have normally exceeded imports by annual amounts ranging from $437 million in 1970 to $5,120 million in 1972. Looking at Japan's overall balance of international payments, however, it is apparent that the country went into deficit in 1973 by as much as $10 billion and ran smaller deficits of $6.8 and $2.6 billion in 1974 and 1975, despite its favorable balance on overseas trade totaling $104 billion in 1975.

Analyzing Japan's foreign trade in generalized terms, some interesting patterns emerge. Using the 1975 statistics as a base, it is evident that on a global basis about 43 percent of Japan's exports and 42 percent of imports are attributable to the "advanced countries" (the United States, Canada, Western Europe, South Africa, Australia, and New Zealand), 48 percent of its exports and 53 percent of imports to the developing countries, and as a special category, 9 percent of exports and 5 percent of imports to the communist countries (People's Republic of China, 4.1 percent of exports and 2.6 percent of imports; the Soviet Union, 2.9 percent of exports and 2 percent of imports). Some of the subcategories involved in this overall analysis are also of interest. In 1974 the United States and Canada accounted for 25.9 percent of Japan's exports and 24.7 percent of its imports. Western Europe as a whole took 15.5 percent of Japan's exports (10.7 percent by the European Community) and provided 8.4 percent of its imports (6.4 percent by the European Community). Australia accounted for 3.6 percent of Japan's exports and a very sizable 6.5 percent of its imports. Among the developing countries, South Korea (4.8 percent of exports and 2.5 percent of imports) and Taiwan (3.6 percent of exports and 1.5 percent of imports) were major trading partners. Southeast Asia as a region accounted for about 11 percent of Japan's exports and 14.6 percent of imports. The Latin American countries took 9.1 percent of exports and provided 4.4 percent of Japan's imports. The Near and Middle East played only a modest role in exports (6.6 percent) but, due to the great and increasing importance and cost of oil, provided an enormous 25.6 percent of

Japan's 1974 imports. The African role was modest (4.2 percent of exports and 2.6 percent of imports); most of the exports were ships to Liberia.

Japan's trading relationships with the United States are obviously of quite special importance. They are summarized in table 3–3. This is the largest overseas trading relationship in world history. Given the relative size and degree of self-sufficiency of the two economies, it is of much greater importance to Japan than to the United States. It is a source of some concern in Japan that the country is dependent on American importers and exporters for slightly more than one-fifth of both its overseas markets and sources of supply. The Japanese government would ideally like to diminish this degree of dependence and to diversify further both its markets and its suppliers. To some extent it has been successful, at least temporarily, in doing this. The United States' share of Japanese exports fell by 5.3 percent from 30.9 percent to 25.6 percent, between 1972 and 1973, by 2.6 percent to 23.0 percent in 1974, and by an additional 3 percent to 20 percent in 1975. The United States' share of Japanese imports also fell from 24.9 percent to 24.2 percent in 1972–73, to 20.4 percent in 1974, and to 20 percent in 1975.

Bilateral trade on this scale (for example, $22,760 million in 1975) is, of course, enormously profitable for both sides. It also inevitably gives rise to numerous and serious problems. In recent years these have centered on charges against Japan by the United States of unfair competition due to lower wage rates and alleged governmental export subsidies, of maintaining the yen at too low a value vis-à-vis the dollar, of unduly restricting the access of American products to the Japanese domestic market, of forbidding or making difficult American equity investments in Japanese enterprises, of dumping, and of unfair competitive practices in third country markets. The Japanese counterclaims have alleged systematic American discrimination against Japanese products, attempts to gain managerial control of critical segments of Japanese industry, actions by state and local governments that infringed Japanese treaty rights, closure or drastic reduction of Japanese access to the American money market, arbitrary and sudden cutoffs of essential supplies, such as soybeans, and unethical extortion of "voluntary agreements" from Japanese businesses to place artificial limits on the volume or

TABLE 3-3
JAPAN'S TRADE WITH THE UNITED STATES
(in millions of dollars)

Year	Exports to U.S.	Percent change over previous year	Imports from U.S.	Percent change over previous year	Trade balance with U.S.
1969	$ 4,958	+21.3%	$ 4,090	+16.0%	+$ 868
1970	5,940	+19.8	5,560	+35.9	+ 380
1971	7,495	+26.2	4,978	−10.5	+ 2,417
1972	8,848	+18.1	5,852	+17.6	+ 2,996
1973	9,460	+ 6.9	9,257	+58.2	+ 203
1974	12,807	+35.5	12,680	+36.8	+ 127
1975	11,160	−12.8	11,600	− 8.5	− 440

Source: Adapted from Japanese Ministry of Finance.
Note: Values on customs clearance basis.

type of their exports to the United States. The attendant controversies have been numerous and often acrimonious. The "textile war" of the early 1970s, for example, was only resolved—temporarily at least—by what amounted to a virtual ultimatum by the United States to the Japanese government. On another occasion, the United States temporarily imposed in 1971 a punitive 10 percent import surcharge on Japanese (and other) exports to this country. There have, therefore, been serious trading problems between Japan and the United States, and it is certain that these will recur in the future. It is a credit to both countries, however, that in all cases they have been able in time to discuss and to settle or at least adjust their economic difficulties on terms tolerable to each side. Ultimately, the enormous mutual benefit to be derived from so vast a trading relationship favors such a process of accommodation.

The Japanese economy is thus heavily dependent on foreign trade. Still, it is by no means unique among major states in the degree of this dependence. If degrees of dependence are expressed in terms of the percentage of gross domestic product (GDP) accounted for by exports and imports, practically all Western European countries have been more dependent in recent years on foreign trade than Japan. In 1974, for example, 54 percent of Belgium's, 26 percent of West Germany's, 18 percent of Italy's, and 16 percent of the United Kingdom's GDP was attributable to exports as contrasted with 12 percent of Japan's. The Japanese ratio was even more favorable on imports, amounting to 13 percent of GDP compared to 57 percent for Belgium, 20 percent for West Germany, 24 percent for Italy, and 21 percent for the United Kingdom. The United States (4 percent) and the Soviet Union are most unusual in their low degree of external dependence. Nevertheless, the survival of the Japanese economy is heavily dependent on foreign trade, and the global conditions and decisions affecting the volume and terms of that trade are largely beyond Japan's sphere of control. Any marked decrease in the global volume of foreign trade is almost certain to affect economic conditions in Japan rapidly. Since 1950, the Japanese economy has become increasingly prosperous, but this should not obscure the fact that the stability of the Japanese economy is notably vulnerable to external pressures and influence. At present, this vulnerability is most pronounced vis-à-vis the United States and, more recently, the oil-producing states of the Near and Middle East. The oil-producing states could bring very substantial economic pressures to bear against Japan and, in the Arab case, have already done so. However, the postwar Japanese economy has not yet been faced with prolonged and serious outside pressures or with a lengthy and deep depression. It is not easy to predict either the economic or the political consequences of such an experience.

Population

The Japanese Government conducts a formal census every five years. The most recent of these indicates that as of 1 October 1975 the population of Japan was 111,933,818. This figure takes into account the retrocession to Japan by the United States in 1972 of control over the prefecture of Okinawa, which added about 969,000 people to Japan's total population. The current Japanese population is, therefore, more than three times that during the Restoration (1867–68) and a little more than double that of 1920.

Japan has the sixth largest population of any contemporary state—ranking behind China, India, the Soviet Union, the United States, and Indonesia, in that order (see appendix 1). This population is distributed, however, over only 372,393 square kilometers of national territory, yielding a 1975 pattern of 297 people per square kilometer. In national terms this is one of the highest population densities in the world, exceeded only by Singapore, the Republic of Korea, the Netherlands, and Belgium. A somewhat more meaningful figure, however, is the distribution per square kilometer of arable land. In 1975 this amounted to 1,982 persons, one of the highest such ratios in the world. In 1975 male members of the Japanese population had a life expectancy at birth of 71.7 years and females of 76.9 years, figures somewhat more favorable than our own and among the highest in the world (see appendix 1).

The postwar population history of Japan is unique (see table 3–4). Immediately after the war, as a result of the demobilization of the armed forces and the repatriation to Japan of about six million Japanese soldiers and civilians resident in other parts of Asia, the national birth rate per thousand of population soared to 34.3, a figure very close to the record high of 36.3 in the 1920s. Thereafter, it declined steadily to 16.9 per thousand in 1961, one of the world's lowest rates. By 1974 it had risen to 18.6 per thousand. Along with this rapid decline in the birth rate has been an equally impressive decrease in the death rate per thousand; it dropped from 14.6 to 6.5 per thousand between 1947 and 1974, largely because of improved medical services and a national health insurance program. These rates compare favorably with those of the United States and the major countries of Western Europe. The result of such developments has been a sharp decline in the rate of natural annual increase of the Japanese population, from a postwar high of 21.6 per thousand in 1948 to a low of 7.0 in 1966. More recently, however, the rate has risen again to 12.1 in 1974. Thus, a population that was increasing by such fantastic annual increments as 4.99 and 3.10 percent in the 1946–47 period of repatriation has in recent years been increasing at a rate of slightly over 1 percent per year. The official projections, which have not been notably reliable in the past, anticipate total populations of 115,972,000 in 1980; 124,744,000 in 1990; and 131,838,000 in 2000.

The abrupt decline in national rates of natural increase is unprecedented in modern demographic experience. It was due in the first instance to the economic hardships of early postwar days plus the enactment in 1948 of a Eugenics Protection Law that legalized abortion and made it readily and cheaply available to persons desirous of limiting the sizes of their families. In a number of recent years there have been more than one million registered abortions in Japan. Adding to these the sizable number of unregistered abortions, the resulting figure may well come close to or surpass the total number of live births occurring annually in Japan. Since 1952, the increasing popularity of contraception as a means of limiting family size has

TABLE 3-4

INCREASE IN JAPAN'S POPULATION, 1920-75

Year	Population	INCREASE OVER PRECEDING CENSUS Number	Percentage	Average annual increase (%)
1920	55,963,053	—	—	—
1925	59,736,822	3,773,769	6.7	1.3
1930	64,450,005	4,713,183	7.9	1.5
1935	69,254,148	4,804,143	7.5	1.4
1940	73,114,308	3,860,160	5.6	1.1
1947[a]	78,101,473	5,561,744	7.7	1.1
1950	84,114,574	5,098,164	6.5	2.1
1955	90,076,594	5,962,020	7.1	1.4
1960	94,301,623	4,225,029	4.7	0.9
1965	99,209,137	4,907,514	5.2	1.0
1970	104,665,171	5,456,034	5.5	1.1
1975	111,933,818	7,268,647	6.9	1.4

Source: Adapted from Office of the Prime Minister, Bureau of Statistics, *1975 Population Census of Japan, Preliminary Count of Population,* Tokyo, December 1975, p. 6.
[a]Due to postwar conditions there was no regular census in 1945. The 1947 count is used in its stead. The population of Okinawa is excluded from the 1947-70 censuses.

reinforced the effect of abortion on the declining birth rate. The rise in the rate of increase in the population between the 1970 and 1975 censuses is attributable largely to what the Japanese call the "second baby boom." Most of the women born during the first postwar "baby boom" around 1947 became mothers during this five-year period.

As a consequence of these developments, the basic nature of Japan's population problem has changed several times in the postwar period, and the resulting political and economic problems have changed accordingly. The initial postwar difficulties associated with an unchecked growth of population were resolved by the late 1950s. They were promptly succeeded, however, by the new problem of a population structure weighted increasingly toward the working population (ages fifteen to sixty), a segment that accounted for 61 percent of Japan's total population by 1960. It was calculated at the time that it would be necessary to find approximately one million new jobs per year to meet the employment needs of this group. For an economy that had only recently recovered from the shock and losses of war, this was a daunting prospect. This problem, however, was solved by the explosive growth of the Japanese economy in the mid- and late-1960s. By the early 1970s, Prime Minister Sato was actually complaining about a labor shortage in Japan, suggesting that the birth rate was too low for the country's economic needs and considering the advisability of positive measures by the government to encourage larger families. At the same time, Japanese firms were beginning to establish assembly plants abroad to carry on the more labor-oriented aspects of production.

The newest version of the Japanese population problem is the increase in the proportion of the population aged sixty-five or more. In prewar times this segment held fairly steady at about 3–4 percent of the population. Between 1950 and 1975, it increased steadily in size from 5.3 million (5.7 percent of the total population) to 8.8 million (7.9 percent). It continues to rise sharply. Furthermore, the entire over-sixty portion of the population increased at a quinquennial rate far in excess of rates for the newborn to aged fourteen (1.6 percent) or aged fifteen to fifty-nine (about 6.5 percent) groups; the actual rate for the five-year period between the 1965 and 1970 censuses was about 19 percent. This shift in the age structure will greatly inflate the national need for programs such as social welfare and old-age and health insurance. A massive change in population balance and characteristics of this sort poses basic problems for both the economy and the polity. They define some of the most basic issues of politics and significantly affect the style as well as the content of the political power struggle. The problem is particularly acute for Japan because the traditional system of care for the aged by their family is only now being supplanted by new and quite inadequate measures of public assistance.

One further aspect of Japan's population structure that deserves notice at this point is the number of households. The significance of such a statistic derives from the traditional centrality of the family in Japanese society and from the greater prevalence in earlier times of "extended" as opposed to "nuclear" families. The nuclear family consists of father, mother, and children; the extended family of this nuclear group plus members of other generations or collateral kin. While it has never been true that families and what the Japanese call "ordinary households" are strictly equivalent groups, it is still possible to gain some insight into the fractionalization of traditional family life, the increasing ascendancy of the nuclear as opposed to the extended family, and by extension, the process of individuation through an examination of the household section of census statistics.

The number of "ordinary households" in Japan and the average number of individuals comprising such households has changed as shown in table 3–5. There has been a steady increase in the number of individual households and a corresponding decrease in their average size. Implicit in

TABLE 3-5

NUMBER AND AVERAGE SIZE OF ORDINARY JAPANESE HOUSEHOLDS, 1920–75

Year	Number of households	Average size of households (number of members)
1920	11,002,901	4.99
1930	12,477,563	5.12
1950	16,425,390	5.07
1960	19,571,300	4.52
1970	26,856,356	3.73
1975	32,143,748	3.48

Source: Adapted from Sorifu Tokeikyoku, *Waga Kuni no Jinko,* 1970, p. 93; and *1975 Population Census of Japan, Preliminary Count of Population,* p. 6.

Note: An "ordinary household" is defined as a group of persons living together and sharing living expenses or one person who occupies a dwelling unit alone.

this is an increase in both the popularity and the normalcy of nuclear family life, which would undoubtedly be considerably more pronounced if housing were cheaper and easier to find in the crowded conditions of postwar Japan. The increase in nuclear families also tells a good deal about the sorts of basic change in the circumstances of daily life that accompany the process of modernization. It has, of course, important consequences for Japan's political system. The older solidarities of political attitudes and behavior that characterized the more stable family and community scenes of earlier times are breaking down, and at the very least, the forces favoring deviance from the more traditional modes of political attitudes, values, and behavior are being substantially enhanced.

BIBLIOGRAPHY

ADAMS, T. F. M., AND IWAO HOSHI, *A Financial History of the New Japan.* Tokyo: Kodansha International, 1972, 537 pp.

ALLEN, G. C., *Japan's Economic Expansion.* London: Oxford University Press, 1965.

ALLEN, GEORGE C., *A Short Economic History of Modern Japan, 1867–1937.* London: Allen and Unwin, 1962, 237 pp.

FRANK, ISAIAH, ed., *The Japanese Economy in International Perspective.* Baltimore, Md.: Johns Hopkins Press, 1975, 306 pp.

HALL, ROBERT B., JR., *Japan: Industrial Power in Asia.* New York: Van Nostrand, 1963, 127 pp.

KAHN, HERMAN, *The Emerging Japanese Superstate: Challenge and Response.* London: Penguin Books, 1970, 274 pp.

KIUCHI, SHINZO, ed., *Geography in Japan.* Tokyo: University of Tokyo Press, 1976, 294 pp.

KOMIYA, RYUTARO, ed., *Postwar Economic Growth in Japan,* trans. Robert S. Ozaki. Berkeley, Calif.: University of California Press, 1966, 260 pp.

LOCKWOOD, WILLIAM W., *The Economic Development of Japan: Growth and Structural Change, 1868–1938.* Princeton, N.J.: Princeton University Press, 1968, 686 pp.

LOCKWOOD, WILLIAM W., ed., *The State and Economic Enterprise in Japan: Studies in the Modernization of Japan.* Princeton, N.J.: Princeton University Press, 1968, 753 pp.

NOH, TOSHIO, ET AL., *Modern Japan: Land and Man.* Tokyo: Japan Publications, 1974, 146 pp.

OHKAWA, KAZUSHI, ET AL., *Agricultural and Economic Growth, Japan's Experience.* Tokyo: University of Tokyo Press, 1969, 456 pp.

OHKAWA, KAZUSHI, AND HENRY ROSOVSKY, *Japanese Economic Growth.* Stanford, Calif.: Stanford University Press, 1973, 327 pp.

PATRICK, HUGH, AND HENRY ROSOVSKY, ed., *Asia's New Giant: How the Japanese Economy Works.* Washington, D.C.: Brookings Institution, 1975, 943 pp.

ROBERTS, JOHN G., *Mitsui: Three Centuries of Japanese Business.* Tokyo: Weatherhill, 1974, 564 pp.

SMITH, THOMAS C., *Political Change and Industrial Development in Japan: Government Enterprise, 1868–1880.* Stanford, Calif.: Stanford University Press, 1955, 126 pp.

TAEUBER, IRENE B., *The Population of Japan.* Princeton, N.J.: Princeton University Press, 1958, 461 pp.

TREWARTHA, GLENN, *Japan: Geography.* Madison, Wis.: University of Wisconsin Press, 1965, 652 pp.

Chapter 4

The Foundations of Politics
SOCIAL STRUCTURE

Any government or political system inherits and has to work with a population possessed of certain basic social characteristics. Its people may be analyzed and described in terms of prevailing social and class structure, social and political mobility, ethnic and religious composition, income distribution, literacy and education, generational differences, urban-rural distribution, and a great variety of other important categories. The particular configurations that these assume in a society at any given time are closely linked to and help define the power structure and the terms of political competition within that society. Of equal importance, they also delineate a large part of the fundamental problems that a political system must face and solve.

Ethnic Characteristics

Japan has a remarkably homogeneous population. Although hybrid in their historic origins, the latest available statistics indicate that of a total population of about 112 million in 1975, only 745,565 (0.7 percent) belonged to registered minority groups. Of this number, 643,096 (86 percent) were Koreans, 47,677 (6 percent) Chinese, and 21,045 (3 percent) Americans. The figures for all other nationalities were insignificant. Although these figures exclude foreigners who have assumed Japanese citizenship (and thus substantially understate the Korean element in the population), there is no other major nation with so small an admixture of identifiable minority elements. Japan is in an ethnic sense 99.9 percent "pure." This helps to explain the strong nationalism frequently displayed by the Japanese in modern times. Their geographical isolation, common language, and long history combine with racial homogeneity to facilitate the development of a very strong "in-group" feeling against foreigners. The result is a nation that, although subject to a number of domestic cleavages, has in the past usually presented a strong and united front to the rest of the world. This same degree of "purity" also affords Japan the most unusual luxury of almost complete freedom from the stresses and problems of ethnic politics that currently afflict so many other societies.

Sectionalism

A distinction must be made between Japan's outward-facing and inward-facing character. Racial homogeneity and nationalism have not precluded the development of political, cultural, and economic sectionalism. Japan's premodern past lies very close to its present; the Restoration occurred just over one hundred years ago. Most of Japan's national history before that was more local than nation-centered. Geography conspired with feudalism and the limitations of premodern communications to insure such a result. The Restoration originally centered around four principal southwestern clans, that is, around specific regions or sections of the country. Until well into the present century, the new system of government established by the Meiji oligarchy was denounced by its opponents as clan-dominated. Sectionalism has thus played a continuous and important role in Japanese political history. Today, sectionalism is still important in an understanding of Japanese politics but in a somewhat different guise. Clan affiliations are largely forgotten, but domestic differences in language, culture, tradition, and economic characteristics and interests reinforce the distinctly regional quality of most politicians' sources of political support in a way that provides a role for sectionalism in the political process. As politicians grow more responsive to local interests and pressures, the importance of sectional considerations may increase rather than diminish. Today, however, they are cast in terms of competitive economic or political advantage rather than traditional loyalties.

Urban-Rural Distribution and Employment Characteristics

Throughout much of Asia, the distinction between city-dwelling and country-dwelling is of fundamental importance. Asian societies are predominantly agrarian, and most of the people are farmers living and working in the countryside. Cities, although by no means new, usually account for minor proportions of the total population. Yet as the modernizing process takes hold in these countries, the urban sector of the population steadily grows in size and changes its social characteristics. Industrialization occurs first in the cities; migrants flow in from the surrounding countryside; foreigners and foreign ideas gain a foothold; and old ways and old social relationships begin to break down. In short, the city becomes the vanguard of change from a traditionally organized to a modern society, whereas the countryside—less directly subject to many of the forces of change—tends to cling more closely to the established and traditional ways. This process has political as well as economic and social consequences. In Japan, for example, the urban population has definitely been more receptive to political innovation than the rural population. Liberalism, socialism, communism, the Clean Government Party, the local autonomy movement, and many other new political movements have been primarily identified with the urban population, at least in their early stages.

The urban portion of the Japanese population has steadily increased. When the first really modern census was taken in 1920, only 18.1 percent of Japan's total population lived in cities. By 1930, this figure had increased to 24.1 percent; by 1940, to 37.9 percent; by 1960 to 63.6 percent; and according to the most recent census of 1975, to 75.9 percent. The Japanese statistic-gathering system somewhat overstates the truly urban segment of the population, but even so, it is still true that in fifty-five years the distribution pattern has altered from one in which more than four-fifths of the population dwelt in the countryside to one in which almost three-quarters lived in cities. By such a measure Japan is more urbanized than France or the United States (see appendix 1). A more meaningful indicator was provided by the introduction of the device of "densely inhabited districts" in the 1960 and subsequent censuses. Even by this more stringent test, however, 57 percent of the Japanese population lived in demonstrably urban areas by 1975 (see table 4–1).

Added importance is given to these statistics by an examination of recent changes in the number and size of Japanese cities. As recently as 1950 there were only four cities (Tokyo, Osaka, Nagoya, and Kyoto) with populations in excess of one million; today there are ten (the preceding four plus Yokohama, Kobe, Kitakyushu, Sapporo, Kawasaki, and Fukuoka). In 1975 they accounted for 20.7 percent of Japan's population. Tokyo is perhaps the world's largest city with an overall population in 1975 of 11,669,167—8,642,800 of whom live within the twenty-three wards (ku) of the city proper. It is interesting to note in the recent census that cities with populations over one million—the true metropolises of Japan—dropped slightly in their share of the total population from 21.6 percent in 1970 to 20.7 percent in 1975, indicating that the very largest cities may be reaching their limits of growth.

The environs of these major cities continue to grow dramatically, however, giving rise to doughnut-shaped rings of areas of very high growth rates. A phenomenon called the Tokaido Corridor or Belt consists of the Tokyo Metropolitan Region (the prefectures of Tokyo, Kanagawa, Saitama, and Chiba with a population of 27,037,267, or 24.1 percent of Japan's total population), the Osaka Metropolitan Region (Osaka, Kyoto, Hyogo, and Nara; 16,772,885, or 14.9 percent), the Chukyo Metropolitan Region (Aichi, Mie, and Gifu; 9,417,461, or 8.4 percent), and Shizuoka (3,308,796, or 2.9

TABLE 4-1

URBAN-RURAL POPULATION DISTRIBUTION

Census year	POPULATION			PERCENTAGE		DENSELY INHABITED DISTRICTS[a]		ALL OTHER DISTRICTS	
	Total	All cities	All rural	All cities	All rural	Population	Percentage	Population	Percentage
1920	55,391,481	10,020,038	45,371,443	18.1	81.9				
1925	59,179,200	12,821,625	46,357,575	21.7	78.3				
1930	63,872,496	15,363,646	48,508,850	24.1	75.9				
1935	68,661,654	22,581,794	46,079,860	32.9	67.1				
1940	72,539,729	27,494,237	45,045,492	37.9	62.1				
1945	71,998,104	20,022,333	51,975,771	27.8	72.2				
1947	78,101,473	25,857,739	52,243,734	33.1	66.9				
1950	83,199,637	31,203,191	51,996,466	37.5	62.5				
1955	89,275,529	50,288,026	38,987,503	56.3	43.7				
1960	93,418,000	59,333,000	34,084,000	63.5	36.5	40,830,000	43.7	52,589,000	56.3
1965	98,281,000	66,919,000	31,356,000	68.1	31.9	47,261,000	48.1	51,014,000	51.9
1970	103,720,000	74,853,000	28,867,000	72.2	27.8	55,535,000	53.5	48,185,000	46.5
1975	111,933,818	84,961,894	26,971,924	75.9	24.1	63,822,648	57.0	48,111,170	43.0

Source: Derived from *1965 Population Census of Japan; 1970 Population Census of Japan; Sorifu Tokeikyoku, Waga Juni no Jinko,* 1970, p. 23; and *1975 Population Census of Japan, Preliminary Count.*

aStarting with the 1960 census, the Japanese government introduced the concept of "densely inhabited districts," defined as a group of contiguous enumeration districts with a population density of 4,000 inhabitants or more per square kilometer lying within the boundaries of a city, town, or village that itself has a population of 5,000 or more inhabitants. This is a more meaningful measure of urban dwelling circumstances than the earlier system that was based on the distinction between political units denominated as cities (*shibu*)—and therefore "urban"—and those denominated as towns or villages (*gumbu*)—and therefore "rural." In fact many parts of areas designated technically as cities (*shibu*) are notably rural.

percent). The result is an almost continuous megalopolitan belt from Tokyo to Kobe with a population of 56,536,409, or 50.5 percent of Japan's total population. These twelve very heavily settled prefectures, therefore, account for over half of the overall population of Japan's forty-seven prefectures. This sort of phenomenon is not unique to Japan. One encounters a similar pattern on a smaller scale in the Boston–New York–Philadelphia–Washington Corridor in the United States.

Since there has been no appreciable change in the Japanese population due to permanent immigration or emigration, the reciprocal of this pattern of rapid growth in the major metropolitan areas has been a heavy drain on the population of the more rural portions of Japan. Most of the increase in urban population has been attributable to domestic migration from the countryside. This process began to slow down in the early 1970s. The 1975 census showed that only five prefectures had actually lost population in comparison with the 1970 census: Akita, Yamagata, Shimane, Saga, and Kagoshima. This was a marked change from 1970, when twenty of the forty-six prefectures had shown a net loss of population compared to the 1965 census (the forty-seventh prefecture, Okinawa, was not returned to Japan by the United States until 1972). This in turn was an improvement over the 1965 census in which twenty-five prefectures showed such a loss. There is a definite geographical pattern for such losses as there is for the gains. The losses concentrate in the poorer and more remote areas. In northern Japan, for example, the prefectures of Iwate, Akita, Yamagata, and Fukushima have had particularly steady losses. In the Chugoku area it has been Tottori, Shimane, and Yamaguchi that have usually lost population, while in Shikoku all four prefectures have lost in the past. With the exception of Fukuoka, the entire island of Kyushu has lost more regularly and more heavily than any other part of Japan. By 1975, however, this phenomenon of net population losses in such areas seemed at least to have slowed down.

A further and more precise insight into the urban-rural characteristics of the Japanese people may be gained from an analysis of their occupational characteristics. The changes are remarkable. For example, in 1920 the total labor force was 26,966,000, and 53.6 percent were employed in the primary or typically rural industries (agriculture, forestry, and fishing), 20.7 percent in the secondary industries (mining, construction, and manufacturing), and 23.8 percent in tertiary or service industries (trade, finance, communications, government, services, and so on). In other words and in occupational terms, more than one-half of the Japanese population was still rural. By 1975 the size of the labor force had increased to 54,380,000. Of this number only 13.9 percent were still engaged in the primary industries, 34.4 percent were in secondary employments, and 51.7 percent in tertiary. Obviously an enormous shift had occurred. Less than one-seventh of the labor force was still engaged in the traditional rural occupations, but more than one-half were in the service industries. A solid one-third were engaged in the secondary industries. Basic changes of this sort in a society's employment characteristics and urban-rural distribution patterns prepare the way for profound shifts in the sociopolitical attitudes, values, behavior, and potentialities of the Japanese people (see appendix 3).

Income Distribution

The economic characteristics of a nation's population vitally affect the country's political attitudes and behavior. Economic dissatisfaction is conducive to political dissatisfaction that may, under appropriate circumstances, lead to political instability and change. In the case of Japan, there can be no doubt that the country's remarkable prosperity in recent years has had a great deal to do with the stability of its political system. Should these economic circumstances change markedly for the worse, corresponding political changes would undoubtedly follow, although it is difficult to foresee their specific nature.

The gross facts of income distribution in Japan are as follows. National income has risen steadily and sharply during the postwar years. During the period from 1948 to 1964, for example, Japan's national income rose from ¥1,961.6 billion ($5.4 billion) to ¥20,522.5 billion ($57 billion), a more than tenfold increase in sixteen years. Not all of this represents a real improvement, however, since it was accompanied by a considerable measure of inflation. If this is compensated for by including changes in the general price index (which until 1964 was based on average prices in the years 1934–36), the real national income increased from approximately ¥9.5 billion ($2.7 billion) to ¥46.6 billion ($13.3 billion), almost a fivefold increase, while real national income on a per capita basis increased in terms of 1934–36 prices and exchange rates from about ¥118 ($34) to about ¥480 ($137), a fourfold increase.

After 1964 the period of explosive growth in the Japan economy got under way with the results set forth in table 4–2. For our purposes, the most meaningful of these figures are those giving gross national product on a per capita basis. Even discounting these for inflation and changes in the value of the yen, it is obvious that the circumstances of the Japanese people have on the average improved markedly in recent years. The 1970 figure, for example, is in real terms about the same as that for Great Britain and substantially better than that for Italy (see appendix 2). Similar cross-national comparisons are difficult for more recent years because of the distorting effects of floating exchange rates, high but differential rates of inflation, and Japan's abandonment of the 1965 base for the calculation of constant prices, but even so, there continued to be notable improvements in real per capita income. The 1973 figures, for example, show an increase of 7.1 percent over those for 1972 after discounting for price increases.

TABLE 4–2

GROSS NATIONAL PRODUCT AND PER CAPITA INCOME, 1965–74
(in billions of dollars)

Item	1965	1970	1972	1973	1974	1975
Gross National Product	$ 88.8	$ 197.1	$ 322.3	$ 407	$ 454	$ 488
Gross National Product per capita	928	1,957	2,949	3,547	4,133	4,432

Source: Adapted from Office of the Prime Minister, Bureau of Statistics, *Japan Statistical Yearbook 1976*; and Morgan Guaranty Trust Company, *Basic Economic Indicators, Japan.*

While there is no doubt that practically all Japanese have benefited appreciably from their country's increasing affluence, these benefits have differed from sector to sector of the population. For example, there are substantial differences from one part of the country to another. To take an extreme case, a 1973 report on the distribution of per capita incomes by prefecture showed a gap of more than ¥832,000 ($2,770) between Tokyo's average of ¥1,417,000 ($4,723) per year and Kagoshima's figure of ¥586,000 ($1,953). Only four prefectures—and these the most metropolitan—had average per capita annual incomes in excess of ¥1,000,000 ($3,333), whereas eight— and these the most rural and remote—had averages below ¥700,000 ($2,333). Thus in terms of average income, it makes a good deal of difference where one lives in Japan. There continue to be marked urban-rural differences with respect to income.

There is also a difference in the monthly earnings of employees of different-sized firms. In 1973, for example, the average monthly wage of workers for firms with 10 to 99 employees was ¥80,000 ($267); for firms with 100 to 999 employees, ¥90,400 ($301); and for firms with more than 1,000 employees, ¥106,500 ($355). There are still significant differences in income attaching to employment by firms of different sizes. However, these are now far smaller than has typically been the case in the modern Japanese economy; they were truly major until the growing labor shortage after the mid-sixties began to increase rapidly the wages of all employees, notably those of the formerly depressed "small and medium industries." In this connection the extraordinary recent increases in the average wages of unionized labor in Japan should also be noted. These were, of course, intended to compensate for the very high rate of inflation. The average wage increase amounted to 20 percent in 1973 and 32 percent in 1974, dropping to about 14 percent in 1975.

The Japanese system of wages is also characterized by quite pronounced generational differences in pay levels. To an unusual degree, wage scales in Japan are directly proportional to age and seniority. In 1973, for example, wages for employees aged eighteen to nineteen started at about ¥62,000 ($207) per month and peaked for males aged forty to forty-nine at about ¥135,000 ($450). Wages fell off very slightly for the group aged fifty to fifty-nine and quite markedly for those over sixty, for whom continued employment is apt to be regarded as a form of social security. There tend to be relatively few exceptions to this gradual escalation of salaries over time, and as might be expected, there is resentment among some younger workers who feel that more recognition should be accorded to performance and less to seniority.

Generational inequities in pay levels are not nearly as pronounced as those in terms of the sex of employees. On the average, the pay scale of women in Japan starts low and remains low. For example, the 1973 average wage level for female employees was ¥56,400 ($188) per month, some ¥51,600 ($172) less than the average of ¥108,000 ($360) received by male workers. Thus, the average male worker was paid almost 48 percent more than the average female worker. In general women are neither highly regarded nor well paid in Japanese industry, although the slow beginnings of change are evident.

Income distribution in Japan, as elsewhere, is obviously stratified in a number of different ways: by geography, by size of firm, by age and seniority, and by sex. In each case, the political consequence is the creation of actual or potential grievances capable of lending themselves to exploitation for partisan purposes. The degree to which these have become real issues in Japanese politics varies greatly. Differences between urban and rural income levels, for example, have long been a major political problem in Japan. They underlie the "military revolts" of the 1930s, while in more recent times they lie at the heart of the highly controversial, and very costly, program of governmental subsidies to the rice farmers of Japan. The women's movement is also something of an issue in contemporary Japanese politics, but it has not been particularly successful in pressing for equal pay for equal work. The same is true for the seniority system. These problems have the capacity to become vibrant political issues in Japan.

Class Structure and Mobility

Despite all the attempts to analyze Japanese society in Marxist or class-oriented terms, it is still impossible to describe with any accuracy the structure of this society on the basis of its social classes. In Japan as elsewhere, satisfactory definitions of precisely what is meant by such terms as upper, middle, and lower classes—or their many variants—are lacking, and there is not enough information to determine what proportions of the population should be assigned to which classes. Insofar as one's class status is a product of socioeconomic status, however, it may prove useful to review the 1975 census findings (see table 4–3).

TABLE 4-3

SOCIOECONOMIC GROUPS IN THE JAPANESE POPULATION
AGED FIFTEEN YEARS AND OVER (1975)

Socioeconomic group	Number	Percent
1. Farmers, fishermen, and associated family workers	7,253,300	8.6
2. Company and corporation executives	1,128,500	1.3
3. Business proprietors	2,998,200	3.5
4. Professionals, engineers, and technicians	2,108,300	2.5
5. Teachers, religious workers, and liberal professions	1,965,600	2.3
6. Managers, administrators, and clerical workers	9,860,800	11.6
7. Sales and service employees	8,742,500	10.3
8. Skilled, semiskilled, and unskilled workers	17,733,700	21.0
9. Protective service workers	737,800	0.8
10. Home job workers	612,200	0.7
11. Pupils and students	7,399,300	8.7
12. Housekeepers	16,707,200	19.7
13. Not employed	7,452,800	8.8
Total	84,700,200	100.0

Source: Adapted from Sorifu Tokeikyoku, *Nihon Tokei Nenkan, 1976*, pp. 32–33.

Whatever may be its precise characteristics, present Japanese class structure is the product of a series of quite unusual historical forces. To begin with, a century ago Japanese society was very rigidly stratified into a four-class hierarchy, ranging from the samurai, or warrior class, at the top through the peasantry and artisans to the merchants at the bottom. Although this ranking frequently did not accord with the actual distribution of wealth or influence in late Tokugawa times, it did represent a very important aspect of the status and value system of the time. It was legally abolished only after the Restoration of 1868. The social and economic tumult of early and mid-Meiji years (roughly 1868–1900) brought with it very considerable changes in class structure.

A new form of hereditary aristocracy was established in 1885. Numerous elements of the old samurai class were ruined, both financially and socially, through their inability to adjust to the new economic circumstances; many others sought refuge in business, the bureaucracy, or the new armed forces and managed to survive in the upper strata. In the countryside, a new sort of status system based on a variety of landlord-and-tenant or landlord-and-laborer relationships began to emerge, while in the cities there was a comparable ferment among the artisan and merchant classes. Out of the period of pronounced social flux and mobility gradually came a new and more modern system of class relationships. Important elements of the old pre-Restoration class system remained, but new avenues of upward social mobility appeared through commerce, industry, the bureaucracy, political parties, or the armed forces. Noble or samurai descent, however, continued to be of appreciable social importance. By the 1930s, this new system was well established.

World War II and Japan's defeat and occupation brought with it another great period of social change that is still in process. At the upper levels of society, the hereditary aristocracy and the military elite were eliminated from positions of leadership. The big business element was shaken up. Many political leaders were purged from politics, at least temporarily. Only the bureaucracy remained largely immune from the most drastic aspects of this great reconstitution of Japan's political elite. At lower social levels, even more massive and important changes have taken place. Before the war, the Japanese middle class was, by Western standards, small in both numbers and sociopolitical importance. Since the war, it has expanded enormously in both size and importance. In the cities, this development has resulted from the postwar development and diversification of Japanese industry, commerce, and government, the improved status and welfare of employees in general, and the economy's growing prosperity since 1952. In the countryside, it has been the product of land reform, technical improvements, and prosperity. As the middle class has expanded, the lower class has diminished. It now constitutes a much smaller proportion of the total population than before the war.

Precise information is lacking, but income statistics, consumers' purchases, the results of polls, biographical data, and a variety of other indicators testify that recent years have witnessed an almost unprecedented amount of upward social mobility in Japan. The specific political consequences of this social surge forward are rather hard to identify, however. Class by itself does not, in Japan, provide a very satisfactory explanation of popular political attitudes or behavior. Major segments of the population are not particularly class conscious politically. Conservative political allegiances are by no means based primarily or exclusively on "the middle class," nor are radical allegiances very closely correlated with "lower-class" or "proletarian" status. In fact, one fascinating aspect of Japanese politics is the extent to which the Japan Socialist and Communist parties derive support from the middle class. Given the general trend of recent developments, moreover, it is improbable that class consciousness will become a major political factor. A prolonged and serious depression or other comparable national disaster could, however, enhance its importance.

Literacy and the Mass Media

Japan is one of the world's most literate nations. Three to four years of elementary education were required for all Japanese children as early as 1886. In 1908, this was increased to six years, and since 1947, nine years of combined elementary and junior secondary education have been compulsory. Practically universal literacy (97–98 percent) and a very high minimum level of modern elementary education are, therefore, the rule. Of all six- to fifteen-year-olds, 99.9 percent are enrolled in the nine-year compulsory curriculum. In addition, Japan has one of the most modern and complete systems of primary and secondary education to be found anywhere in the world (see appendix 4). About 82 percent of Japanese children take some schooling beyond the compulsory level. In 1974, for example, there were 4,499 senior secondary schools, with a total enrollment of 4,270,943 students; 505 junior colleges with an enrollment of 330,360 students; and 410 colleges and universities with a total of 1,659,338 students. About one out of four Japanese aged eighteen to twenty-one was regularly enrolled in a college or university. This figure of about 23 percent of the age group compares favorably with the American figure of 31 percent and considerably exceeds the comparable French (15 percent), English (13 percent) and West German (11 percent) statistics. It is interesting to note also that the sex ratios of Japanese students in the elementary, lower secondary, and higher secondary schools are practically equal. At the junior college level, female students constitute about 84 percent of the student body, while this proportion is reversed at the college and university level where 80 percent are male. Practically all students in the technical colleges are male. By prewar standards, however, the number of female students has increased about nineteen times.

This high level of national educational attainment is one of Japan's great strengths. By 1970, for example, 51.6 percent of the entire population aged fifteen and over had completed the compulsory years of education, 30.1 percent had completed higher secondary schools or their equivalent, and 8.4 percent had completed a junior college or college education. These are proportions exceeded only in the United States. These high levels of education have important consequences for both politics and Japanese society in general. To an unusual degree the Japanese educational system operates on a basis of demonstrated accomplishment and merit. While no system eliminates completely the educational advantages conferred by family wealth or high socioeconomic status, the Japanese system has succeeded in doing so to an unusual degree. Higher and specialized education of excellent quality is still relatively cheap and generally accessible in Japan, and the admission standards involved are ruthlessly and fiercely meritocratic. Indeed, the popular complaints about higher education in Japan today center less upon its quality than upon the cruelty to children entailed in the long series of grueling entrance examinations, known as "examination hells." These start with kindergarten and continue through college and must be successfully passed before a student can be admitted to one of Japan's more prestigious universities—which, incidentally, tend to be public rather than private. Careers in the national higher bureaucracy are highly valued in Japan. They are open—again on the basis of rigorous entrance examinations—only to the most outstanding graduates of Japan's finest universities. These strictly merit-oriented standards make it possible for brilliant students from poor families to have more frequent access to high-level positions than is common in many other societies. The same standards insure a very high level of intellectual capacity and talent in Japan's higher bureaucracy.

Japan's consumption of the mass media is correspondingly high (see appendix 4). In 1973, for example, the Japanese were purchasing 537 daily newspapers per one thousand people, a figure in excess of the United States' figure of 300. In 1971, the Japanese published 26,595 separate titles of new books and reprints, a figure substantially in excess of that for the United States. Japan also produced more feature length films than any other country in the world. Practically every household had a radio, and 82 percent had a television (42 percent were color). Japan is literally saturated by the outpourings of the mass media, most of which devote a considerable amount of space or time to subjects directly or indirectly related to politics. Whatever their political views and behavior, the Japanese are exposed to a substantial amount of political information and stimulation, even by the most advanced Western standards.

It is important to note that much of what the average Japanese reads in the press is critical of the government and its policies. The relationships between government and the printed media in Japan are complex and interesting. The press is largely national to an extent unknown in the United States. Three major daily papers dominate the national market: the *Asahi* and the *Yomiuri* with circulations in excess of six million each, and the *Mainichi* with a circulation of about 4.5 million. These three papers blanket the entire country. The closest American analogy would probably be the *New York Times,* which is nationally read but has a circulation of only 843,000.

In general the Japanese press conceives its mission as involving systematic and continuous criticism of the government in power. Seldom does one encounter words of praise or confidence concerning governmental performance, capacity, or plans. To a degree this vested hostility is moderated in practice by the close personal relationships that often develop between Japanese reporters and the politicians and bureaucrats of the party or ministry in which they specialize. Japanese reporters specialize to a far greater extent than is customary elsewhere; the Diet and every ministry has regularly assigned to it a group of particular reporters from the major papers who constitute that agency's "press club." Only these reporters have routine and favored access to the personnel and news of that particular agency —a cause of constant complaint by the foreign press representatives stationed in Japan. The effect of this close relationship seems to be, in some cases at least, a moderation of the types and intensity of the criticism carried by the press. Still, the overall tone is with few exceptions distinctly antigovernmental.

The political content of television differs from the press in the sense that the emphasis on politics in news telecasts is considerably less intense and the treatment more factual and neutral. To some extent, however, this relative neutrality is compensated for by the number and popularity of what the Japanese call *zadankai,* panel shows with a political focus. These often tend to be antigovernmental in content and emphasis. The use of television in connection with election campaigns is, by American standards, almost completely colorless. A very limited amount of television time is allocated by law to each candidate, and no one can buy or otherwise acquire more for campaign purposes.

Generational Differences

Japan provides a fascinating laboratory for the investigation of hypotheses about the generational aspects of politics. Unfortunately, however, surmises and specious generalizations far exceed the number of solidly documented studies in this field. The case for a generational explanation of Japanese political attitudes and behavior is, however, both obvious and unusual. Prewar Japan had a predominantly authoritarian political system. This was systematically reinforced by an educational system designed to support the status quo. Then came World War II, defeat, and the Allied Occupation that lasted for almost seven years. The American authorities introduced into Japan a new and unprecedentedly democratic political system and bolstered it with an educational system explicitly designed to inculcate democratic attitudes, values, and behavior patterns into the nation's youth. Some thirty years have passed since the inauguration of these new political and educational systems, and they have in most essentials taken firm root in Japan.

The generational implications of these experiences are plain. Anyone born after 1940 has grown up and been educated in a postwar Japan that is different in many important respects from its prewar status. Their political socialization was very different than that for their parents. It is also possible that Japanese born after 1916 and thus in their twenties at the outset of the occupation were extensively influenced by the new attitudes and institutions of postwar Japan. Exponents of this view hold that those Japanese who had passed their more formative years by the advent of the "New Japan" were, therefore, less apt to be deeply influenced by the new democratic ideology. While this is doubtless an oversimplification, it is evident that World War II and its immediate aftermath constitute an enormous watershed in the political socialization of the average Japanese and that it is quite reasonable to expect that this difference in personal experiences should be reflected in differing political attitudes and behavior patterns.

There is an alternative hypothesis, however, that also deserves notice. This maintains that political attitudes and behavior are equally or more the product of life cycle than of generational causes. The most common expression of such a viewpoint asserts that young people tend to have relatively radical or innovative political attitudes and values but that they gradually lose these and become relatively conservative as they age and acquire more of a stake in the existing order.

The available evidence relating to either the generational or the life cycle hypothesis leaves a good deal to be desired. It is widely believed in Japan that members of the wartime and postwar generations—sometimes defined as children born since 1937—are considerably more apt to have socialist or communist political views and allegiances than are their elders. Estimates vary with the commentator and the particular youth group under consideration. One study claims that 41 percent of the twenty- to twenty-four-year-old age group voted in favor of left-wing—or, as they are called in Japan, "progressive"—political programs and parties in the 1958 general election. Others say that a majority of the new voters coming of age every year vote socialist or communist at their first opportunity. A poll taken after the 1963 general election, however, showed only 32 percent of the twenty- to twenty-four-year olds voting for socialist candidates.

Based on a poll taken in conjunction with the 1967 general election, the situation seems to be considerably more complex than this. When a sample of 1,295 voters identifying with either the Liberal Democratic Party (the conservative group in power) or the Japan Socialist Party (the principal left-wing opposition party) was stratified by age groups, the results depicted in table 4–4 emerged. In 1967, the allegiance of voters aged twenty through thirty-nine was far from consistent. Socialist support peaked among those aged twenty to twenty-four and thirty-five to thirty-nine. This was offset, however, by Liberal Democratic Party majorities among those aged twenty-

TABLE 4-4

PARTY IDENTIFICATION AND AGE
(percent)

Voting choice	Age groups							
	20–24	25–29	30–34	35–39	40–49	50–59	60–69	70+
Japan Socialist Party	47.9	39.9	43.9	45.3	31.8	33.0	22.4	11.6
Liberal Democratic Party	40.3	49.0	44.8	38.7	51.3	56.3	65.7	83.7

Source: Adapted from Akira Kubota and Robert E. Ward, "Family Influence and Political Socialization in Japan," *Comparative Political Studies* (July 1970), p. 145.

five to twenty-nine and thirty to thirty-four. After forty (persons born in 1927 or earlier), however, a strong and steadily increasing preference for the candidates of the Liberal Democratic Party is manifest. Thus, in this sample at least, there is a high correlation between the older age brackets and conservative political party allegiance. The evidence, however, is variable and confused with respect to the party identifications of voters below forty, and the findings are ambivalent with respect to either the generational or the life-cycle hypotheses. Neither can explain all the cases involved.

More attention has been paid to the political views and behavior of Japanese college and university students—and of their teachers as well—than to any other element of the population. It is quite obvious that two organizations that reflect the political views and activities of many students are themselves rather rigidly and militantly Marxist: *Zengakuren* (the National Federation of Student Self-Government Associations) and *Nikkyoso* (the Japan Teachers' Union). Many college and university students, although a minority of their age group, are among the most vocal, active, and sometimes violent supporters of left-wing causes. The political sympathies of other elements of the youth group—such as rural as opposed to urban youth, or high school as opposed to college students, or young workers as opposed to students in general—are less certain. Polls indicate that the "progressive" parties and candidates have the support of a very substantial segment of the younger voters, especially among the student and urban youth contingents.

The reasons for this phenomenon are debatable. Some observers note that political interests and activities—often radical or revolutionary in nature—are a part of the student tradition in Asia. Some simply say that radical political views are characteristic of youth in most modern societies, especially in disturbed times. Others attribute this radicalism to the influence of the allegedly unsettling and ill-advised changes in the national school system introduced by the Allied Occupation and of the radical sympathies and indoctrination of many of the present teachers. The available evidence is inconclusive, however.

Religious Affiliations

For most Japanese, religious attitudes and persuasions do not seem to have an appreciable effect on their political attitudes or behavior. This is a rather surprising development because of the political uses to which prewar Shinto was put, because of the seeming importance of organized religion in postwar Japan, and because many Westerners expect a people's religious affiliations to affect their politics. The symbols of religion are everywhere in Japan—temples, shrines, priests, and pilgrims. The average Japanese is a registered member of some faith and is usually a member of two faiths, the Buddhist and the Shinto, at the same time (only about 0.5 percent of the population is Christian). This dual allegiance, however, normally carries with it rather modest doctrinal and spiritual commitments. Religious considerations do not seem to be influential in the average person's decision making, particularly political decisions.

There are, of course, exceptions to this generalization. The political militancy of national Shintoism before the war, with its emphasis on the divine descent of the emperor, on Japan's world mission, and on the citizen's duty to be unquestioningly loyal and obedient, is found today in a scattering of small right-wing bands. A few of the "new religions" have strong political views or programs that they strive to impart to their followers. The *Sokagakkai* is the most notable of these. It claims a membership of more than sixteen million, but sophisticated observers are inclined to place its active or meaningful membership at somewhere between three and five million. The *Sokagakkai* has also established its own political party, the *Komeito* or Clean Government Party, that is currently the third largest group in the House of Councilors and the House of Representatives. The official relationship between the religious movement and the *Komeito* was formally severed in 1972, however, and the party's candidates now present themselves in an ostensibly secular guise. This is the only significant political party in Japan that has explicitly religious antecedents or connections.

BIBLIOGRAPHY

ABEGGLEN, JAMES C., *Management and Worker: The Japanese Solution.* Tokyo: Kodansha International, 1973, 200 pp.

ALLISON, GARY D., *Japanese Urbanism: Industry and Politics in Kariya, 1872–1972.* Berkeley, Calif.: University of California Press, 1975, 276 pp.

ANESAKI, MASAHARU, *History of Japanese Religion.* Tokyo: Tuttle, 1963, 423 pp.

ANESAKI, MASAHARU, *Religious Life of the Japanese People.* Tokyo: Kokusai Bunka Shinkokai, 1970, 122 pp.

BEARDSLEY, RICHARD K., ET AL., *Village Japan.* Chicago: University of Chicago Press, 1972, 498 pp.

BENEDICT, RUTH, *Chrysanthemum and the Sword.* Boston: Houghton Mifflin, 1946, 324 pp.

BUNCE, WILLIAM, *Religions in Japan.* Tokyo: Tuttle, 1976, 194 pp.

COLE, ROBERT E., *Japanese Blue Collar: The Changing Tradition.* Berkeley, Calif.: University of California Press, 1971, 300 pp.

DORE, RONALD P., *Aspects of Social Change in Modern Japan.* Princeton, N.J.: Princeton University Press, 1971, 474 pp.

DORE, RONALD P., *British Factory, Japanese Factory: The Origins of National Diversity in Employment Relations.* Berkeley, Calif.: University of California Press, 1973, 432 pp.

DORE, RONALD P., *City Life in Japan: A Study of a Tokyo Ward.* Berkeley, Calif.: University of California Press, 1973, 472 pp.

DORE, RONALD P., *Education in Tokugawa Japan.* London: Routledge and Kegan Paul, 1965, 346 pp.

DUKE, BENJAMIN C., *Japan's Militant Teachers: A History of the Left-Wing Teachers' Movement.* Honolulu: University Press of Hawaii, 1973, 236 pp.

FUKUTAKE, TADASHI, *Japanese Rural Society,* trans. R. P. Dore. London: Oxford University Press, 1967, 230 pp.

HADLEY, ELEANOR M., *Antitrust in Japan.* Princeton, N.J.: Princeton University Press, 1970, 528 pp.

HIRSCHMEIER, JOHANNES, AND TSUNE-HIKO YUI, *The Development of Japanese Business, 1600–1973.* Cambridge, Mass.: Harvard University Press, 1975, 340 pp.

HUNSBERGER, WARREN S., *Japan and the United States in World Trade.* New York: Harper and Row, 1964, 492 pp.

ISHIDA, TAKESHI, *Japanese Society.* New York: Random House, 1971, 145 pp.

LEBRA, TAKIE S., ET AL., *Japanese Culture and Behavior: Selected Readings.* Honolulu: University of Hawaii Press, 1974, 459 pp.

LEVINE, SOLOMON B., *Industrial Relations in Postwar Japan.* Urbana, Ill.: University of Illinois Press, 1958, 200 pp.

MASSEY, JOSEPH A., *Youth and Politics in Japan.* Lexington, Mass.: Lexington Books, 1976, 235 pp.

MORIOKA, KIYOMI, *Religion in Changing Japanese Society.* Tokyo: University of Tokyo Press, 1975, 252 pp.

NAKANE, CHIE, *Japanese Society.* London: Weidenfeld and Nicolson, 1972, 232 pp.

PASSIN, HERBERT, *Society and Education in Japan.* New York: Columbia University Press, 1965, 347 pp.

ROHLEN, THOMAS P., *For Harmony and Strength: Japanese White-Collar Organization.* Berkeley, Calif.: University of California Press, 1974, 285 pp.

THURSTON, DONALD R., *Teachers and Politics in Japan.* Princeton, N.J.: Princeton University Press, 1973, 337 pp.

VOGEL, EZRA F., *Japan's New Middle Class: The Salary Man and His Family in a Tokyo Suburb.* Berkeley, Calif.: University of California Press, 1971, 313 pp.

VOGEL, EZRA F., ed., *Modern Japanese Organization and Decision Making.* Berkeley, Calif.: University of California Press, 1975, 180 pp.

WHITE, JAMES W., *Sokagakkai and Mass Society.* Stanford, Calif.: Stanford University Press, 1970, 376 pp.

WOODARD, WILLIAM P., *The Allied Occupation of Japan 1945–1952 and Japanese Religions.* Leiden: Brill, 1972, 392 pp.

YOSHINO, M. Y., *Japan's Managerial System: Tradition and Innovation.* Cambridge, Mass.: MIT Press, 1968, 292 pp.

YOSHINO, M. Y., *The Japanese Marketing System: Adaptations and Innovations.* Cambridge, Mass.: MIT Press, 1971, 319 pp.

Chapter 5

The Foundations of Politics
POLITICAL CULTURE

Politics also has its psychological and cultural dimensions. Ultimately, what men do politically is determined by what they think and feel and by their perception of what is desirable, what is feasible, and what is safe for themselves, their families, and their communities. The political decisions involved are sometimes reached rationally and consciously, but usually they seem to be based on a combination of reason and a broad range of dimly intuited assumptions about authority, government, politics, the state, and the nature of a good society. These beliefs and assumptions, whether explicitly held or vaguely apprehended, constitute the psychological and cultural foundations of a political system. They differ remarkably from society to society and from time to time. Their appeal, their authority, and the extent of their acceptance have a potent effect on the stability and the effectiveness of the political system concerned. Such qualities as patriotism, self-discipline, and public interest spring from these sources. Collectively, and without pejorative intent, we often find ourselves referring to these basic beliefs and assumptions as the political myths of a society or, in more neutral and compendious terms, as its political culture.

In modern times, the political culture of a society seldom commands universal allegiance. It changes, and the attitudes of people toward it also change. At any given moment, some portion of the population is apt to dissent more or less strongly from any particular proposition generally held by the population. This is definitely true of postwar Japan. Before its defeat, the nation was far more unified in support of its political culture and myths

58

than it is today. The major watershed in this respect was the year 1945. Defeat, the Allied Occupation, and the overall course of postwar liberalization and democratization have discredited many of the prewar beliefs in whole or in part. In many ways, Japan is today a nation in search of a new and more satisfactory political culture. This complicates our problem because it is hard to tell which aspects of the political culture are now obsolete, which are on the way out, and which will probably retain viability and appeal for substantial segments of the Japanese people. The present situation, therefore, is unclear and can only be described in mixed and qualified terms.

Collectivity and Hierarchy

Some aspects of a people's political culture are so fundamental, so deeply ingrained in the collective psyche, that they take precedence over and almost predetermine the basic forms of social organization that emerge in that society. In Japan the closely associated traits of collectivity and hierarchy play such a role. The attitudes and values involved are subtle but profound in their consequences. They are perhaps best explained by means of contrast.

Americans, in particular, have long been exposed to historical, philosophical, and economic forces and circumstances that combine to exalt the role and the rights of the individual in society. Traditionally, their religions have taught them to believe that everyone has an immortal soul and a consequent duty to "save" it through the performance of good works and living a virtuous life. Americans have inherited a system of economic beliefs and practices that exalt the role and social value of the creative individual entrepreneur. American history emphasizes that the United States' strength and affluence were won by an unprecedented upsurge and emancipation of individual talents and energies encapsulated in the phrase "rugged individualism." American folk heroes are distillations of this imagery: Daniel Boone, Davy Crockett, and the frontiersmen who "won the West." Thus, Americans have a political system that was fundamentally conceived as a means of insuring and protecting certain basic individual and local rights against incursions by the national government. Although there are many qualifications that distinguish theory from practice, it is still correct and very important to note that American political culture predominantly chooses to exalt the role and rights of the individual at the expense—in descending order—of those of the national government, the local governments, the social institutions in general, and ultimately, even the family.

Considering Japanese political culture against this background, the foundations are quite different. The role, importance, and rights of the individual are far less salient in all contexts. In social, historical, economic, and philosophical terms, the prime unit upon which larger social structures and institutions are built is the family, or, more accurately, the *ie* or household. The household unit is elemental; traditionally it is valued above the individual in all meaningful contexts. If there should be conflict between household interests and individual interests, it is the individual who should give way.

Individuals gain identity, status, and fulfillment as loyal members of a household who dutifully and effectively serve the collective interests involved. The Japanese term "household," incidentally, differs from the Western concept of "family" in two ways. First, the range of kinship relationships represented in such a unit is apt to be more extensive than simply a nuclear family composed of parents and immature children. For example, viewed from the standpoint of a mature eldest son, it may also include his parents, his unmarried sisters, and some or all of his brothers and their families as well as his own children. Second, traditional Japanese "households" frequently also contain unrelated retainers and servants as well as family members. In both philosophical and practical terms, the gap that divides a household-based society from one that exalts the role and rights of the individual is very wide. The salience of the household in Japanese society is reflected in practically every meaningful sphere of social action or organization. The earliest histories of Japan were written in terms of households and multiples of interrelated households called "clans." Religious obligations were perceived and phrased in familial terms. The economy was organized and traditionally worked in household units in cities and in the countryside. Social status, rank, and privilege was basically a function of birth and familial status more than of individual achievement. The folk heroes of Japan were above all else dutiful sons dedicated to the effective performance of their household obligations, ardent in their defense of household interests, and skilled and fearless in these pursuits. It follows that the Japanese evolved a political system built upon agglomerations of households stratified and organized for purposes of local and national governance.

The primacy and salience of the household is one fundamental characteristic of Japanese political culture. This collectivity receives classic recognition in the household or family, but it also ramifies from this basic level and is encountered at all other levels of organized social interaction in Japan. The Japanese operate in group rather than individual contexts to a far greater and more systematic extent than is true of American society. They are simply more comfortable and, they feel, more effective acting collectively rather than alone. This is different from American behavior, but it differs only in degree, not qualitatively. The practical and visible consequences of this preference for collective action are encountered everywhere in Japanese society today as well as in the past. Japanese political parties and the real social structure of a Japanese governmental office or ministry are characterized by "factionalism"—a pejorative term implying a deviation from the harmony and unity that should (in Confucian thought at least) characterize society as a whole and its major components. Factionalism in this sense means that within the party, office, or ministry there exists a number of identifiable and continuous groups seeking to advance their collective and personal interests in some degree at the expense of those of other competing groups. Factions or groups are everywhere in Japanese politics. This is true to such an extent that some claim that the real key to understanding Japanese politics lies in a capacity to identify and assess the interests and relative strengths of the factions or groups that comprise the real operational units of the Japanese political scene. Again this is not qualitatively different from politics in the West. It is just that in Japan the groups involved are more omnipresent; more persistent; more pervasive in their demands upon their members' time, energies, and loyalties; and perhaps less issue-oriented in many cases than their Western equivalents.

If collectivity is one fundamental trait of Japanese political culture, the other equally fundamental and salient characteristic is hierarchy within collectivity. If a group of any sort is more than a passing and adventitious rabble, it must have some form of organization. The organizational possibilities range widely from classical democracy to totalitarianism. Progressing along an organizational spectrum, the degree of hierarchical structure —that is, the degree of authority and control exercised by superiors over subordinates within the group—increases until at the totalitarian end of the spectrum it theoretically becomes absolute. On such a spectrum the Japanese group is usually characterized by a substantial degree of hierarchy but with qualifications and adaptations that appreciably moderate in practice what otherwise might seem to be quite authoritarian procedures.

Hierarchy in Japan begins with the family or household. Every household has a head who is traditionally the oldest living male of the senior branch who has not yet retired from this office. In theory—and until fairly recent time in law as well—his powers were absolute in family matters. In practice, they were almost always tempered by persuasive models of what constituted a virtuous rather than a tyrannical exercise of household authority and by a complex interplay of personalities, household roles, and relative intelligence and skills of other household members, both male and female. Beneath this household head other members were hierarchically ranked with males having precedence over females and older members over younger.

Beyond the household group, today as in the past, hierarchical structuring is normal. In all Japanese groups, age and seniority are matters of great importance. Among the senior members, one individual is normally recognized as the group leader. Closely associated with him are a group of ranking elders, and distributed beneath these are structured ranks of juniors trailing off to the most junior and recent members. There is a clearly established and formal hierarchy generally recognized by all concerned and within which each member has a clear sense of his own position and perquisites. For anyone familiar with the Japanese language and social customs, this hierarchy is readily identifiable by the members' modes of address and speech and manners of deportment when interacting within the group.

Nevertheless, the authority that is theoretically implicit in the leaders of such a group is tempered in practice by several countervailing factors. One is simply the passage of time and the access of new political, legal, and social circumstances in Japan since the Restoration (1868) and, more particularly, since the advent of the present Constitution (1947). Times have changed in Japan as elsewhere, and the total political and social system has adapted in many ways to new and more democratic standards. Other forms of qualifying the authority of group leaders are more traditional but no less effective. For example, because the original model of authority within groups is based on the Japanese family or household, it should be exercised in ways that are both humane and demonstrably in the group's collective interest. To a degree that is often surprising to outsiders, a great deal of what might be called "intrafamily egalitarianism" enters into personal relationships within a Japanese group. The term "egalitarianism" must not be overconstrued in this context. It refers not to formal position in the group's hierarchy but to the belief that all group members, however junior, have a right to be heard on an issue and to have their opinions taken into account in the resultant decision-making process. On this basis, all group members have a recognized right to participate and to be heard and, depending on their personalities and the circumstances of the particular case, often exercise this right to a degree that would be surprising in many comparable American contexts. Factors such as these, together with the fact that the prosperity of groups is usually related to their harmony, size, and cohesiveness, substantially temper the quality and impact of the degree of hierarchical structure and authority that characterizes most Japanese groups.

It is helpful when observing or analyzing any aspect of Japanese society to keep these closely associated characteristics of collectivity and hierarchy in mind. Together they provide a way of looking at both social organization and social action in Japan that clarify many structures and procedures that otherwise appear exotic or unreasonable by Western or, specifically, American standards.

Legitimacy

How do the Japanese view their form of government from the standpoint of its legitimacy? Does its authority over them seem to be based on some right and proper title, or is it simply a result of the government's control of such instruments of mass coercion as the police and the armed forces? The mass of the population, now as before the war, does not seem to entertain serious doubts or reservations on this score. The average Japanese seems to conceive of government in general, including his or her own, as part of the fundamental order of things; it is as natural as the family system, after which the earlier Japanese political system was modeled in both Tokugawa and post-Restoration times. This is quite a different basis for legitimacy from the theories of social contract or general will encountered in the West, but it seems reasonably efficacious in Japan.

The basic assent on the part of the Japanese people to their form of government, however, is no longer as general as it was before the war, when the entire conception was more closely identified with the "divinity" of the emperor. Today, for example, the legitimacy of the government is challenged by dissident Marxists, by those who regard the present form of government as imposed upon a helpless Japanese people by the Allied Occupation, and by those on the extreme right who advocate a return to imperial rule in Japan. At present, however, these continue to be minority elements and sentiments. What has undoubtedly changed, however, is the intensity of the views held by many Japanese with respect to the legitimacy of their government. The external manifestations of such views, such as loyalty and patriotism, were once marked by unusual degrees of passion and ardor in prewar Japan but now seem to be characterized by far lower levels of emotional loading or even by apathy. Challenges to the system are also much more common.

It is impossible to speak of legitimacy in connection with the Japanese political system without considering the role of the emperor. We must be concerned with those mythical or symbolic elements in Japanese culture that affect the political solidarity of the Japanese people. Apart from the fluctuating issues and controversies of current politics, what basic attitudes of and assumptions by the Japanese people make for national political unity or consensus? What attitudes produce conflict and dissension? One of the factors that increases national cohesion is the insular nature of Japan, which gives the Japanese a common identity and unites them against all outsiders, all non-Japanese. To this must be added the role of the emperor and the imperial family as a unifying symbol.

Before 1945, the official myth—systematically contrived in early Meiji times from bits and pieces of ancient Japanese history and rigorously instilled into the people by all possible means—was that the emperor was descended in direct and unbroken line from Amaterasu-omikami, the pre-eminent goddess of the sun and that rule over Japan was divinely entrusted to him through his ancestors. Under these circumstances, the emperor was —in crude translation—"divine," or as the Japanese say, he was a *kami*. A more appropriate modern rendering would be that he was a superior and awe-inspiring personage of more than natural attributes. The official interpretation proceeded from this basis to state in vague and deliberately mystic and mystifying language that the emperor was somehow fused with the Japanese "state"; the two concepts could not, in fact or theory, be disentangled from one another because they mutually informed and gave meaning and substance to each other. Somehow, the emperor was the "state" and, as such, was a "divinely" descended, all-powerful, sacred, inviolable, and absolutely sovereign figure. This was the basic theory of the state in post-Restoration Japan, known officially as the doctrine of *kokutai* or "the national polity." It was also the basis for numerous assertions, official and otherwise, that the Japanese were a unique and superior race with a "divine" mission to spread the blessings of their culture to lesser breeds of men, especially in Eastern Asia.

This entire belief is apt to appear spurious, fantastic, and quite incomprehensible to Westerners, but in fact it is little if any more nonsensical than other political myths that have commanded the impassioned support of millions of dedicated followers within the twentieth century. How well do the mythical bases of Italian Fascism, German Nazism, Russian Communism, or in a different genre, the social contract aspects of democratic theory withstand rigorous logical analysis? In any event, this interpretation seems to have been either actively believed or passively accepted by a substantial majority of Japanese before the war, and as a consequence, the emperor became the basic symbol of the legitimacy and the unity of the state. Public authority was wielded in his name and with his sanction, governmental acts were construed to be manifestations of his will, and the loyalty and patriotism of most of the people were fiercely and sincerely focused on his person; all this was despite the fact that in practice the emperor actually possessed very little political power and usually had limited influence on the formulation or execution of public policy.

Since Japan's defeat and the enactment of a new Constitution in 1947, the legal and theoretical position of the emperor has been drastically changed, although his actual power remains negligible. Early in 1946, he formally and publicly renounced any claims to divinity or superhuman status that might have been made on his behalf. The new Constitution carried this further by stripping him of all vestiges of sovereign power and political authority of any sort; it specifically declared him to be no more than "the symbol of the State and of the unity of the people, deriving his position from the will of the people, with whom resides sovereign power." Thus, the prewar position of the emperor has been completely inverted. Nevertheless, he remains the single most powerful symbol of the political identity and unity of the Japanese people. He is a different sort of symbol to be sure—less awesome and more human and democratized—but he is still the focus of most popular political loyalties, although these too seem to be considerably less ardent and demonstrative than before the war.

The imperial institution has undergone some remarkable changes in postwar Japan. Before the end of the war, for example, a systematic campaign was launched by government and court officials to humanize and popularize the emperor as a person. Following the war there were a series of unprecedented tours throughout Japan featuring an emperor, notably ill at ease and at a loss for conversation, visiting farms and factories and engaging in uncomfortable dialogues with his equally embarrassed subjects. The campaign reached a peak with the lengthy and lovingly chronicled romance of Crown Prince Akihito that culminated in his marriage to a commoner, Shoda Michiko, in 1959. The lives and activities of the imperial family continue to be a topic of substantial interest to the Japanese press and people, but it is very difficult to assess the quality of the popular feelings involved. Certainly any imputations of divine or awe-inspiring status are confined to small and unrepresentative minorities today. Sentiments of low-keyed affection, approval of the continuities symbolized by the imperial institution, and simple acceptance of the situation seem to be more commonly held viewpoints. There are also people who challenge the imperial institution. Many younger Japanese and numerous intellectuals favor the abolition of the monarchy, charging that it is outdated, anachronistic, and useless. Until, however, it can be replaced in the minds and hearts of most Japanese by some other equally efficacious symbol of their unity and nationhood, it might prove to be dangerous to eliminate the emperor.

Nationalism

Another basic factor contributing to the political solidarity of the Japanese people is their nationalism. Prior to 1945, the ardency and aggressiveness of Japanese nationalism had long been one of the most conspicuous features of Japanese culture. It provided the strongest sort of mass support for both the domestic and foreign programs of the Japanese government and, in particular, for the series of generally profitable overseas campaigns and wars that began with the Sino-Japanese War of 1894–95 and culminated disastrously with World War II. Defeat and postwar developments in general have worked strange changes in the quality of Japanese nationalism, however. What was a strong flame now seems to be a dim and flickering light. Prewar martial and aggressive qualities seem to have been replaced by a general spirit of pacificism and internationalism and by an absorption with commercial and peaceful pursuits.

Some observers—including many Japanese—conclude that Japanese nationalism is a dead or dying force or that it is in the process of being replaced by a new spirit of internationalism, but such a judgment seems premature. Japan's national circumstances since the war have been markedly peculiar and, in general, have not been conducive to the reemergence of Japanese nationalism. To begin with, there were the massive facts of defeat, devastation, and national collapse, both economic and spiritual. This was attended by about seven years of Allied military occupation, followed by a period of very close attachment to the United States in international affairs. These were also years during which Japan was a constitutionally disarmed nation, supporting only the weakest of military establishments masquerading under the name of "self-defense forces." During this postwar period, Japan did not really play a prime or prominent role on the international scene. In foreign policy, it operated along only limited lines and from an unusually protected and secure position on the fringes of the Western camp.

This sheltered or removed quality and a widespread and sincere desire to avoid becoming involved in any military or diplomatic arrangements that could lead to war have convinced many Japanese that no real threat to their national security exists at present. It is perhaps this feeling that accounts for the recent quiescence of Japanese nationalism. Nationalist sentiments often flourish only against a background of some real or apprehended threat to the national security or to expansionist ambitions. Most Japanese today have no overseas ambitions and many—perhaps unrealistically—see no real threat from abroad.

These circumstances, however, have gradually been changing. The renascence of national pride, for example, may well have begun in the early 1950s with the victories of the first Japanese swimming teams to compete abroad following the war. Events such as the 1964 Tokyo Olympic Games and Osaka's "Expo '70" were partially intended to demonstrate the renewed vitality and status of Japan to the outside world. The "economic miracle" was another event in which most Japanese took great and justified pride. In pace with these symbolic steps, the real influence and stature of Japan in world affairs also increased rapidly, especially after 1965. It was, however, a curiously lopsided or incomplete international status that was involved. Lacking aggressive military power of any significance but at the same time possessing the third largest aggregation of economic power in the world, Japan was literally a new species of great state in modern times; it was the first case of a nation possessing wealth and technological capacities to opt voluntarily out of the power struggle and to elect to concentrate its foreign policies and activities on the economy. Still, Japan's enormous accomplishments along these lines brought a resurgence of national pride and confidence. For many it was enough to be citizens of one of the world's richest and most prosperous states. For some it seemed either necessary or desirable to take the next step and to supplement and protect Japan's economic accomplishments with military strength on a scale more appropriate to their country's needs and capacities.

It is possible in this framework to speak of a revival of nationalism in contemporary Japan, taking great care to specify just what is involved. For most Japanese it consists of regaining collective confidence based primarily on pride in the enormous vitality and creativeness of Japan's people and economy. Many of those who feel this pride and enjoy their new national status also strongly support the pacificism and continued disarmament—relatively speaking—of Japan. There are others, however, whose nationalism is more classic. Very few harbor anything even remotely resembling the aggressive nationalist sentiments of prewar days. Nevertheless, they do feel that present day Japan suffers from a lack of patriotism, discipline, and national pride; that a state that is both wealthy and disarmed is a dangerously vulnerable anomaly in the modern world; and that Japan should, therefore, both rearm and strive to inculcate her citizenry with more positive sentiments of loyalty, discipline, and service to the country. So far such sentiments seem to be held by only a relatively small minority, but a serious and sustained national crisis could cause them to spread. Nationalism is not dead in Japan; it has simply experienced a change of character and mode of expression.

Underlying and unifying all forms of revived nationalist sentiments in Japan is a very strong and almost universally shared sense of the uniqueness of being Japanese. Fundamentally the term "nationalism" means a sense of identity, of belonging to the same group that, for all its internal differences, is somehow different from other national groups. Sociologists speak of this as an in-group feeling shared on a national scale. All nations by definition have this feeling, but it is held with different degrees of consciousness, intensity, and uniformity. Among major Western states, for example, the Italians might fall toward the less conscious, less intense, and less uniform end of a spectrum measuring degrees of nationalist feeling. The Japanese to the contrary would probably fall very high, quite possibly at the top of a spectrum for great modern states and their peoples. This is not, however, patriotism or the fierce, aggressive nationalism that characterized the prewar Japanese people; it is the intensely held in-group feeling widely shared among the Japanese people and is a sense of the uniqueness of their national experience, their culture, and their language that clearly sets them apart from all other peoples. The essence of this feeling is captured in the Japanese word for foreigners; they are *gai-jin*, literally "people outside." Foreigners are outside the explicit and well-known boundaries that demarcate the Japanese from all other peoples of the world. In most other societies it is possible for a foreigner, an "outsider," given time, dedication, and talent, to become and to be accepted as truly "naturalized," as an "insider" in his or her new nationality. Many doubt that this is possible for any foreigner seeking to gain acceptance as a Japanese. The cultural barriers, reinforced by Japan's unique degree of racial homogeneity, are simply too great.

Monism versus Pluralism

Some peoples conceive of government as a supreme and exclusive form of social organization whose power and authority should, when legally exercised, override and control almost all competing claims. Such governments in modern times are apt to play a very positive and extensive role in their societies. Others think of government as one among a number of social organizations—such as the family, the church, and a variety of economic, professional, and cultural organizations —possessed of a unique and, for some purposes, superior type of power and authority but with no right to control or perform all social functions within its boundaries. Governments so conceived tend to play a more restricted role in their societies and to leave many major functions largely to other social organizations. For our purposes, the first is referred to as a monist and the second as a pluralist view of government and its functions. The Japanese have traditionally adopted a monist view.

The concept of either individual or institutional rights as in any way removed from or immune to governmental control is completely alien to the Japanese tradition. No real or meaningful sphere of private decision or action was legally or theoretically recognized in Japan until the enforcement of the present Constitution in 1947. It was generally assumed that government could do whatever in fact it had the power and the inclination to do. This right was qualified on occasion by authoritative statements as to how a virtuous ruler or government should deport itself, but these were often of more theoretical than practical consequence. Since 1947, the law has changed in this respect, but it takes time for legal changes to affect popular attitudes and behavior. There has been, however, a fairly steady increase in the disposition of people and groups in postwar Japan to challenge the correctness and propriety of governmental policies and actions. There are entire areas in which governmental action is either precluded or substantially inhibited by adverse public sentiment; these include control of labor disturbances, student riots, and political demonstrations in general and regulation of school curricula and of the content or style of the media. The contrast with prewar Japan in these respects is obvious.

The sphere of private rights and of freedom of individual and group decision and action has been greatly expanded in postwar Japan and, in practically all cases, at the direct cost of governmental rights and actions. Also, there has been an unprecedented upswing of new organizations and interest groups that have added greatly to the pluralist potentialities of Japanese society. This situation is still essentially in flux, and postwar Japan has yet to achieve even a reasonably stable compromise between the spheres of governmental rights and action and of private rights and actions. It is probably true, however, that no government has or, perhaps, ever will.

Nevertheless, the basic issues involved have yet to be faced in Japan, and the present circumstances represent more a concatenation of tactical and *ad hoc* decisions on both sides than a more reflective agreement on the respective roles of governmental and private initiative. The lack of such a philosophical base is probably one of the prices a society pays for the "importation"—though the term scarcely does justice to the circumstances of the Allied Occupation that did the actual importing—of so many of its basic political institutions.

Egalitarianism

The traditional Japanese conception of equality is closely related to their monistic views of government. Are men generally regarded as political equals, possessed of basically the same rights and responsibilities, or are some regarded as superior or more privileged than others? The answer is complex. Historically, of course, Japan had an unequal, or elitist, society. Relatively few people, all in the upper classes, had any political rights. Under these circumstances, political equality was a concept that simply did not occur to the Japanese. There was nothing in their experience and apparently little in their aspirations to sustain such a notion. After the Restoration, however, the idea of political equality was borrowed from Western writings by some of the early party leaders and political thinkers, but it was usually applied in a highly restrictive fashion to members of the "better" classes only. Gradually, however, the concept of equal political rights was expanded. Today, all adult Japanese subjects have substantially equal political and legal rights. This particular type of equality has, therefore, been established in Japan.

In political attitudes and behavior, however, vestiges of traditional elitism still survive. There is still a tendency among sizable segments of the population—particularly among farmers and the poorer and less-educated urban classes—to regard politics as beyond their sphere of concern. Their inclination is to look to someone more sophisticated and experienced than they are for advice on political decisions of all sorts. As a consequence, the politically influential person, often a respected local figure whose political advice is widely followed, is a common phenomenon in Japan. Such individuals, in effect, control sizable elements of the Japanese electorate on a highly personalized basis. This practice, of course, seriously detracts from the real significance of the equality that is legally guaranteed to all electors. This situation is scarcely unique to Japan.

One further aspect of egalitarianism in Japan that is traditional in origin but still widely encountered today is the practice of consensual decision making. In a group's search for consensus, not all participants may be equal, but each one is regarded as having the right to participate, to speak, and to be heard. This system of wide consultation does a great deal in practice to relax the hostilities and tensions that might otherwise beset a hierarchically organized society.

Personalism

There are two major types of political allegiance, programmatic and personal. Programmatic allegiance is based on considerations of policy; personal allegiance on affection for or loyalty to a particular political leader. In modern nontotalitarian states, both types are usually present to some extent. Classifying societies in terms of the degree to which their members' political allegiances are determined by programmatic or personal considerations, Japan would rank toward the personal end of such a scale. Until rather recently, political programs—reasonably intelligible and meaningful statements of policy—did not have much to do with determining the political attitudes and behavior of the vast majority of Japanese.

With the advent, after the war, of sizable Socialist and Communist parties that provided some measure of real policy choice to the voter, this situation was somewhat altered, and it seems probable that the policy or programmatic content of Japanese politics is still slowly increasing. On balance, however, the mass of the population seems more responsive to personal than to policy appeals and loyalties. Politics in Japan has always been a highly personalized process, in which individual, family, and clan relationships have been of predominant importance. The aspirant to political office normally joined *someone* rather than some cause or policy-oriented movement. In general, this continues to be the case—both within the seemingly more modern and program-oriented left-wing parties as well as in the more traditional conservative ones. As a consequence, the nation's prevailing image of politics is predominantly personal rather than programmatic.

Political Participation

In making an analysis of a people's political culture, it is important to know how they regard acts of political participation. Are such acts considered the exclusive prerogative of a particular social class, or does the average man regard himself as having some significant rights of participation in the political decision-making process? Again, for Japan the verdict must be mixed. The Japanese have traditionally looked upon politics as an activity reserved for the upper classes. In post-Restoration times, this restriction was somewhat abated by the grant of a very limited and sterilized suffrage in 1890 and by its subsequent expansions. It was not until 1925, however, that universal manhood suffrage was introduced. Because of the very limited authority of the elective lower house of the National Parliament, this did not really mark the advent of effective popular participation in politics. Particularly in the case of the peasantry, there seems to have been little effective assimilation of the concept of the vote as a means of participating in and controlling major public decisions. Government continued to be something that was done to such people by their superiors, rather than something done in any part by themselves. It is hard to accustom a people to the idea of effective political participation when they have for so long regarded politics as the exclusive domain of their superiors.

Again, defeat and occupation were crucial in the Japanese national experience. In 1945 just after the Allied Occupation got under way, adult women were enfranchised. The voting age was also reduced from twenty-five to twenty. Many more public offices were made elective, including both houses of the Parliament established by the Constitution of 1947. At the same time, the actual and potential power attaching to these new elective offices and bodies was enormously increased. In this sense, the acts of voting and political participation were given new and real meaning in Japan—not for the first time but certainly on an entirely new scale.

It has taken time for the Japanese voters to accustom themselves to these new institutions and enhanced possibilities of effective popular participation. They have gradually done so with results that are generally comparable to those of the "advanced" Western nations having democratic forms of government. Vestiges of the older practices and traditional relationships frequently appear in certain contexts, but basically the Japanese both vote and participate in interest groups to a degree comparable to that in the West. They also profess in polls and elsewhere to have a sense of their own political efficacy—that is, of the collective importance of their votes and of the influence of the electorate on government. A complete account would require a great deal of qualification of these generalities. For example, apathy and ignorance in matters political are no less common in Japan than elsewhere. Nevertheless, Japan now has a vastly more participant political system than was the case before the war, and in general, this degree of popular participation has produced consequences comparable to those that took place earlier in the West.

Political Violence

Peoples vary, too, in their conceptions of the role of violence—an extreme form of political participation—in domestic politics. In the United States, it is usually denied that violence has any proper place in politics, although developments in the civil rights and ethnic controversies of recent years cast some doubt upon this. Assassination, in particular, seems to most of us a particularly reprehensible political tactic. The Japanese political record is a strange mixture of docility and violence. Japan's history was strongly militarist in its values, of course, for many centuries prior to 1945. Violence and the use of armed force to accomplish political ends have a long and honorable tradition, which is by no means limited to pre-Restoration times. The phrase "government by assassination" gained broad currency in Japan as late as the 1930s and with considerable justification. Furthermore, it is hard to deny that a very large segment of the populace viewed with tolerance, if not active approbation, the allegedly patriotic assassinations of those days. Such approbation was even more probable if an assassin expiated his crime in the traditionally approved fashion of suicide, preferably by *seppuku* (that is, *hara-kiri*), or if he protested sincere and patriotic motives.

This type of sincerity is of the greatest importance in Japanese politics. If one acts sincerely, that is, through pure and personally disinterested motives, and if one is willing to pay an appropriate price for such action— such as suicide or execution in more serious cases—there is in Japan a traditional inclination to approve, or at least to "understand," both the actor and his act. It is hard to say that this attitude has completely disappeared in postwar Japan. The violence of numerous "demonstrations" by opposition elements both in the streets and on the floor of the National Diet would seem to indicate that it is still alive. "Sincerity" continues to excuse a great deal in Japanese politics.

Decision Making

Different peoples also have different views about how political decisions should be made, and these affect the form and operations of their political system. In the United States, for example, public issues are usually decided by an adversary process in which representatives of competing political groups present alternative proposals to the public or their representatives. A majority or plurality of the group then decides the issue, usually by voting, and the defeated minority is expected to acquiesce in the decision or, at least, to engage only in legally recognized forms of protest against it. The traditionally approved form of decision making in Japan is quite different from this. It operates by consensus, that is, by unanimous consent or a close approximation. When an issue is posed before a group for decision, the problem is discussed at length but in a nonadversary context. Care is taken to minimize open conflict or debate between the sponsors of alternative solutions. Instead, the group will talk around the issues until at last a compromise solution acceptable to all parties emerges. This is then formulated by some senior member as a proposal for action that is then accepted by the group by unanimous agreement.

In such a process, there is no open confrontation of groups or parties, no voting in the sense of distinguishing yeas from nays, and consequently, no open identification of majority and minority elements. The "face" of all participants is guarded, and no one is labeled as being opposed to the solution adopted and, thus, as having broken the harmony of the group or community. Obviously this is, in theory at least, quite different from the system in the United States that assumes the existence of majority and minority elements on any serious problem and tries to build a constructive role for the minority into the decision-making system. The Japanese system abhors the element of contention involved in the Western system, has no place for open minority elements, and prefers to proceed by compromises that permit at least the show of unanimity.

This traditional preference for decision by consensus has, of course, long been breaking down in Japan. Particularly in postwar times, the creation of a semi-British type of parliamentary structure and procedure has introduced open partisan debate, voting, and other adversary techniques into the National Diet. Still, behind the scenes at the national level and far more openly at the local level, it is surprising to see how strong the traditional preference for decision by consensus is. When the opposition forces in Japanese politics complain so bitterly against "tyranny by the majority," they are saying, in effect, that majorities, even when acting by a perfectly legal process, have no right to make a decision that ignores or overrides the views of the minority. The appeal is clearly to the traditional Japanese doctrine of decision by consensus. Not infrequently, aggrieved minorities resort to violence and rioting in support of such an interpretation.

Two other characteristics of the Japanese system of decision making are related to consensus. One is the Japanese preference for collective decisions rather than individual ones. The Japanese seem to feel much more comfortable with decisions that are the product of committees or groups than with those of a single leader. The difference is, of course, one of degree, but there is decidedly less emphasis on individual "leaders" and "leadership" as a means of decision making in Japanese culture than there is in the United States. Japan's political system is even more committee-ridden and group-oriented than is that in the United States. From this system flows the second characteristic. In Japanese politics, blurred compromises often take the place of forceful decisions. This again is true of many modern political systems, but the role of consensus and committees in Japan makes it particularly conspicuous there. Thus clear-cut decisions are difficult to achieve in Japan on any but the most urgent issues.

Tradition versus Change

All societies, including even the most tradition-bound, are constantly changing. It is therefore somewhat misleading to pose tradition versus change as if the former implied a rigidly static and unchanging community. Nevertheless, societies differ greatly in their rates of change, the areas and sequences in which change takes place, and most importantly, in their views of the possibility and desirability of change. In Japan, there has certainly been a spate of profound and basic changes during the last century and especially since its defeat in 1945. Japanese culture as a whole has definitely not been inhospitable to change. Despite this, however, a surprising amount of tradition survives in Japanese culture, perhaps more in attitudes, values, and behavior patterns than in institutions and more in the political sector of the society than elsewhere. A struggle has been going on since the end of the war between traditional and modernizing elements in the Japanese political system, and this has profoundly affected national attitudes toward the possibility of political change.

Postwar Japan has seen a rapid acceleration of change. In prewar politics, the balance of power normally lay with conservative and traditionally oriented forces that were opposed to any significant alterations in the basic institutions or power relationships of the Japanese political system. Postwar Japan has experienced a thorough shaking up of these earlier power relationships, and circumstances far more favorable to political change and innovation have appeared. Although segments of the population are still apathetic in their attitudes toward further political and social transformation, a process of fermentation has been set in motion. More and more Japanese have come in fragmentary but important ways to conceive of politics as amenable to some degree of popular influence and control, and in so doing they are reaching the conclusion that political change is a natural or, at least, possible goal of political life. This is quite a change from the political apathy, conservatism, and traditionalism that so successfully opposed political innovations in prewar times. It is also a very important fact about current Japanese politics.

The Japanese people are in the process of changing their minds about so simple but basic a proposition as the possibility and desirability of political change. It is still too early to say what the results will be. The developments may or may not in the long run be democratic or progressive, but the Japanese no longer regard the existing political situation as a part of the order of things, as fixed and unalterable. A more activist attitude has gained currency. Japan's political leaders are aware of this and have been adjusting their policies and actions accordingly, thus introducing profound changes in both the style and content of Japanese politics.

BIBLIOGRAPHY

ANDERSON, RONALD S., *Education in Japan: A Century of Modern Development.* Washington, D.C.: Department of Health, Education, and Welfare, 1975, 409 pp.

ARIMA, TATSUO, *The Failure of Freedom: A Portrait of Modern Japanese Intellectuals.* Cambridge, Mass.: Harvard University Press, 1969, 296 pp.

MARUYAMA, MASAO, *Thought and Behavior in Modern Japanese Politics.* London: Oxford University Press, 1963.

MORRIS, IVAN S., *Nationalism and the Right Wing in Japan: A Study of Postwar Trends.* London: Oxford University Press, 1960, 476 pp.

PATRICK, HUGH, ed., *Japanese Industrialization and Its Social Consequences.* Berkeley, Calif.: University of California Press, 1976, 505 pp.

RICHARDSON, BRADLEY M., *Political Culture of Japan.* Berkeley, Calif.: University of California Press, 1974, 271 pp.

Chapter *6*

Political Dynamics

INTEREST GROUPS

Between the foundations of the Japanese political system described in the last four chapters and its formal decision-making apparatus lies a gap that is bridged in practice by several types of political agents. In this and the following three chapters, four major types of such agents are distinguished: political interest groups, political parties, elections, and political leaders. In most societies, these serve as links between the population, which has certain historical, ecological, social, and ideological characteristics, and the official machinery of government. They bring the great welter of public interests and desires to the attention of the government, which is then called on to deal with these demands. These agents thus serve to transform interests and issues into political action—a role of the greatest political importance.

As societies grow more complex and modern in their social, economic, and political characteristics, the promotional and regulatory interests and activities of their governments also expand. More and more individual and group actions are significantly affected by the decisions and actions of legislators and bureaucrats, and as a consequence, public interest in and involvement with government increase. In democratic societies, the public's desire and ability to influence such governmental decisions also increase. One way in which this is done is through the popular election of legislators to represent the interests and desires of their constituents. However, this alone is not adequate under modern circumstances. No one legislator can even begin to represent effectively the variety of urban, rural, industrial, commercial, financial, labor, women's, local, national, social, cultural, and other interests represented by a geographically defined constituency of several hundred thousand people. To compensate for this deficiency, interest groups provide a second level of popular representation and a more precisely focused means of representing the views and interests of a particular group to political parties, legislators, administrators, or the general public. No society lacks some form of interest-group activity, but in premodern societies such activity is normally inclined to be more personal, episodic, private, local, and diffuse, whereas in modern societies it is more apt to be systematic, impersonal, continuous, public, and focused.

Types of Interest Groups

In postwar times the nature of Japanese interest groups has changed as rapidly as the country's economic structure. Such groups have long existed in Japan; for example, merchants' associations in the Tokugawa Period were large, well-organized, and influential agencies with effective access to the political authorities of the time. Similarly there were farm, business, and labor organizations in prewar Japan that were sometimes national in scope and that in varying degrees represented their members' interests before national and local governmental agencies. It was not until postwar times, especially the 1950s and 1960s, that Japanese society reached that point of saturation by interest group activities that characterizes the United States or the Western European nations.

The prevalence of interest groups differs somewhat in salience from one social sector to another. They are, for example, not as numerous in the countryside as in the major cities. They are not, however, absent or unimportant in rural Japan. Agricultural cooperatives with legal authorization have existed in Japan since 1900. The postwar legislation authorizing and encouraging such cooperatives dates from 1947. Local branches of the national Agricultural Cooperative Association exist in every farming village and area in Japan. Their membership includes practically all agricultural households, about twenty million individuals. Practically the entire membership shares a keen interest in such highly political matters as the level of government subsidies in support of the prices of agricultural commodities, official regulations governing the sale and price of agricultural land, governmental policy with respect to import tariffs or other means of protecting Japanese farmers from foreign competition, the price of fertilizers and agricultural machinery, and differences between standards of living in the cities and in the countryside.

These are all issues of great practical importance to the Japanese farmer. For example, the price of rice to the Japanese consumer is two to three times the price at which it could be purchased abroad and made available on the Japanese market. Rice is still a basic staple in the Japanese diet. Japan grows all the rice it consumes—more than it needs in fact—primarily because for many years the government has supported the grower's price at wholly unrealistic and steadily increasing levels. Every year when the special budgets are compiled there is a major confrontation between the Ministry of Finance, which wants to keep the budget as low and non-inflationary as possible, and the organized farming interests of Japan, which want and demand the highest possible price for the producers. Thousands of farmers descend upon Tokyo to demonstrate in the streets and represent their interests to Diet members from rural election districts, while millions sign petitions urging larger rice subsidies, usually in the name of raising rural living standards to levels more closely approximating those in the cities. The Diet delegation of the Liberal Democratic Party with a heavy quota of members from farming districts is, after a good deal of bitter internal debate, supportive of this cause, and as a result, the government eventually capitulates and agrees to a substantial rise in the subsidy and, thus, in the market price of rice. In the 1975 fiscal year, this program cost about $2.5 billion. The same is true with respect to the government's recent campaign to increase the degree of Japan's self-sufficiency in basic foodstuffs. On a value basis this ratio, 90 percent as recently as 1960, had sunk to 72 percent by 1972. The decline was even more abrupt in caloric terms; by the 1970s, Japan was importing about one-half of its food supply. In an attempt to improve these circumstances, the government is paying handsome subsidies to domestic producers of soybeans, wheat, and corn as well as rice. The consequence has been the creation of vast differences between the cost of the imported and home-grown products. For example, in the 1974 fiscal year, the price per bushel for imported soybeans was $7.35, for domestic $17.77; for imported wheat $5.17, for domestic $12.41; and for imported corn $3.92, for domestic $8.62. Similarly it has been exceedingly difficult politically for the Japanese government to carry out its international commitments to open the Japanese domestic market to foreign competition in such items as imported oranges or lemons because of strenuous and very effective opposition from organized Japanese citrus growers.

Japan does not, therefore, lack interest groups operating nationally in a well-organized, highly sophisticated, and heavily financed manner on behalf of rural interests. Such groups may not be as numerous or complex as those in the cities, but they have been very effective in obtaining what they want from a sympathetic and politically accessible party in power. Prominent among those associated with the Agricultural Cooperative Association (*Nokyo*) have been such bodies as the National Federation of Agricultural Cooperative Purchasing Associations (*Zenkoren*), the National Federation of Agricultural Cooperative Marketing Associations (*Zenhanren*), the National Federation of Agricultural Cooperative Mutual Insurance Associations (*Kyosairen*), and the Japanese Forestry Association (*Nichirinkyo*). All of these support political causes and are said to provide financial support for favorably disposed candidates for political office. In addition to the preceding semipublic associations, there are also several farmers' unions, usually of left-wing political persuasion, and other even more sharply focused agricultural interest groups such as the National Farmland League, which in 1965 succeeded after a prolonged struggle in extracting from a very reluctant government upwards of $402 million in compensatory payments for some

1.6 million ex-landlords whose farm lands had been confiscated in the course of the occupation-sponsored land reform program of the late 1940s.

It is in the cities, however, that systematically organized and active interest groups really come into their own. The Minami District of Osaka City is a fairly typical example. The district office issues annually a listing of organizations within its boundaries that in some way direct their activities toward the public. It took seventy closely printed pages in a recent edition simply to list the names and top officers of these groups and their branches. The entire city may in this way be viewed as a web of such groups organized along both geographical lines (for example, by shopping districts, streets, or blocks) and functional lines (by industry, trade, or specific interest). Particularly active in local, and sometimes in national, politics are such groups as the Red Cross Service Organization (*Nisseki Hoshidan*), the Federation of Housewives (*Shufuren*), the League of War Widows (*Mibojinkai*), and many others. A list of this sort could go on indefinitely.

The really major operators, however, are the representatives of organized business and organized labor. The Japanese refer to business interests collectively as the *Zaikai*, especially in a political context. The term translates literally as "financial world." The media impute enormous power, political as well as economic, to the *Zaikai*. Indeed they and others sometimes speak of "Japan, Incorporated" or describe the Japanese political system as a tripartite division of power among organized business, the Liberal Democratic Party, and the professional bureaucracy. In more specific terms then, who or what interests comprise the *Zaikai*? Most often the reference is to a vast and somewhat amorphous collectivity, the most conspicuous leaders of which freely translate as the "Big Four Economic Groups." These are the Federation of Economic Organizations (*Keidanren*), the Committee for Economic Development (*Keizai Doyukai*), the Federation of Employers' Organizations (*Nikkeiren*), and the Japan Chamber of Commerce (*Nissho*).

The Federation of Economic Organizations is the most important and powerful of these groups. It is the spokesman for really big business in Japan; its membership is limited to about seven hundred of the country's largest corporations and upwards of one hundred industrial, financial, and commercial associations of business interests. Its function is to provide a mechanism for big business to discuss its common concerns, seek a consensus, and represent its views to the government, political parties, bureaucracy, and the general public. It also frequently represents and speaks for Japanese business interests abroad. The federation has routine and frequent communication with the Japanese government in its spheres of concern, particularly with the Ministry of International Trade and Industry. It systematically attempts to influence governmental policies along the lines it favors. It was very influential, for example, in the selection of Ikeda Hayato as Prime Minister in 1960. On the other hand, it failed in its very serious effort to obtain this post for Fukuda Takeo in 1972 when Tanaka Kakuei won the party presidency and hence the premiership. Thus, the federation is influential but within limits more exigent than are usually thought to be the case. It speaks only for big business; it can do that only on occasions when it can achieve consensus within that community—often a difficult or impossible task; and normally its influence is limited to economic matters in a fairly narrow sense of that term. Politically, the federation is a strong, but not very satisfied, supporter of the Liberal Democratic Party. Its members supply the bulk of the party's campaign and operating funds. Given the economic persuasions of the opposition parties, this is hardly surprising. For years the federation has been urging internal party reforms, especially an end to factionalism, upon the leaders of the Liberal Democratic Party. To date, it has been unsuccessful in this effort.

The Committee for Economic Development, named after its American counterpart, was originally formed by a group of younger business leaders in Japan who were interested in studying and in adapting for use in Japan modern managerial techniques developed abroad. They were relatively liberal politically and enjoyed a reputation as "Young Turks." The committee has been active in Japanese politics and has rather consistently pressed for reforms within the Liberal Democratic Party and in the system of financing political campaigns. It is neither as prestigious nor as influential as the Federation of Economic Organizations.

The Federation of Employer's Organizations concentrates almost exclusively on problems of labor relations viewed from management's standpoint and includes over sixty thousand member firms. The Japan Chamber of Commerce is the overall representative of both large and small business in Japan and has a membership of about two hundred fifty thousand firms. Among so diffuse a membership, disagreements on policy are numerous, and an effective consensus is difficult to achieve. When it can agree on a policy, the chamber lobbies with government on its members' behalf. A more active and effective spokesman for small business interests exists, however, in the Federation of Medium and Small Enterprises. In general, however, small business interests are neither as well represented nor as influential in Japan as those of big business.

Some background on organized labor and interest group activities is helpful. The most recent figures place the overall size of the Japanese labor force at about fifty-three million, with about forty-five million in secondary and tertiary industries. Of these forty-five million, about twelve million (27 percent) belong to labor unions. This fraction has changed very little in recent years. By American standards the unions involved are somewhat unusual. They are organized not along craft or industrial lines but on the basis of enterprises; that is, a given union normally consists of workers in a particular plant, mine, or factory except for higher management. Also, enterprise unions do not usually include all workers at such plants but only that fraction, often about 35 percent at larger plants, that enjoys the status of permanent or lifetime employees. The other or untenured employees are not usually members of the local enterprise union. The situation is one that ordinarily gives rise to divided loyalties on an employee's part between the firm and his union. This is enhanced by the paternalism of Japanese business in general, the absence of labor mobility, and the extent to which the employee comes to perceive his own long-term economic and social interests as identified with the continued prosperity of his employer. Enterprise unions are aggregated into national unions based either on common corporate ownership, such as the Sumitomo Metal Workers' Union, or a shared profession, such as the Japan Teachers' Union. A substantial number of these national unions also participate in still larger national federations or councils of unions of which the most important are the General Council of Japanese Trade Unions *(Sohyo)*, the Japanese Confederation of Labor *(Domei)*, the Federation of Independent Unions *(Churitsuroren)*, and the National Federation of Industrial Organizations *(Shinsanbetsu)*. At present these four federations have a membership totaling just over eight million, that is, about 67 percent of all unionized labor or about 15 percent of the total Japanese labor force.

The largest, most important, and most politically active of these federations is the General Council of Japanese Trade Unions *(Sohyo)*, with a membership of about twenty-two thousand unions and 4.3 million individual members. Well over half the members belong to unions of governmental employees, such as the All-Japan Union of Prefectural and Municipal Workers and the Japan Teachers' Union, or of employees of semigovernmental corporations, such as the National Railway Workers and the Joint Council of Telecommunications Workers. The General Council is a militant and very active force in Japanese politics. It is the principal source of organized popular support for the Japan Socialist Party. Its political program is forthrightly and ardently socialist. Its foreign policy stance has been neutralist and strongly opposed to the Security Alliance with the United States and to any measures of rearmament by Japan. Many of its members work for the government, and thus, it is inclined to use political means for the accomplishment of its goals, which notably include the right of government employees to strike. The General Council is also the chief organizer of an annual event known in Japanese as the *shunto* or Spring Struggle. At a set time each spring, practically all of unionized labor in Japan joins forces to demonstrate and bring pressure on both private employers and the government to raise their wages. These efforts have been generally successful and sometimes spectacularly so, especially during the years when the annual rate of inflation in the Japanese economy was very high. In 1974, for example, the average raise for unionized labor was almost 30 percent, and in 1975, about 20 percent. Recession reduced this to 8 or 9 percent by 1976, however. Given the effects of inflation, the real gains of labor were substantially less than these nominal percentages would indicate.

The second largest national federation of Japanese labor unions is the Japanese Confederation of Labor *(Domei)*. It is composed of some eleven thousand six hundred unions and about 2.2 million members, that is, about 19 percent of the total membership of Japanese unions. This membership is drawn almost entirely from private industry, particularly manufacturing, transport and communications, and textiles. The confederation is much less political than *Sohyo*, the General Council of Japanese Trade Unions, and more active in the promotion of the economic interests of organized labor. It has, however, taken an official stand as the principal supporter of the Democratic Socialist Party.

There are two other national federations of unions as well. The first is the

Federation of Independent Unions *(Churitsuroren)* that has a membership of about thirty-eight hundred unions and 1.3 million individuals, about 11 percent of the total. The second is the National Federation of Industrial Organizations *(Shinsanbetsu),* a much smaller organization with only two hundred unions and about seventy thousand members. Neither of these has a formal association with a particular political party, although in general both oppose the ruling party on many issues. In addition to these four national federations of unions, there are a sizable number of unaffiliated unions and smaller groupings that collectively have almost four million members.

Despite the explicit and exclusive commitments of *Sohyo* and *Domei* to the support of the Japan Socialist and the Democratic Socialist parties respectively, it would be a serious mistake to assume that their federations effectively control the votes of all, or perhaps even a majority, of their members. Available data are not conclusive but suggest that large numbers of union members vote for conservative candidates or are apathetic and frequently do not vote at all in national elections. In spite of such deviations from official policy, however, these federations routinely provide the strongest and most important organized political support for these two opposition parties.

While big business and big labor are undoubtedly the largest, most conspicuous, and politically active interest groups in Japan, there are a variety of other organized interests that also merit notice. Practically all professions have national organizations to represent their interests. The medical profession, for example, is tightly and very effectively organized for the accomplishment of political goals. About three-fourths of the country's medical practitioners belong to the Japan Doctors' Association. Japan has a national health care system that regulates the practice of medicine in a number of ways that affect the average doctor, including setting permissible fees for medical services under the plan. The association has been extremely active in its endeavors to induce the Ministry of Health and the government to raise these fees, at one time going so far as to organize a one-day nationwide strike by doctors.

Women's interests receive political representation in Japan through associations such as the Housewives' Association, the Japan Mothers' Conference, the All-Japan Federation of Local Women's Organizations, and the women's organizations maintained by all of the major political parties. The Housewives' Association has been especially active and moderately effective in a number of local contexts relating to educational and consumer issues and sometimes on national issues of pacificism and disarmament as well. In formal representational terms, however, women have not done as well. In the first postwar general election, thirty-nine women were elected to the House of Representatives. Their numbers have steadily declined since then to six in the 1976 election. They have done somewhat, but not much, better in the upper house. The same trend may be seen in town and village elections, although there have been some increases in the female membership of assemblies at the prefectural and large city levels.

The most conspicuous recent interest groups have been what are collectively called "residents' movements" *(jumin undo)*. These usually focus on environmental, consumer, or civic issues. Common examples are antipollution movements, boycotts of color television sets as a protest against overpricing and of foods containing cyclamates on health grounds, or mass demonstrations against industries that have contaminated local water supplies or fishing grounds. The degree of air pollution in major Japanese cities is impressive even by American standards. Large numbers of citizens have become actively and effectively concerned about it, and partially as a result of this pressure, the government has been induced to develop and enforce an entire program of ameliorative measures that are gradually making impressive inroads on this massive problem.

Local governmental interests in Japan have also found it useful to organize nationally in order to represent their collective interests as effectively as possible to various branches of the national government. The principal interest involved, of course, is a massive annual effort to increase the share of the national revenues allocated to local governments. The six associations of this sort are the National Association of Prefectural Governors, National Association of Chairmen of Prefectural Assemblies, National Association of City Mayors, National Association of Chairmen of City Assemblies, National Association of Town and Village Mayors, and National Association of Chairmen of Town and Village Assemblies. All of these maintain permanent representation in Tokyo.

Interest Groups in Politics

Japan thus has a large and increasing complement of interest groups. Our knowledge of their structure and activities is incomplete, but the following generalizations might be ventured. At both the national and local levels, the majority of them seem to be involved in politics. Their involvement is of at least three different types. The first is electoral in nature, stemming from the fact that the secret of success at the polls lies in skillfully appealing to units or blocks of voters and in garnering adequate financial support. To the practical politician, an interest group represents primarily a potential and accessible bloc of votes plus a source of campaign contributions. Many interest groups are not loath to play such a political role for selected politicians in return for preferred access to his or her attention and influence once he or she is in office. In one arena or another, then, the average Japanese interest group does support candidates for election to local or national office.

The general effectiveness of such support is not known, but in particular cases it is quite obvious that certain members of the National Diet owe their seats almost entirely to the support of certain interest groups. One study, for example, concluded that 59 of the 467 members elected to the lower house in 1963 were there primarily as the representatives of particular unions—14 for *Nikkyoso* (the Japan Teachers' Union) alone. This practice, of course, represents an extreme variant of the more normal situation in which a given interest group is simply one of many groups supporting a particular candidate. In the case of these labor unions, they constitute a sort of ad hoc political party and support their own candidates for office.

A second type of action by interest groups is directed toward particular political figures, primarily high-level administrators. In Japan, the relations between the ministries and high administrative offices of the national government and their organized public clienteles are apt to be very close, for example, between the Ministry of Agriculture and Forestry and the organized farm groups throughout Japan or between the Ministry of International Trade and Industry and the organized business groups that it ostensibly regulates. In fact, the ministry, to simplify its administrative relationships with such clientele groups, is sometimes responsible for their establishment in organized form. The resultant relationship is complex. Once in existence, such an organization performs the functions of a political interest or pressure group, but its representations are made to a group of officials in Tokyo with whom it maintains the closest and most cordial of relationships. This is particularly true of interest groups of a business, agricultural, technical, or professional nature. Labor unions and left-wing affiliated interest groups are apt to have more difficult problems of access.

One aspect of the relations between government and business in Japan that has attracted much attention and criticism is the common practice of firms providing postretirement employment for former bureaucrats. A study by Professor Chalmers Johnson describes the system in some detail.[1] Members of the Japanese higher bureaucracy uniformly retire at a very early age—between fifty and fifty-five. For most this creates the need of further employment, since pension arrangements are inadequate. Those seeking such employment normally have four possibilities: (1) a position in a particular private profit-making enterprise (movement by a bureaucrat to such a position is called *amakudari* or "descent from heaven"); (2) employment by a public corporation or enterprise such as the Japan Monopoly Corporation, the Japan Highway Public Corporation, or the Japan Housing Corporation (known as *yokosuberi* or "sideslipping"); (3) a position with one of the many national trade associations that represent various Japanese industries, such as the Iron and Steel Federation of Japan or the Petroleum League of Japan; or (4) running for election to the National Diet, usually the House of Councilors in the national constituency (called *chii riyo* or "position exploitation"). Only the first of these transitions is regulated by the Japanese equivalent of conflict-of-interest laws, but these laws are in practice very casually interpreted and almost never enforced. As a consequence, "colonization" of private and semipublic enterprises by former bureaucrats of high rank is very common. Between 1970 and 1973, for example, there was an average of 179 *amakudari* transfers each year. Such movements to important positions in private business are most easily managed by career bureaucrats from those ministries having important regulatory and licensing functions with respect to particular businesses—for example, the Ministry of Finance, Ministry of International Trade and Industry, Ministry of Construction,

---

[1] Chalmers Johnson, "The Reemployment of Retired Government Bureaucrats in Japanese Big Business," *Asian Survey*, vol. XIV, no. 11 (November 1974), 953–65.

Ministry of Agriculture and Forestry, Ministry of Transportation, and National Tax Agency. In general, the higher the bureaucrat's preretirement post, the easier the transfer and the more important and lucrative the new position is apt to be. Former vice-ministers (the highest post in the professional civil service) do best of all. Johnson's list of examples of the postretirement positions of former vice-ministers of the Ministry of International Trade and Industry is particularly impressive in this respect. Their new jobs included the presidency of the New Japan Steel Corporation (Japan's largest corporation), the Toshiba Electric Company (ninth largest), and the Japan Petrochemical Company, the vice-presidency of the Arabian Oil Company, and executive directorships in the Tokyo Electric Power Company and Nippon Kokan.

There is a great deal of debate in Japan over the consequences of this practice. In general the reputation of Japan's higher civil service for honesty and integrity in office is very good, and it seems quite doubtful that much outright corruption or malfeasance in office results. This conclusion is reinforced by the fact that individuals do not normally solicit the positions in private enterprise to which they move. This is done in their behalf by the chief of the secretariat of their ministry as a means of facilitating early retirements and is a normal aspect of the Japanese personnel management system. There can be no doubt, however, that the inside knowledge and personal relationships of these ex-bureaucrats are of practical value to their new employers. It is probably also true that their presence in important positions in private industry makes it easier for the government—their own successors and juniors in high ministerial offices—to exercise what the Japanese call "administrative guidance" over the business policies and practices of major Japanese firms and industries. Such a system, of course, guarantees ready and preferred access of business viewpoints to the appropriate governmental authorities and vice versa. Finally, it should be noted that the practice of *amakudari* may well be on the wane, partly because of increasing resistance by the normal staff of some, but not all, private firms to having government interlopers brought in over their heads. This does not apply, however, to the allied practice of *yokosuberi* in which the enterprises concerned are really supported by public funds and, in some measure, are intended as a means of taking care of the employment needs of retired bureaucrats.

A third type of political action by Japanese interest groups takes the form of direct public pressure. There are traditional antecedents for this; indeed, in some instances *seppuku*, or ritual suicide, was one such form of protest. The recent florescence of a variety of "citizens' movements" have given new shape and popularity to direct action by interest groups. These take the form of group-sponsored boycotts of certain products, large public demonstrations in front of the National Diet, the mobilization of public sentiment against pollution and the responsible industries, or sometimes violent obstruction of unpopular projects.

The political targets of most Japanese interest groups have traditionally been the government administration rather than the legislature. Executives and bureaucrats, rather than legislators, have made most of the important decisions in Japanese politics and administration, or if they have not made them, they have at least interpreted and applied them, which is apt to be of equal importance. Since the war, the political role of the House of Representatives has gradually increased in importance. Interest groups are perhaps paying greater attention to the legislature and its committees, but their stress remains heavily on the higher bureaucracy. Members of the legislature still seem to serve primarily as intermediaries between interest-group representatives from their constituencies and high officials of the national government and, perhaps to some degree, as a means of bringing favorable budgetary or other pressures to bear on such officials.

Extensive or reliable information about the predominant style of Japanese interest-group activities before bureaucrats and legislators is not available. The press is largely convinced that in many cases the lobbies depend heavily on corrupt and illegal techniques. Public trials and investigations have demonstrated the truth of such claims in specific cases, but there is not enough evidence to generalize about more serious forms of bribery and corruption. Quite obviously, the minor corruptions represented by *geisha* parties, elegant meals, and expensive entertainment for important individuals flourish in Tokyo as in other capitals. Equally obvious, and perhaps more serious, is the practice of providing positions for retired bureaucrats. There does seem to be a tendency, however, for some of the major Japanese interest groups to place increasing emphasis on "educational materials" and appeals for broad popular support. These probably forecast a shift away from the older and more personalized techniques of influence.

Political interest groups have definitely established a firm and expanding role for themselves in the Japanese political system. On balance, they have almost certainly enabled many interests to have more effective representation in the government than was previously the case. In this sense, they have probably advanced, if largely inadvertently, the cause of more popular and responsible government in Japan. Indeed, the degree to which they flourish today is one of the basic factors distinguishing the postwar from the prewar political scene in Japan. More needs to be done, however, to give all interest groups equal access to the government; at present some groups undoubtedly get preferential treatment. To a certain degree this is inevitable in a party system of government, but if some interest groups are consistently denied access to the government, the long-term political consequences might be very serious.

BIBLIOGRAPHY

COOK, ALICE H., *An Introduction to Japanese Trade Unionism.* Ithaca, N.Y.: Cornell University Press, 1966, 216 pp.

HARARI, EHUD. *The Politics of Labor Legislation in Japan: National-International*

Interaction. Berkeley, Calif.: University of California Press, 1973, 221 pp.

HEIDENHEIMER, ARNOLD J., ET AL., *Business Associations and the Financing of Political Parties: A Comparative Study of the Evaluation of Practices in Germany, Norway, and Japan.* The Hague: Martinus Nijhoff, 1968, 247 pp.

KRAUSS, ELLIS S., *Japanese Radicals Revisited: Student Protest in Postwar Japan.* Berkeley, Calif.: University of California Press, 1974, 192 pp.

STESLICKE, WILLIAM E., *Doctors in Politics.* New York: Praeger Publishers, 1973, 302 pp.

YANAGA, CHITOSHI, *Big Business in Japanese Politics.* New Haven, Conn.: Yale University Press, 1968, 371 pp.

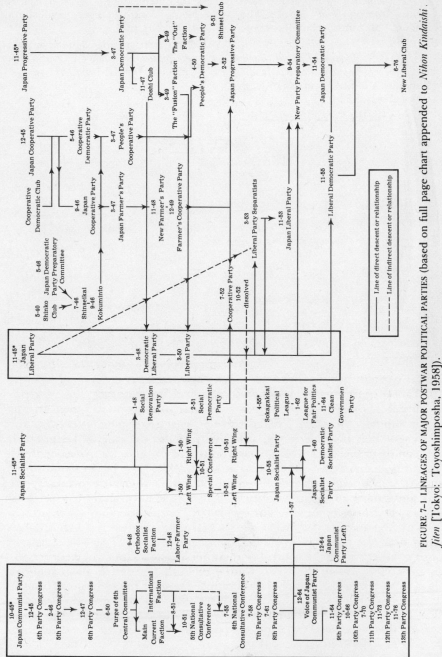

FIGURE 7–1 LINEAGES OF MAJOR POSTWAR POLITICAL PARTIES (based on full page chart appended to *Nihon Kindaishi Jiten* [Tokyo: Toyoshimposha, 1958]).
*Numbers indicate date of party's establishment, that is, 10–45 is October 1945.

Chapter *7*

Political Dynamics

PARTIES

Political parties are among the most conspicuous of political agents or actors. They are primarily instruments for the mobilization of political support and votes and for choosing among aspirants for public office. Parties are not a postwar innovation in Japan. In one form or another, they have existed since at least 1874. The antecedents of the present conservative party, the *Jiyuminshuto,* or Liberal Democratic Party, can be traced back to the early 1880s and those of the *Nihon Shakaito,* or Japan Socialist Party, go back to at least 1925. The Japan Communist Party, *Nihon Kyosanto,* was established in 1922. It is, therefore, primarily the status and power of Japan's political parties that have altered in postwar times. From groups competing for the control of membership in the prewar House of Representatives that possessed largely negative and carefully restricted political power, they have advanced since 1947 to the status of groups competing for the control of membership in a House of Representatives that has become the basic source of both legislative and executive authority in a new and more democratic system of national government. The difference is of vital importance. The role and importance of Japan's political parties have fluctuated with the role and importance of the lower house of the National Diet. The postwar development of these political parties is described in figure 7-1.

This discussion of the organization, programs, and general characteristics of Japan's political parties is limited to the six parties that are most important at present—the Liberal Democratic, New Liberal Club, Socialist, Democratic Socialist, Communist, and Clean Government parties. Although it is not certain how long a given constellation of parties will survive the constant pressures for fission and reconstitution, these six parties represent the major types of organization, programmatic appeals, support patterns, financing, and leadership that have characterized Japan's postwar political parties.

The Liberal Democratic Party (*Jiyuminshuto* or LDP)

In one form or another, the Liberal Democratic Party or its predecessors have ruled Japan since the inauguration of the new Constitution in 1947. Through its various factions it is a lineal descendant of the prewar *Seiyukai* and *Minseito* parties that—also in various guises—trace their histories back to the early 1880s and that in time gradually came to play an influential, though never a dominant, role in prewar Japanese politics. Since 1947 there has been only one insignificant exception to the unbroken record of Liberal Democratic Party rule. This occurred during a nine-month interim from May 1947 to March 1948 when a socialist, Katayama Tetsu, held the prime ministership. The illusion of Socialist Party rule created by this development was meaningless, however, since the government was based upon a very tenuous coalition with a conservative party that effectively negated any possibilities of socialist innovation.

The Liberal Democratic Party emerged in its present form in November 1955 as a result of an amalgamation of the Liberal and Japan Democratic parties. The merger has aptly been described as a shotgun marriage caused more by the imperatives of electoral strategy than by any more spontaneous or constructive initiatives within the two conservative parties. The hitherto separate left and right wings of the Japan Socialist Party had in the preceding month merged into a combined party, and the conservatives anticipated highly adverse consequences at the polls if they were to remain divided in the face of a combined socialist opposition.

Against this background it is useful to note the pre–1955 antecedents of the Liberal Democratic Party as depicted in figure 7–1. Note particularly the number, variety, and complex interrelationships of the lineages involved. This historical diversity has contemporary relevance in terms of the pronounced internal disunity of the party today. Perhaps its most salient characteristic is the prominence and importance of factions within the party. Figure 7–1 demonstrates clearly that there is nothing new about this phenomenon. If one thinks of Japanese political parties as arrayed on a spectrum that in very crude and approximate terms runs from left-wing to right-wing political views and ideologies—which is the way that practically all Japanese political commentators view them—or, alternatively and more usefully, as divided into the "ins" and the "outs," then that portion of the spectrum that would be designated respectively as the "conservative" (versus the "progressives") or the "party in power" (versus the "opposition") has habitually been fragmented and in internal disarray. This was true before World War II as well as since. Incidentally, it is at least equally true of the "progressives" or "opposition." The professional practice of politics in Japan is highly personalized; it functions primarily through individual personal relationships of very substantial value and importance to those involved and is aggregated for operational purposes into hierarchically structured and relatively small and cohesive groups. This is true to such an extent for the Liberal Democratic Party that some commentators regard it as more a coalition of parties than as a single party composed of a number of factions. This is probably an overstatement.

Within the party, factions are not stable but, viewed over their history, undergoing a continuous process of change. Defining a faction as an hierarchically structured element of a political party composed of Diet members united for the sake of advancing their own political careers, a shared ideology, or some political program, it follows in practice that as factional leaders die or lose influence and fund-raising capacity, as the balance of power within the party shifts, or as the times and salient issues change, the individual factions flourish, attenuate, split, or combine. Old factions die, and new ones are born.

Within the Liberal Democratic Party, factions differ in many respects. For example, their numbers at any given time have varied widely from eight to as many as twelve or thirteen. In size an individual faction may range from as few as four members to as many as sixty or seventy. All are elected members of either the lower or upper houses of the National Diet. Not all Diet members belong to a faction, although the great majority of them do. Some factions, especially the larger ones, draw members from both houses, and others from only one. Each faction is led by a prominent, influential, and usually senior politician who normally aspires to and considers himself an active candidate for the party's presidency and, hence, for the prime ministership—in the long run if not in the short. Leadership within a faction is usually achieved by varying combinations of political skill and influence, seniority, and connections in the business world that insure a reliable source of large-scale funding for the insatiable needs of the faction and all its members. Occasionally great personal or family wealth is a factor as well. Even by American standards, the costs of supporting a major faction for campaign and everyday purposes is enormous. In the Liberal Democratic Party, factions have usually been based on considerations of individual career advantage and personal ties and loyalties rather than on principle or policy. More recently, however, there have been some signs of an increasing concern with issues and policies that are occasionally backed by entire factions, although they have more often given rise to interest or pressure blocs whose membership cuts across factional lines.

Under these circumstances the balance of power within the party—and, consequently, the immediate explanation of most party appointments and, to a lesser degree, policies—is determined primarily by shifting combinations and agreements among the leaders of these factions. It normally takes a common front among an effective majority of them to carry any important decision. As a result, their leaders are very important figures. Four or five of them in combination can normally make or break a Cabinet. Thus, a successful party president and prime minister must accommodate himself to their advice and wishes; party leadership is really more a collegial than an individual matter; and most major decisions taken by the party on issues of policy or appointment represent rather complicated compromises. On most important questions, a sizable and organized element within the Liberal Democratic Party is certain to be actively dissatisfied with prevailing party policy on grounds of intraparty gamesmanship, if not on principle or policy. Such opposition, although it may occasionally abstain or absent itself from the Diet, is seldom carried so far as to produce a vote against the party line. This might lead to the disintegration of the party that, at present, only a few really seem to desire. The existence of a constant and organized minority does serve to keep the party in a volatile and uncertain state. Decisive or durable individual leadership over a period of time is very difficult under these circumstances.

These factors also give rise to what is in practice one of the most important structural aspects of the Liberal Democratic Party; these are two constellations of factions known as the mainstream and antimainstream groups. These initially came into being in connection with the election of a party president who, because the Liberal Democrats have been the majority party, automatically has become prime minister of Japan. In order to become party president, a particular factional leader must put together by complex means a coalition of factions commanding a majority vote in party conferences held, since 1971, every three years (instead of every two years as had formerly been the case). This winning coalition is called the mainstream group, and its opponents the antimainstream group. The choice ministerial posts in the Cabinet and a wide and intricate series of other patronage-type rewards within the gift of the prime minister then accrue to the leaders and senior members of the factions comprising the mainstream group. Becoming a prominent member of such a winning coalition is thus the path to political advancement. In order to keep a necessary minimum of peace and order within the party, however, some less desirable posts and patronage are reserved for leading members of the antimainstream group. Furthermore, the composition of the mainstream group is not necessarily stable. If the particular party president and prime minister remains in power for any significant length of time—and he normally does—the component factions of the mainstream group are usually reconstituted one or more times.

Despite its great strength at the polls, the Liberal Democratic Party is not a truly mass membership organization. Although possessed of a national apparatus that looks most impressive on an organization chart, the party's formal membership is relatively small. In November 1975, for example, it claimed a total registered membership of 1,157,811. Of these, however, only 345,575 were actually dues-paying members. Indeed, at the local level formal party membership is a vague and not too meaningful category. Despite this, the party maintains branch organizations in every prefectural capital and in many cities, towns, and villages. Most of these seem in practice, however, to be more closely identified with the political fortunes of particular local Liberal Democratic politicians and Diet members than with those of the party as a whole.

The heart and head of the Liberal Democratic organization are in Tokyo, where the vast majority of the party's business is transacted. In fact, for purposes of most policy decisions and day-to-day business, the party is almost exclusively controlled by its higher membership normally resident in Tokyo. The party's central organization is complex. Ultimate authority in a formal sense is wielded by a party congress composed exclusively of professional political leaders. The congress meets annually in Tokyo and every third year selects a party president, the most eminent and powerful of party posts. As long as the Liberal Democrats are the majority party, their president almost automatically becomes prime minister of Japan. Under normal circumstances a party president may be reelected for a second three-year term. It would, however, take a two-thirds vote by all of the party's Diet members—a most improbable event—to authorize a third term. The group that participates in the annual party congresses is currently limited to all Liberal Democrats from both houses of the National Diet, four representatives from each of the party's forty-seven prefectural branch offices, and one representative from each prefectural party youth group and women's group. Despite its ostensibly plenary authority, the actual importance of party conferences is not great. They largely legitimize decisions reached earlier by the party leadership.

In addition to its annual congresses, the Liberal Democratic Party has an elaborate hierarchy of party posts and functionaries. Most important of these after the president are the vice-president and the secretary-general. The secretary-general is a senior party leader usually from the president's own faction but sometimes from an allied mainstream faction. Of great importance also are the thirty-member Executive Committee and the Policy Affairs Research Council and their chairmen. The former is responsible for overall party management and major policy decisions, while the latter researches and recommends legislative policy and stands, operating through a variety of subcommittees. All members of both groups are Diet members, predominantly from the lower house. In addition to these bodies, there are a number of other formal party committees on organization, finance, public relations, and so on and one informal group known as the Leaders' Meeting centering about the president, the secretary-general, and the chairmen of the Executive Committee and the Policy Affairs Research Council.

Through this organizational apparatus and its adjunct committees, the party determines its policies and attempts to translate them into legislative actions through its delegations in the National Diet. Once agreement has been reached within party circles, the discipline imposed on its members in the Diet is very strict. Voting conformance is practically automatic, under pain of expulsion from the party.

The leadership of the Liberal Democratic Party—as represented by its members holding seats in the lower house of the National Diet—may also be analyzed in terms of the members' social and professional backgrounds. An official survey of the membership of the House of Representatives that sat from 1972 to 1976 yields the following information that is fairly typical for recent years. Of the 271 successful Liberal Democratic candidates, only

2 were women (0.7 percent). There were 242 (89 percent) incumbents, while another 3 (1 percent) were former Diet members temporarily out of office at the time of the 1972 general election. Thus only twenty-six (10 percent) of the Liberal Democratic delegation were really new candidates —what the Japanese call "new faces." The group was, therefore, highly professional; in fact, they had on the average already served five and one-half terms in previous Diets. Their average age was about fifty-seven, and 75 percent were university graduates. Most (92 percent) were born in the prefecture in which they ran for office. In terms of career backgrounds, the three most numerous categories represented were company executives, former members of prefectural or local assemblies (professional party politicians), and former bureaucrats in the national service. In at least thirteen cases they were sons or sons-in-law who had run successfully for seats previously held by their fathers or fathers-in-law, thus establishing a sort of dynastic effect.

Related to personal characteristics are the districts from which these successful candidates were returned and their chief political characteristics. In earlier postwar times, the Liberal Democratic Party was often described as rural- rather than urban-based. This claim, while always an exaggeration, had some substance in the sense that the most faithful and reliable sources of Liberal Democratic strength were found in the countryside. As the demographic characteristics of postwar Japan changed steadily from rural to predominantly urban, however, some changes had to occur in the support characteristics of the Liberal Democratic Party if it were to remain in power. These shifts may be viewed in several ways. One is to divide Japan's 130 electoral districts into four categories, metropolitan, urban, semirural, and rural, and to analyze the distribution of Liberal Democratic support at the polls in these terms. Professor J. A. A. Stockwin has made a very interesting calculation on this basis.[1] He showed the following on the basis of the general elections of 1958, 1967, and 1972: (1) Liberal Democratic plus independent (concealed Liberal Democratic) support in metropolitan electoral districts has declined steadily from 48.4 percent to 32.1 percent of the total vote; (2) in urban districts the decline has been much less sharp, from 66 percent to 56.8 percent; (3) in semirural districts it has fallen from 65 percent to 61.7 percent; and (4) finally, in rural districts it has risen from 67.4 to 70.8 percent.

An official Japanese source performing the same sort of calculation for only the 1969 and 1972 general elections classified election districts by the percentage of their labor force engaged in primary industries (farming, fishing, and forestry): I = less than 10 percent, II = 10–19 percent, III = 20–29 percent, IV = 30–39 percent, and V = more than 40 percent. The stratification involved is quite similar to Professor Stockwin's and ranges, of course, from most urban (I) to most rural (V). The overall findings are in general similar. They show a slight decrease of Liberal Democratic support from 31 to 30 percent of the vote in the most urban areas, while Liberal

[1] J. A. A. Stockwin, *Japan: Divided Politics in a Growth Economy* (New York: Norton, 1975), p. 100. At the time of Stockwin's writing there were only 124 electoral districts.

Democratic strength remains stable at 61 percent of the vote in the most rural areas.[2]

The conclusions are obvious. In these two general elections the Liberal Democratic Party has derived an average of 32.5 percent of its seats from rural areas, 32 percent from urban areas, 26 percent from semirural areas, and only 9.5 percent from metropolitan areas. In a society characterized by heavy urban growth at the expense of the countryside and by a proliferation of metropolitan areas, the demographic grounds for Liberal Democratic concern over their ability to remain the majority party clearly emerge. It is equally apparent, however, that the Liberal Democratic Party is by no means a rural-based party. It is also very strong—especially versus any single opposition party—in urban and semirural areas, and it still controls a majority of the seats in all categories except the metropolitan, where it controls about one-third. Although steadily losing popular support by small decrements in recent elections, the Liberal Democratic Party is still a formidable force.

The almost complete absence of reliable information about party finances in Japan does not inhibit public discussion of them, usually in rather sensational terms. The general assumption about the Liberal Democratic Party is that a very substantial measure of control over its policies is wielded by its financial supporters and that these are to be found almost exclusively in the ranks of big business, particularly among the *zaikai,* or great cartels of Japan. Few persons familiar with Japanese politics would deny that the party's connections with big business are very close or that the bulk of its support comes from business firms and associations. The details of this relationship and the extent of the influence or control over party policies by business interests are very vague and imprecise. The average commentary on the subject tends to overestimate the unity of the political views and programs of "big business" and, consequently, to oversimplify the Liberal Democratic Party's relationship to business.

Party politics, particularly election campaigns, are still very expensive in Japan as elsewhere. A vague and understated idea of the size of the funds involved can be gained from the official reports of political contributions that the parties are required by law to file with the Local Autonomy Ministry. Few would vouch for their literal accuracy, however, and the most recent figures are not readily available. An official survey by the Ministry of Home Affairs shows that in 1975 the Liberal Democratic Party reported an income of ¥18.8 billion ($62.9 million), and this was not an election year. The *Mainichi* newspaper estimated Liberal Democratic election expenditures for the July 1974 House of Councilors election at a total of ¥41 billion ($136.6 million), ¥26 billion of which ($86.6 million) allegedly came from party leaders (who in turn received most of this from business sources) and ¥15 billion ($50 million) from the business community. Average campaign expenses for individual candidates in the national constituency were estimated by the *Asahi* newspaper at ¥18 million ($60,000) and in the local constituencies at ¥9.9 million ($33,000). However, these relate only to actual expendi-

[2]Japan Institute of International Affairs, *White Papers of Japan, 1971–72* (Tokyo: East West Publications, 1973), p. 255.

tures during the thirty-day legal period and not to the far larger amounts spent over the preceding year or more that were actually for campaign purposes.

The sources of these funds are in general well known. A large part were major contributions from the Citizens' Association *(Kokumin Kyokai)*, a separately incorporated fund-raising arm of the party that duns business firms for campaign purposes. Other parts came directly to Liberal Democratic Party headquarters or to factional leaders in the form of gifts from particular major businesses. In the 1974 House of Councilor's election, these contributions were so large and the use of money for electoral purposes so blatant as to arouse strenuous criticisms from the media and public that seemed to disadvantage the Liberal Democratic Party at the polls.

The program of the Liberal Democratic Party, of course, changes with the issues that are current at any given time. It also represents the product of numerous compromises and is in many respects as cautiously vague in its stands and promises as are the programs of major parties in the United States. It is not, by American standards, a notably conservative document. During a recent upper house election, for example, it called for a variety of measures related to price levels and to the control of inflation, including a system of incentives to encourage savings in order to restrain general demand and a promise to hold down the soaring costs of land. An education section combined advocacy of higher salaries for teachers with statements deploring the political activities of the *Nikkyoso*, the national teachers' union, and recommending the cultivation of morality through classroom means. Farmers were assured of increases in government subsidies for their rice crops, while the elderly and indigent were promised larger welfare pensions and child care allowances. Measures to insure an adequate supply of energy and to conserve existing sources were given considerable prominence. In the field of foreign policy, the party strongly endorsed alliance with the United States and bolstering of measures for more adequate self-defense. These are not especially controversial measures in Japan. They are for the most part rather general and vague responses to generally felt and serious economic problems. The anti-*Nikkyoso* and pro-moral education plank is controversial and represents an appeal to fairly widespread concern over the obvious politicization of the national teachers' union and its alleged consequences in the classroom. The foreign policy plank, while traditional for the Liberal Democrats, also differs sharply from the stands of several opposition parties. By Western standards, however, the Liberal Democratic Party is not particularly "conservative" in either its policies or practice. Like most of its counterparts in other democratic societies, it has co-opted numerous social policies and stands initially advocated by its "progressive" opponents.

As indicated earlier, the party's principal current problem is maintaining its attenuating status as "the majority party" or, if not, devising a coalition with elements of the opposition that would at least enable it to remain the dominant force on the political scene. This includes the possibility of some measure of disintegration and recombination of the Liberal Democratic Party as presently constituted—for example, a defection of the party's more liberal elements and the formation of a new moderate party in combination with the Democratic Socialists and the right-wing membership of the Japan Socialist Party.

The New Liberal Club (*Shin Jiyu Kurabu* or NLC)

On 25 June 1976, an event occurred that may well be premonitory of just this sort of disintegration and recombination of the Liberal Democratic Party. Six dissident Diet members of the Liberal Democratic Party, led by Kono Yohei, formally submitted their resignations to the party's secretary-general. Five of those concerned held seats in the House of Representatives, one in the House of Councilors. Later in the day they met with the press and announced the formation of a new political group to be called the New Liberal Club. This was said to be preparatory to the establishment of a new conservative political party. In the ensuing general election on 5 December 1976 for the House of Representatives, Kono and his associates advanced a slate of twenty-five candidates and succeeded in polling 2.3 million votes (4.18 percent of the total) and securing seventeen seats. For a totally new party, this was a remarkable feat, testifying in particular to the disillusionment with the Liberal Democratic Party on the part of conservative voters who were seeking a means of protest without either abstaining or voting for "progressive" candidates.

The New Liberal Club was obviously inspired by its leaders' disgust with the disunity, bickering, and ineffectiveness of the Liberal Democratic Party. In their statement to the press they strongly denounced the Liberal Democratic Party as "a gerontocracy bent on back-room power struggles" (three of the six dissidents were in their thirties) and claimed that its senility and ineptitude was a serious threat to the preservation of a democratic political system in Japan. They committed themselves to the establishment of new and higher standards of political morality and to the sponsorship of programs that would eliminate the social inequities that had developed within the Japanese capitalist system. They made completely clear, however, the fact that their fundamental beliefs were conservative and that they hoped to preserve, not replace, the capitalist system. They also favor the existing joint security relationship with the United States.

There has not yet been time to evaluate the New Liberal Club's political record in practice. The development represented by their defection from the Liberal Democratic Party and subsequent success at the polls, however, could well be a harbinger of some more massive realignment of the conservative and middle-of-the-road political forces in Japan. There can be no doubt that mounting popular distaste for the incessant factional strife within the Liberal Democratic Party and for certain aspects of its recent performances in office together with sheer boredom after more than thirty years of rule by essentially the same group have brought about a situation in which a sizable number of conservative voters are seeking a responsible political alternative. They are not comfortable with the parties of the left that seem to a sizable segment of the electorate to be hopelessly disunified and unpromising in their platforms and prospects. The situation, therefore, could be ripe for a major restructuring of the party scene in Japan.

The Japan Socialist Party (*Nihon Shakaito* or JSP)

Although socialist and left-wing political parties existed in Japan before the war, they were of small electoral or parliamentary significance. Only since 1945 have they constituted major opposition for the dominant conservative groups. For one brief nine-month period in 1947–48, they were even able to obtain the leadership of a weak coalition Cabinet for their leader, Katayama Tetsu. The Japan Socialist Party in its present form dates from October 1955, when its formerly separate left- and right-wing factions were merged into a single party. The party remains more or less unified, although a portion of the right-wing contingent seceded in January 1960 to form the Democratic Socialist Party.

An examination of table 8–2 clarifies the shifting electoral fortunes of the Japan Socialist Party since World War II. Before the party split into separately organized left- and right-wing groups in January 1950, its record at the polls varied widely from 26.2 percent of the vote and 30.7 percent of the seats (in the general election of 1947) to only 13.5 percent of the vote and 10.3 percent of the seats (in 1949). Following its recombination in 1955, it attained a postwar peak of popularity in the 1958 general election when it polled 32.9 percent of the vote and 35.5 percent of the seats. Thereafter, the trend has been downhill and the party has been unable to break—or even to approximate breaking—what used to be called the "one-third barrier" (obtaining more than one-third either of the popular vote or of the seats in the lower house). Despite these shortcomings, the Socialists remain, by a factor of about 2.2 in terms of seats, the largest opposition party in Japan. They have recently held an average of about one-quarter of the seats in the lower house.

It is worth considering the effects of thirty-odd years of oppositional status on a political party in a democratic system. For all practical purposes the brief nine-month period in which a Socialist Party leader served as prime minister can be ignored. His was a coalition government in which the Socialists held no independent authority. To say the least, thirty years in the political wilderness of the powerless is bound to be a decidedly frustrating experience, particularly so since it was quite clear throughout most of this time that the party's future chances of coming to power were little better than their past ones. Throughout this period they lacked any access or title to national political posts of real importance; they could enact no legislation unless, as sometimes happened, it caught the fancy of and was preempted by the Liberal Democrats; they had no meaningful patronage powers; and their access to and influence with the national bureaucracy was vastly inferior to that of the party in power. Without practical assets of this sort or some realistic prospect of acquiring them in the reasonably near future, it is extremely difficult to hold any party together. One must, therefore, seek other means of doing so.

The Japan Socialist Party has found these other means in a combination of two factors. The first is ideology. By the standards of most of its Western European counterparts, the Japan Socialist Party is an anachronism. It has undergone little of the tempering of doctrinal orthodoxy by practical political considerations that has been notable in the history of European socialist parties. There is a rigor and intensity about the ideological commitments of many Japanese socialists and, consequently, a vehemence with which they conduct their intraparty feuds and debates that is distinctly reminiscent of the nineteenth century elsewhere. Despite bitter internal disagreements on doctrinal grounds, however, there has been sufficient commonality of viewpoint and ideology to enable the party to stay together since 1955 under circumstances that would doubtless have led to discouragement and disruption in a less committed group.

The second factor making for party cohesion has been the discovery of the political potentialities of "extraparliamentary procedures," in reality a form of political blackmail. This takes the form of a variety of tactics not anticipated by normal parliamentary practice. These include the well-known "cow's-walk," a device for slowing the vote-taking process in the Diet to practically a halt by deliberately dilatory modes of voting on the part of Socialist—and other opposition—Party members absenting themselves en masse from committee and plenary sessions and, in the case of legislation deemed of exceptional importance, mounting sometimes violent demonstrations in the Diet building or in the streets. The party claims in such instances to be protesting what it calls "the tyranny of the majority"; it appeals to the traditional Japanese belief that important decisions should be made by consensual rather than adversary means and accuses the Liberal Democrats of riding roughshod over the rights of the minority. The party in power normally strives to avoid serious confrontations of this sort because it fears a hostile press and adverse public reaction. Thus, when the Socialists and the opposition parties in general can unite on an issue, they are able to exercise a type of effective legislative veto on some issues despite the fact that their parliamentary strength alone would be inadequate for this purpose. This also helps the party survive in the difficult role of a seemingly permanent opposition and legitimizes in its own and others' eyes an occasional recourse to violence on a scale sufficient to arouse concern among those who prefer the normal parliamentary means of conducting the public business.

Against this background it is not surprising to find that the Socialist Party, while a formally unified group like the Liberal Democratic Party, is also in fact a congeries of competing factions. In some respects these resemble their analogues in the Liberal Democratic Party. They are hierarchically structured groups centering around an acknowledged leader; they involve strong personal attachments and loyalties; they offer a path for personal career advancement within the party and improved financial support at election time; and they compete strenuously, and sometimes bitterly, with one another for power in and control over the determination of party strategy and policy. They also differ from factions in the Liberal Democratic Party in two very important respects. First, they are competing in a power vacuum so far as the prizes of office and real political payoffs are concerned. These go to the party in power and its factions. Second, the role of ideology is very prominent in determining the composition and agenda of factions within the Socialist Party. In general, it is possible to array the six or more Socialist Party factions that have usually been identifiable in recent years along a spectrum running from left to right in doctrinal terms. The most stable and important of these have been the Socialist Society and the Sasaki faction at the left end of this spectrum, the Katsumata faction in the center, and the Eda faction on the right, although all three of these leaders lost their seats in the 1976 general election. There are also a number of members who belong to no faction.

The particular occasions for controversy among the factions of the Socialist Party have, of course, varied over time. Many of them have prewar antecedents. Among the more notable have been the 1950 Peace Treaty, the Security Treaty with the United States, relations with the Soviet Union and, more recently, with the People's Republic of China, the means by and the pace at which a socialist society is to be achieved in Japan (evolutionary and democratic versus revolutionary and violent strategies), relations with the Japan Communist Party, and the highly practical issue of whether the Japan Socialist Party should be based solely on the proletariat and proletarian causes or should seek some broader and more promising popular base. These controversies within the party have been responsible for the defection of the sizable group of right-wing socialists who founded the Democratic Socialist Party in 1960, for the continued weakness of the right-wing elements remaining within the party, notably the Eda faction, and for the curious circumstance that the recent policies of the Japan Socialist Party have often been to the left of those of the Japan Communist Party.

The explanation for these developments lies not only in the party's tortured intellectual history but also in two other factors. The first is simply the fact that they have never had an opportunity to exercise political power in a legal and responsible context. Prolonged oppositional status seems to breed an oppositional mentality that, for lack of constructive extramural opportunities for satisfying action and fulfillment, appears to breed and thrive on intramural strife. The second and more immediate factor is the relationship between the Japan Socialist Party and Japanese labor unions. For campaign staff and organization, the Socialist Party is almost totally dependent on union support. This dependence is also very heavy for financial support and party personnel. Furthermore, it is concentrated upon a single massive national confederation of unions known as *Sohyo* rather than diffused over a larger number of separate unions.

Sohyo is a national confederation of labor unions; its largest and most important components are public service unions whose members are either directly in government employment or work for semigovernmental monopoly corporations in fields such as railroads, telephone and telegraph, or tobacco. It is the largest organization of this kind in Japan. Membership in its various unions totals more than 4.3 million. The political preferences of *Sohyo* are decidedly left-wing, and it is the most radical of Japan's major labor union confederations. Its programmatic interests are also relatively narrow and specific. It officially supports the Japan Socialist Party and provides a volume and variety of services without which it is doubtful that the party could survive in anything approximating its present status. With this role goes a degree of influence and sometimes control that can be quite uncomfortable for the party. In practice *Sohyo's* influence has served to bolster the power of left-wing elements within the Socialist Party and to insure the espousal of radical views and policies to a degree that makes more moderate Socialists distinctly uncomfortable.

It is perhaps not surprising to find under these circumstances that the Japan Socialist Party, like the Liberal Democratic Party, is not a mass organization. Claimed party membership in recent years has averaged only about fifty thousand, and it is doubtful if even that figure is really very meaningful. Most of those involved are probably semiprofessional local politicians and organizers operating from a labor union base on behalf of Socialist candidates. They are apt to be more responsive to their unions' interests and influence than to the party's. Professor Stockwin's analysis of the demographic basis of Socialist Party support at the polls is useful.[3] The distribution of the Socialist vote is surprising. In comparing the 1958 general election with two recent ones it emerges that the Socialists have lost strength in the metropolitan areas (a decline from 19 percent of their seats to 13.5 percent), have stayed the same in urban areas (a steady 31 percent of their seats), and have gained a bit more support in the semirural and rural areas (from 25 to 27.5 percent and from 25 to 28 percent of their seats respectively). Despite the rather unremarkable percentile changes involved, it should be remembered that the actual number of seats held by the Socialists decreased steadily from 166 in the 1958 election to 118 in 1972. These findings are substantially confirmed by the analysis based on percentages of the labor force involved in the primary industries (farming, fishing, and forestry) previously described with respect to the Liberal Democratic Party. This describes the vote in terms of areas ranging from the most urban to the most rural. The Socialist vote in two recent general elections varied very little from one area to another; it actually lay between 18 and 23 percent in each of the five types in one case and between 20 and 23 percent in the other. Socialist support is, therefore, quite equably distributed in terms of an urban-rural continuum and is rather low—about 20 percent on the average—at all points on that continuum.

Despite the dwindling fortunes of the Socialist Party in general elections, it has been improving its position in local politics. As of 1975, for example, 1 of 47 prefectural governors and 17 of 643 city mayors officially proclaimed themselves to be Socialists. In actuality at least 8 other governors, including those of Tokyo, Kanagawa, Osaka, and Kyoto (four of Japan's largest and most important prefectures) were in effect Socialists, while seven of Japan's ten largest cities had "progressive" (Socialist) mayors. In these cases the Socialist candidates were, in contradistinction to their record in general elections, doing best in Japan's most metropolitan settings. They obviously hope that the record established by these Socialist governors and mayors

---

[3]Stockwin, *Japan*, p. 167.

will be so attractive as to gain for the party new support in national elections as well.

Like the apparatus of their Liberal Democratic rivals, that of the Japan Socialist Party is highly centralized in Tokyo, where an elaborate party headquarters is maintained. The party has no president but is headed by the chairman of its central executive committee. Its administrative chief is the secretary-general, and the chairman of its control committee also plays an important role in the party. Ultimate authority within the party resides theoretically in an annual party congress, which is usually a far more lively and controversial affair than its Liberal Democratic counterpart. The congress elects the party's chief officers, and it debates vociferously such long-standing policy issues as whether the party should represent national interests or class interests, that is, those of the industrial and peasant proletariats; what attitude it should adopt toward Communists and the Japan Communist Party; and what relationship the party should maintain with the unions and federations of unions that provide the bulk of its support. In addition to the party congress, the conference of party members who hold seats in the National Diet also plays an important role in the party councils. As with the conservatives, this body—once a party policy has been established—is under rigid obligation to provide loyal and unanimous voting support for the party's legislative program in both houses.

The Japan Socialist Party does not command the financial resources or support that the Liberal Democratic Party does. The available official figures, for example, show a total party income of only $3,780,666 in 1975. This is misleading, however, because it represents only party income as such and fails to account for the income of particular factions or factional leaders, and more important, it ignores the great variety of free manpower and services that the party obtains from its union supporters. The *Sohyo* unions are the largest source of support for the party. Surprisingly, however, some large and important business firms also give token contributions to the Socialist Party.

The party's program is, of course, in some degree tailored to the issues of the moment. In a recent House of Councilors election its main planks were as follows. The national budget should be restructured to give priority to the needs of the citizenry. Public utility rates should be frozen for a three-year period. Individual incomes up to ¥2,350,000 ($7,833) a year should be exempt from taxation. Corporate taxes should be increased, and large wage increases granted. Compulsory education should be completely free of charge, and the current entrance examination system for high schools and colleges should be eliminated. Members of boards of education should be publicly elected, and government control of education should be abolished. Farmers should be guaranteed their production costs plus at least a minimum income beyond that. Farmers should also be given rights of collective bargaining, and the agricultural cooperatives should be democratized. In the social welfare field a minimum pension of ¥60,000 ($200) a month should be guaranteed, and welfare payments should be linked to rises in the cost of living. Social insurance premiums should be lowered, and the medical care system drastically revised. The energy industries should be realigned and rationalized, and new sources of energy developed. Finally, in the area of foreign affairs the party platform advocated a basic policy of nonalignment, neutrality, and peace. Economic cooperation with the developing nations was to be strengthened, the Security Treaty with the United States scrapped, and the Self-Defense Forces disbanded. Friendly relations should be promoted with all neighboring countries. It is difficult to say to what extent this represents the policies that the Japan Socialist Party would actually follow should it ever come to power. There are certain electoral advantages that flow from the circumstance of being permanently out of power—and a degree of irresponsibility in the formulation of party programs is one of them. It is safe at least to say in the present case that there would be very substantial difficulty in performing some of the Socialist recommendations.

Thus, the Japan Socialist Party today is somewhat farther from the possibility of forming its own government than was the case in the late 1950s. Like the Liberal Democratic Party, it has fairly steadily lost strength at the national level since the mid-fifties, and its principal problems today are how to prevent further losses to the Japan Communist Party or the Clean Government Party while at the same time holding its own ranks together.

The Japan Democratic Socialist Party (*Nihon Minshu Shakaito* or DSP)

In January 1960, the heated dispute over both doctrinal and tactical issues that had long been seething below the surface of the Japan Socialist Party came to a boil. The party split in two in a break of the sort that has been common among Japanese political parties on both the left and right. On this occasion, the extreme right-wing faction of the party, led by Nishio Suehiro and a few members of the Kawakami faction, walked out and established a party of its own known as the Japan Democratic Socialist Party. At the time, the dissidents had the support of about thirty-five Socialist members of the lower house of the National Diet, a number that increased to forty before the general election of November 1960. They fared poorly in this election, however, and emerged with only seventeen seats, a drastic reduction in their parliamentary strength. They improved this holding to twenty-three seats in the 1963 general election, to thirty in 1967, and to thirty-one in 1969 but dropped to nineteen in 1972. In 1976 they managed to increase their holdings to twenty-nine seats through improved campaign strategies, but even so, their share of the popular vote has long remained stable at about 7 percent. Their long-term prospects are, therefore, dubious.

The level of popular support for the Democratic Socialist Party's candidates has never been particularly impressive. In fact it has been almost static from the outset in the sense that its total popular vote has consistently ranged between 3 and 3.6 million, that is, between 6.3 and 8.7 percent of the valid votes. Prior to the 1972 general election, the bulk of this support —42 or 43 percent usually—came from metropolitan constituencies.[4] With

[4]Stockwin, *Japan*, p. 171.

the loss of most of their following in Osaka when Nishio Suehiro retired, this fraction sank to only 16 percent, leaving the party primarily dependent on support from urban constituencies. Prior to 1972, between 26 and 30 percent of their votes came from semirural and rural constituencies combined. This rose to 37 percent for their much smaller number of seats in 1972.

Most of the Democratic Socialist members of the lower house are longtime professional politicians. Professor Stockwin found that they had on the average been elected to this office five times as of 1972. Thus, they had at least twelve years of parliamentary service and were experienced campaigners with reliable campaign organizations and financial backing. Like their colleagues in the Socialist Party, their main source of organized support was the unions. In their case, however, it was not *Sohyo* but a second, smaller, and more conservative national federation of unions known as *Domei*. The *Domei* group includes largely private industrial unions with an aggregate membership of about 2.2 million compared to Sohyo's 4.3 million. Its politics are much more conservative than *Sohyo*'s, and it normally and officially supports Democratic Socialist candidates.

The organization of the Democratic Socialist Party resembles that of the Socialist Party. At the head of the party is the chairman of its central executive committee, and a secretary-general is in charge of party administration. A party congress possesses ultimate authority, and in practice, the council composed of its members holding seats in the National Diet wields a good deal of influence. There has been evidence of some factionalism in the party, but this has not become a serious problem. So small a group cannot really afford the luxury of internecine strife. Party membership is small, amounting in 1976 to about forty thousand members.

The Democratic Socialist Party has espoused a moderate and pragmatic type of socialism, seeking to occupy the middle ground between the Liberal Democrats and the Socialists. They advocate a type of welfare state in which a very sizable sector would operate as a free enterprise economy but subject to state supervision and regulation in the public interest. In a recent election, for example, the party's platform called for such items as the freezing of public utility charges for a three-year period, a ten-year plan for the attainment of self-sufficiency in food supply, a negative income tax to support increased welfare payments, energy saving, the development of undersea resources on Japan's continental shelf, compulsory education through senior high school, and reforms in the university educational system. In foreign affairs the party called for friendly but equal relations with the United States, revision of the Security Treaty to permit an American military presence in Japan only in times of national emergency, improved relations with the Soviet Union and the People's Republic of China, and a halt to further increases in Japan's military strength. These are policies that to many Japanese seem to lack color, drama, and popular appeal. They may have been selected not so much on their merits but because they represent a compromise between the program of the Liberal Democratic Party and those of the Socialists and Communists. There is also a belief that this is a "party-in-waiting" rather than a truly autonomous force on the Japanese political scene—the waiting in this case being for a series of events that will lead either to a coalition with the Liberal Democratic Party or, more desirably, to a breakup of both the Liberal Democratic and the Socialist parties and the subsequent formation of a new party based on the Democratic Socialists, left-wing elements of the Liberal Democratic Party, and right-wing elements of the Socialist Party. The Democratic Socialists have long made clear their opposition to cooperating with the Communist Party in almost any political context.

For the Democratic Socialists the problems of the future are simple and formidable. Can they survive? If they do, how can they exercise any real political influence on national policies? The answers to both questions are probably dependent upon the emergence of some form of coalition government in which they would play a role. There is little doubt that they would be willing to discuss seriously the terms of such a coalition with either or both the Liberal Democrats and the right-wing Socialists.

The Japan Communist Party (*Nihon Kyosanto* or JCP)

The Communist Party has been a legal political party in Japan since General Douglas MacArthur released its leaders from prison in October 1945. Although its top leaders went underground for a time during the Korean conflict, the party has run candidates in every general election since 1946. In the early postwar years, the party's electoral fortunes peaked in the 1949 general election when many Socialist voters switched to the Communist ticket because of scandals involving Socialist leaders. As a consequence the Communist Party received almost three million votes, about 10 percent of the total, and won thirty-five seats in the lower house. This success was fleeting, however, for in the 1952 election Communist candidates polled fewer than one million votes (2.6 percent of the total) and won no seats at all. Thereafter they did not gain more than 1.1 million votes or three seats until the 1963 and 1967 general elections when they received 1.6 and 2.1 million votes respectively (4 and 4.8 percent) and five seats on each occasion. After that their electoral fortunes improved markedly until 1976. In the 1969 election they won 3.1 million votes (6.8 percent) and fourteen seats; in 1972, 5.4 million votes (10.5 percent) and thirty-eight seats. In the 1976 general election, however, while continuing to poll well over five million votes (10.4 percent of the total), they won only seventeen seats, a loss of twenty-one seats. This puts the Communists in a tie with the New Liberal Club for last place in the House of Representatives—following the Liberal Democrats, the Socialists, the Clean Government Party, and the Democratic Socialists. In the House of Councilors, where they held a total of twenty seats in 1976, they are in fourth place.

Professor Stockwin's analysis indicates that on the average between 50 and 60 percent of the support for Communist candidates has come from metropolitan areas, 20 to 30 percent from urban areas, 10 to 20 percent from semirural constituencies, and only 5 percent from rural areas.[5] In

[5] Stockwin, *Japan*, p. 169.

national elections, therefore, the Communists are obviously strongest in Japan's largest cities. The popular bases of Communist strength differ from those of the Socialist and Democratic Socialist parties in the respect that they lack any consolidated union support comparable to that afforded their rivals by *Sohyo* or *Domei*. While no national federation of unions stands behind the Communists, the party is strong in particular unions, especially those on the left wing of the *Sohyo* group such as *Nikkyoso* (the Japan teachers' union) in which many individual union leaders and members undoubtedly support Communist candidates in spite of *Sohyo*'s official support of the Japan Socialist Party. This longstanding policy of *Sohyo* is in fact a major source of contention between the Socialist and Communist parties. The latter's supporters regularly attempt at *Sohyo*'s annual conventions to gain acceptance for the principle of "freedom of political party choice," that is, freedom for *Sohyo* officials and members to support openly Communist as well as Socialist candidates should that be their preference. They have recently succeeded in this endeavor.

The real secret of the recent electoral successes of the Japan Communist Party, however, lies in the quality of its current organization and leadership. In a structural sense the party's officers are directed by a triple-tiered hierarchy of committees of diminishing size and increasing authority. Formal power is vested in a Central Committee of 168 members (120 regular and 48 alternate). Above this stands a thirty-eight-member Presidium (elected by the Central Committee) and, at the top, a fourteen-member Standing Committee of the Presidium that actually controls the party. The party's elder statesman, Nozaka Sanzo who was eighty-four in 1976, serves as chairman of the Central Committee. Actual leadership lies with Miyamoto Kenji who is chairman of both the Presidium and the Standing Committee. Of great importance also is the party Secretariat (headed by Fuwa Tetzuzo in 1976).

The Communist Party differs from all other Japanese political parties except the Clean Government Party because it is, by Japanese standards at least, a mass party. In 1976 it claimed to have slightly more than three hundred thousand registered party members. Theoretically these represent the party's hard core. Beyond these members are supposed to lie a more fluctuating group of fairly reliable party sympathizers. Shifts in this larger group of core plus periphery are usually measured in terms of the circulation figures for the party's daily newspaper, *Akahata*. These currently amount to 550,000 for the daily and 1,950,000 for the Sunday edition. While impressive, these circulation figures are by no means remarkable by Japanese standards. The *Asahi*, for example, has a morning and evening daily circulation of almost eleven million, and the *Yomiuri* has upwards of ten million. In this connection it might be noted that the Communist Party's publications are a highly lucrative venture, providing the party with an annual income second only to that of the Liberal Democrats ($33,580,333 in 1975).

The party has in the past experienced serious internal rifts. These were acute enough in the mid-1960s, when the party was rent with disagreements over the issue of what policy to adopt toward the Communist Party of the Soviet Union and the Communist Party of the People's Republic of China, to lead to the establishment of two small independent Communist parties that still exist. These are the pro-Soviet Voice of Japan *(Nihon no Koe)* Party and the pro-Chinese Japan Communist Party (Left). The former was led by Shiga Yoshio, once a leading member of the Japan Communist Party. It continues to follow a pro-Soviet line but seems to have only about four hundred members. The somewhat larger Japan Communist Party (Left) with about one thousand members has recently split into two factions that disagree about the wisdom and desirability of Peking's recent policy of détente with the United States and confrontation with Moscow.

In practice the Japan Communist Party operates on a variety of fronts, often through mass organizations in which its members play leading or, at least, prominent roles. One of the less known and most successful of these has been the Democratic Youth Organization *(Minseido)* that has an estimated membership of two hundred thousand and branches in all prefectures. This serves as a recruiting device for the party and a potent means of influencing organized student and youth activities on college campuses and elsewhere. The Communist Party is also active and influential in the councils of *Sohyo,* especially its more left-wing and activist unions. The party plays a leading role in the peace movement in Japan, operating in this case through an organization known as the Japan Council against Atomic and Hydrogen Bombs *(Gensuikyo)* that is supported and largely controlled by the party. It also sponsors three well-known international friendship associations for Japan-Korea, Japan-Soviet, and Japan-China relations.

Like its counterparts in Italy and France, the Japan Communist Party has been energetically supporting candidates in local elections at the prefectural, city, town, and village levels with reasonably encouraging results. In the 1975 elections of prefectural governors, for example, the party's candidate won in Osaka in a three-way race against rivals sponsored by the Liberal Democrats and by a coalition of the Japan Socialist, Democratic Socialist, and Clean Government parties. In eight other prefectures, including Tokyo and Kanagawa, the Communist Party was part of the coalition of "progressive" parties that supported the winning gubernatorial candidate in either the 1975 or earlier elections. The party has also done reasonably well in electing members of prefectural, city, town, and village assemblies. As of September 1975, it controlled 3,144 seats in such bodies out of a total of 73,615 positions. This compares quite favorably with the local electoral record of the Japan Socialist Party and is better than that of the Clean Government Party. In general, however, the 1975 local elections were a disappointment and a setback for the Communist Party. Its candidates (usually the candidates of "progressive" coalitions involving the party) for governor won in only three prefectures, it secured eight fewer seats in prefectural assemblies than in the preceding round of local elections, and the number of prefectural assemblies in which it held no seats increased from three to seven. In contesting for posts at the local level, it has been the uniform practice of Communist candidates to ignore or deemphasize ideological and doctrinal issues in favor of basic problems of the locality such as inflation, jobs, transportation, welfare, schools, and bureaucratic abuses or ineptitude. These stands have proven quite popular.

Like communist parties elsewhere, the Japan Communist Party has had continual difficulty in living down its own postwar record and relating advantageously to other political parties. Its dominant relationship with the party in power is, of course, one of strong opposition on selected issues. This is to be expected. It is relations with the other opposition parties that cause problems. There are numerous instances in which it might be collectively advantageous for the opposition parties to present a joint front against the Liberal Democratic Party. In practice, this is exceedingly difficult to do except on a highly ad hoc basis because of the deep suspicions of the Communist Party harbored by most of the other parties and a feeling that in practice cooperative efforts tend to redound more to the Communists' benefit than to their own. Relations are worst between the Communists and the Democratic Socialists. Anti-Communism is a basic tenet of the Democratic Socialist Party. Despite some recent overtures involving the *Sokagakkai,* the parent body of the Clean Government Party, and the Communist Party, relations between that party and the Communists have been uniformly very poor, and in very few cases has any cooperation proven possible. The situation is more complicated for the Japan Socialist Party. Its left-wing elements strongly endorse and press for cooperation with the Communists in a number of contexts. Its right-wing elements normally oppose such cooperation with equal vehemence, thus adding one more discordant issue to the long list of internal problems that beset the Socialist Party.

The problem of how to relate to senior communist parties and governments abroad has historically been vexing for the Japan Communist Party. Until the early 1950s, the party was under effective and obvious Russian influence. With the success of the revolution in China and the rise of the People's Republic of China, Peking's influence over the party began to increase. With the Sino-Soviet break in 1959–60, an obvious and acute problem of divided loyalties was posed for the Japanese party. It chose Peking and actively and openly supported the Chinese cause against Moscow in international communist circles. Neither stance—subordination to Moscow or to Peking—was popular with the Japanese public, and the party paid a heavy price at home for both of its external loyalties. In 1965, therefore, the party confronted this problem and began increasingly to assert its status as a "national" or autonomous communist party; thus it was among the earliest of communist parties to adopt a posture that has recently become more fashionable. At present the Japan Communist Party's fraternal relations with its brethren in both China and Russia are frequently tense and acrimonious. The party does not hesitate to assert its independence of foreign influence or control on all possible occasions and presents itself to the public as a Japanese, not an international, institution. These problems of relationship and status within the communist family have not significantly altered the Japanese party's policy of hostility toward the United States. American imperialism is still regarded as the principal international enemy of Japan. The party's platform has consistently and vehemently urged the abrogation of the Security Treaty between Japan and the United States, the immediate elimination of American bases, and the neutralization of Japan, hopefully with international guarantees.

In domestic policy, the Communist Party advocates nationalization of the energy industries, self-sufficiency in and higher prices for farm products, a new land reform program, large increases in welfare and social security payments, a comprehensive program of medical care, stabilization of food prices, no taxation of incomes less than ¥2,150,000 ($7,166), and a halt to inflationary governmental spending. Here, as at the local level, the party is obviously emphasizing basic problems of daily life rather than ideological appeals. It has for some time renounced a policy of achieving power by violent means.

Now that the Japan Communist Party has solved—for the time being at least—the vexatious matter of their autonomy vis-à-vis Russian or Chinese influence or control, the party would seem to have two fundamental problems in the future. The first revolves around its ability to dispel the widespread suspicion and mistrust with which it is regarded by many Japanese. A recent poll showed that 41 percent of the respondents could "never like" the party. Such views are very widespread, and despite the fairly impressive record that the party has had at the polls in recent years, there is a serious question as to whether it, like the Japan Socialist Party, will not encounter—if it has not already done so—an inflexible and fairly small limit of public support. Many feel that it cannot hope to win at the polls more than 50 of the 511 seats in the House of Representatives. Others think that it peaked at 38 seats in 1972. The second problem is one of relationship with the other opposition parties. Given the strong aversion of the Democratic Socialist Party, the Clean Government Party, and important elements of the Socialist Party to any formal cooperation with the Communist Party, it will be difficult for the Communists to participate in any coalition government that might emerge if the Liberal Democratic Party should fall from power. If this is the case, it raises serious questions about the long-term wisdom and practicality of the party's current policies, assuming that the Japan Communist Party actually expects some day to achieve power, or a share therein, by parliamentary means.

The Clean Government Party (*Komeito* or CGP)

Religious sects have not normally organized their own political parties in Japan, although there have been religious overtones to the programs of some of the right-wing or ultranationalist parties both before and since the war. The Clean Government Party is unusual, therefore, in the sense that until recently it explicitly represented one of the "new religions" of Japan, the *Sokagakkai* or Value Creation Society. The faith was established by Makiguchi Tsunesaburo in about 1930, ostensibly as an offshoot of the long-established *Nichiren* sect of Buddhism. It did not really achieve national importance until the mid-1950s, but today it is without a doubt the most energetic, militant, and widely discussed religious movement in Japan. It claims a membership of sixteen million, and even its critics are willing to grant it something in the neighborhood of ten million.

Sokagakkai first entered politics in the Tokyo local elections of 1955 and succeeded in returning several of its members to seats in the prefectural and ward assemblies. In the upper house election of 1956, it elected 3 of its candidates to the House of Councilors. In 1959, 5 more of its members were elected to the upper house and 293 to various local assemblies throughout the country. These successes continued in the 1962 and 1965 House of Councilors' elections, with nine victories in the former and eleven in the latter. The Clean Government Party is now the third largest in the upper house.

In January 1962, *Sokagakkai* established a separate political branch called the League for Clean Government *(Komei Seiji Remmei)*. In 1964 this was transformed into an official political party called the Clean Government Party *(Komeito)*. The party ran a very effective campaign during the 1967 general election and returned twenty-five of its thirty-two candidates to the lower house. In 1969 it increased this number to forty-seven. It fell back to twenty-nine seats in the 1972 general election but advanced to fifty-five in 1976. It is, therefore, the third largest party in the lower house behind the Liberal Democrats and the Socialists.

In 1971 the Clean Government Party severed all official connection with *Sokagakkai* in an attempt to establish its status as a normal and secular political party rather than as the political arm of a somewhat militant religion. It is not at all evident that the maneuver has accomplished this aim for the Japanese public in general. Nevertheless, one should now distinguish between the religion with its ten million adherents and the party that claims a membership of only forty thousand. Incidentally, not all members of the faith vote regularly for candidates of the Clean Government Party. In fact, the decline in the party's vote from 5.1 to 4.4 million between the 1969 and 1972 general elections was at the time widely attributed to the defection of *Sokagakkai* members displeased by the new secular and autonomous status of the Clean Government Party. However, the party's vote came back to 6.1 million in 1976.

The party has shared at least one characteristic with the Japan Communist Party. As long as it was closely associated with *Sokagakkai*, it was a mass-based party in a society in which such parties were unusual. The sect itself is elaborately and very effectively organized throughout Japan with overlapping and hierarchically structured units based on geography, on age cohorts, on shared interest groups, and fundamentally, on small neighborhood cells or groups that bring together activist members who are the missionaries of the religion with their immediate converts in that area. This network readily lends itself to campaign as well as to devotional and other purposes. Until 1971 at least, there is reason to believe that this national network was the electoral apparatus of the Clean Government Party. Since then, it is difficult to determine the extent to which this continues, despite the ostensible break between the two organizations. The adverse results of the 1972 election would seem to indicate at least a decline in the intensity and efficacy of the support at the polls extended by the *Sokagakkai* apparatus.

It is difficult to classify the Clean Government Party's policies with precision. The party has sometimes referred to itself as "neo-socialist," but in practice its statements and programs have little to do with orthodox Marxism. Initially it pressed for the "purification" of politics, including fair elections. This is still an important theme. Beyond this, it has been closely identified with a variety of programs to improve the quality of life, the cost of living, social security, and the general well being of less affluent Japanese citizens. In a recent election, for example, the party platform called for lower public utility rates, moves against profiteering, tax reductions for smaller enterprises and compensatory increases for larger ones, exemption from income tax for citizens earning less than ¥2,000,000 ($6,666) per year, opposition to government control of education, promotion of life-long education, old-age pensions for all, free medical care for the aged, stabilization of oil supplies, increased subsidies for farmers, and self-sufficiency in the principal food crops. Like the Communists, they emphasize the quality of life approach to the electorate, though it is far from clear as to how they hope to realize these goals. In foreign affairs, the party has recommended abolition of the Security Pact with the United States; the conclusion of a non-aggression pact with the United States, Soviet Union, and People's Republic of China; the establishment of a neutral and non-nuclear zone in Asia and the Pacific; the prohibition of nuclear armaments; and the conclusion of a peace treaty with the Soviet Union after solving Japan's problems of disputed territory in the Kuriles now occupied by the Russians.

The Clean Government Party shares with all other opposition parties in Japan the basic problem of limited electoral horizons. Despite a sizable following, the party's suspected relationship with the militant *Sokagakkai* sect makes it politically unacceptable to many Japanese. Has it, therefore, any more promising prospects than those already achieved, or has it reached the highest point of popularity and support given its limited appeal to the Japanese voter? Many believe the latter to be the case. If they are right, then further progress is probably dependent on the party's participation in a coalition government that might eventuate should the Liberal Democratic Party lose its majority and, therefore, its capacity to govern alone.

General Characteristics of Japanese Parties

There are several characteristics of the general political party situation in Japan. First, none of the parties—except perhaps the Clean Government and Communist parties—are truly mass membership organizations. They notably lack solid bases in popular involvement and support. They normally operate in Tokyo and among circles limited almost exclusively to professional politicians and administrators. They are essentially parliamentary parties. Their prime focus of interest is the lower house of the National Diet and what goes on there. Only during election campaigns do they engage in massive and sustained contact with the people. They are increasingly aware of the unsatisfactory nature and the dangers of this sort of relationship with the electorate and are seeking more meaningful forms of association. So far they do not seem to have found them. This is true of both conservative and progressive parties, with the previously mentioned exceptions.

Second, the two largest parties are internally disunited. Both the Liberal Democrats and the Socialists are really congeries of factions held together primarily by the tactical requirements of effective campaigning and parliamentary competition. Within both parties there is a great deal of disagreement on major issues of policy and program. Neither the Liberal Democratic Party nor its several factions may be said really to have a basic program. The party's politics are pragmatic and professional rather than ideological. The Socialists, primarily ideological in their orientation, share some common theoretical ground among themselves but differ so fiercely over the all-important means of translating theory into practice that they are at least as disunified as their opposition. Indeed, it seems to be easier for the practical conservatives to reach agreements on particular political issues than for the more theory-oriented progressives to do so. The results of such a situation are constant instability and strife within each party. The first concern of a party leader must be the careful nursing of the factional coalition that supports him in power; the loss of even one element may well be fatal to his leadership. These are not circumstances conducive to strong, continuous, or courageous party leadership. As a consequence, although the parties —or, more specifically, their leaders—increasingly discuss and suggest national policies and formulate these as bills for parliamentary adoption, the policies are almost certain to represent the end product of an elaborate series of compromises. Between the two largest parties, the fundamental differences in their political orientation produce a marked and dangerous lack of common ground. A rigorous, theoretical approach to politics confronts a hostile and pragmatic approach. The terms and levels of discourse are different, and on issues judged to be basic, both sides are inflexible. Pitched battles rather than parliamentary processes are frequently the result.

It should also be clear that Japan does not have a two-party system in the American sense. Only once since 1945, and then briefly, have the Socialists been able to form a Cabinet—and that was a weak coalition. Instead, Japan has a multiparty system in which one party, the Liberal Democratic Party, has been constantly in power. There is no present indication that the Japan Socialist Party's circumstances will undergo a marked improvement in this respect. In fact, if anything, their prospects of gaining power have on the whole been steadily deteriorating since 1958.

Considering the weakness of the Socialist Party and the fierce hostilities, suspicions, and rivalry that beset the five opposition parties collectively, some understanding of the basic immobilism of Japanese party politics begins to emerge. The Liberal Democrats and their predecessors have been able to rule without interruption since 1948 partly because of a lack of any credible alternative. Despite this advantage, the Liberal Democratic share of the popular vote has declined steadily from 57.8 percent in the 1958 general election to 41.8 percent in 1976. Adding to these figures the proportion of the vote for independent candidates that really should be counted for the Liberal Democrats, the party's total was somewhat improved to 46 or 47 percent. That was still dangerously less than a majority. It is really the superior campaigning skills of the party that have maintained for it a working majority in the lower house. In the 1972 election, for example, the Liberal Democratic Party was able to translate 46.8 percent of the popular vote into control of 55.1 percent of the seats—this does not include the eleven successful independent candidates who joined the Liberal Democrats immediately after the election (see table 8–2). After the 1976 election, however, this ruling margin—even after some thirteen victorious independents were added—had shrunk to 51.2 percent of the seats (262 of a total of 511). Adding to this dwindling measure of success at the polls the adverse consequences of a succession of highly publicized scandals involving Liberal Democratic leaders, the apparent ending of the boom economy so long sustained in Japan, the impact of an unusually prolonged recession, a hostile press, the advent of the New Liberal Club, and sheer public boredom with the party after some thirty years in power in one guise or another, it is now conceivable—some would say probable—that the Liberal Democrats will fail to obtain a working majority of the seats in the lower house in some election in the near future. Somewhat less serious, but probably more imminent, would be a similar loss in the House of Councilors.

Should either of these events occur, Japan would be faced with the prospect either of a certainly unstable minority government or of the need to patch together some sort of coalition government with a working majority. The preceding sections have dealt with the problems of forming such a coalition from the present opposition parties as long as the Liberal Democratic Party retains anything approximating one-half of the seats. The remaining alternatives are clear. Either several of the existing parties could split up and recombine into a new majority party—probably the left wing of the Liberal Democratic Party, the New Liberal Club, and all or some elements of the Democratic Socialist, Clean Government, and Japan Socialist parties—or the present Liberal Democratic Party could enter into a coalition that would insure it the dominant position in the group with one or more of the previously mentioned parties. Of the two, the latter alternative currently seems a bit more probable in the near future. It is difficult to see, however, how such a development would improve the quality of governance in Japan. It would probably serve to make decisions and actions even more difficult and time-consuming than they are at present.

BIBLIOGRAPHY

BECKMANN, GEORGE M., AND OKUBO GEN JI. *The Japanese Communist Party, 1922–1945.* Stanford, Calif.: Stanford University Press, 1969, 453 pp.

BERGER, GORDON M., *Parties Out of Power in Japan, 1931–1941.*

Princeton, N.J.: Princeton University Press, 1977, 413 pp.

COLE, ALLAN B., ET AL., *Socialist Parties in Postwar Japan.* New Haven, Conn.: Yale University Press, 1966, 490 pp.

FUKUI, HARUHIRO. *Party in Power: The*

Japanese Liberal Democrats and Policy Making. Canberra: Australian National University Press, 1970, 301 pp.

LANGER, PAUL F., *Communism in Japan: A Case of Political Naturalization.* Stanford, Calif.: Hoover Institution Press, 1972, 112 pp.

SCALAPINO, ROBERT A., *Democracy and the Party Movement in Prewar Japan: The Failure of the First Attempt.* Berkeley, Calif.: University of California Press, 1975, 471 pp.

SCALAPINO, ROBERT A., *The Japanese Communist Movement, 1920–1966.* Berkeley, Calif.: University of California Press, 1967, 412 pp.

SCALAPINO, ROBERT A., AND MASUMI JUNNOSUKE, *Parties and Politics in Contemporary Japan.* Berkeley, Calif.: University of California Press, 1962, 190 pp.

STOCKWIN, J. A. A., *The Japanese Socialist Party and Neutralism.* Melbourne: Melbourne University Press, 1968, 197 pp.

THAYER, NATHANIEL B., *How the Conservatives Rule Japan.* Princeton, N.J.: Princeton University Press, 1969, 349 pp.

TOTTEN, GEORGE O., III, *The Social Democratic Movement in Prewar Japan.* New Haven, Conn.: Yale University Press, 1966, 455 pp.

Chapter *8*

Political Dynamics

ELECTIONS

Japan has had a national election system since 11 February 1889, although in the beginning the suffrage was drastically restricted by tax and residence qualifications to a very small portion of the adult male population. Thereafter, it was gradually liberalized; universal manhood suffrage was adopted in 1925, and universal adult suffrage in December 1945. Prior to World War II, however, general elections were not of primary political importance in Japan. They determined membership in only the lower house of the Imperial Diet, or Parliament, and that house played only a subsidiary and carefully controlled role in the making of public policies. Since Japan's defeat and the enactment of a new Constitution in 1947, however, this situation has changed radically. Elections are now a fundamental aspect of the Japanese political system.

There are many levels and varieties of elections in contemporary Japan, but by far the most important and dramatic are the general elections of the entire membership of the House of Representatives, the lower house of the National Diet that has steadily increased in significance in postwar Japan. Control of a majority or plurality of its seats is tantamount to control of the entire national executive and administrative machinery of the state, and in practice, it is victory in a general election that determines which party will succeed in achieving this cherished goal. As a consequence, general elections are both tense and gala occasions in Japan. Tremendous sums are expended—legally and otherwise—on campaigning, publicity, entertainment, and other means of garnering votes and support. All the media of modern mass communications are called into play, and the public is incessantly entreated and harrassed in noisy attempts to gain its support for this or that candidate and party. When on election day the Japanese voter finally declares his choices, it is a decision of the gravest political consequence; it is comparable in importance to the results of a British general election or the combination of presidential and congressional elections in the United States.

The Electoral System

Among the several levels and types of elections that exist in Japan today, the general elections for the House of Representatives are the primary focus here. There are at the national level, in addition to these, elections of several different types: (1) those that determine membership in the House of Councilors, that is, the upper house of the National Diet, (2) regular referendums on the holders of Supreme Court justiceships, and (3) special referendums or elections on proposed constitutional amendments, although postwar Japan has not yet had such a case. At the local level, the governors and assemblies of prefectures and the mayors and assemblies of cities, towns, and villages are regularly chosen by public election, and provision is also made for special types of elections or referendums in connection with initiative and recall measures. These other national or local elections are not, however, truly central to the Japanese political process in the same degree as are the general elections of the House of Representatives. They are described briefly at a later point.

The present general electoral system in Japan is based on the Public Offices Election Law of April 1950 that consolidated several earlier laws in this field. It guarantees the right to vote to practically all Japanese citizens, male or female, who have reached the age of twenty. Candidates for office must be twenty-five. In the case of the House of Representatives, the Constitution prescribes four-year terms for all members. In fact, with the exception of the 1972–76 period, no postwar Diet has served this full term; the Cabinet has always dissolved the lower house at some earlier date and thus brought about general elections at intervals ranging from six and one-half months to three years and eight months. For the purposes of such elections, the membership of the lower house was set at 467. With the thirty-first general election in January 1967 it became 486. With the return of Okinawa to Japanese sovereignty, this number was raised in the 1972 election to 491. On 4 July 1975 an additional 20 seats were added, bringing the total number of seats in the House of Representatives to 511. Candidates are returned from 130 (124 before the 1976 general election) "medium-sized" election districts; each district returns from three to five members, with the exception of the special district of the Amami Islands that is represented by a single member. Despite the fact that several members are returned from all but one of these districts, each elector casts only one vote. The system has no multiple voting or proportional representation. It is technically a multimember constituency, single vote system. Campaigning is legally restricted to a period of thirty days preceding the election, and almost all facets of campaign practice—including finance, personnel, campaign offices, speeches, advertising, and publicity in general—are rigidly, although somewhat ineffectively, regulated by law.

This type of electoral system gives rise to a number of problems and practices that are unfamiliar in the West. It produces a wide range of rather exotic problems for the practical politician. If, for example, a major party is conducting a general election campaign in a given election district that returns five members, how many candidates should it run—five, four, three, or fewer? If it runs too many in proportion to the party's probable popular support in that district, it takes a serious risk of dividing the party's strength too many ways and thus of losing one or more seats to less powerful parties and candidates who mass their smaller total support behind just one or two candidates. If it runs too few candidates, it is wasting those votes that exceed the number required to elect this smaller number of candidates, and this excess may be enough to elect still another candidate. The problem is complicated further by the fact that most major party contenders really run as candidates of a faction within their party rather than of the party itself. For this reason party candidates usually compete more keenly and bitterly with other candidates nominally of their own party—but actually from other factions—than they do with the ostensible opposition.

Once having determined the optimum number of candidates for a given district, how does the party insure an optimal distribution of its total vote among its several candidates? Any excess votes polled by the party's strongest candidates over the number required to insure their election can only detract—and perhaps disastrously—from the votes available to the party's weaker candidates in that district. This creates problems in the proper apportionment of the vote. The system thus contains a sort of built-in bias in favor of weaker parties and candidates. It forces the majority party to calculate its chances optimistically and constantly tempts it to run too many candidates, thus splitting its strength. At the same time the system encourages weaker parties to concentrate their smaller support more effectively behind one or two candidates. These are problems not encountered in single-member constituencies in the United States.

Many Japanese, especially in the Liberal Democratic Party, feel that this electoral system maximizes factionalism and disunity within a political party, adversely affects the quality of leadership that parties can provide for the country, places a premium on local as opposed to national electoral issues and on considerations of personality rather than of policy, and is conducive to an unnecessary and highly undesirable amount of electoral corruption and campaign abuses. As a consequence there is a good deal of current discussion of possible changes and improvements through the adoption of a small district, single member, single vote system or some modified version of this incorporating features of proportional representation. Politically, however, few institutions are more difficult to change than electoral systems, and it has not yet been possible to obtain the needed degree of consensus, even within the ranks of the majority party. Despite this, almost every year witnesses well-publicized proposals for the revision of the electoral system. These are invariably so controversial and so hazardous to the political fortunes of present Diet members that, if seriously pressed, they would lead to major disruptions of the parliamentary process. Under these circumstances the proposals are either voluntarily withdrawn by the government or scaled down to a point of innocuousness that is acceptable to both the government and major elements of the opposition. What minor progress has been achieved falls in this latter category.

The Japanese electoral system, like that of the United States, has failed to keep abreast of large-scale shifts in residence within Japan. Until July 1964, there had been no reapportionment of seats to compensate for the much more rapid growth of population in the cities than in the countryside. The population of the city of Tokyo, for example, more than doubled in the ten years between 1950 and 1960, whereas that of many of the more rural prefectures and election districts actually declined. Yet there had been no increase at all in the number of members representing Tokyo in the House of Representatives. As a consequence, the actual political value of a Japanese elector's vote varied enormously depending on where he lived. It was worth, for example, approximately three times as much if he was a resident of Hyogo Prefecture's rural and stable Fifth Election District than if he lived in Tokyo's First District. Periodically a reluctant government makes half-hearted attempts to cope with such inequities, invariably through the device of adding new seats to the existing quota for the most overpopulated and underrepresented districts without at the same time withdrawing seats from the most underpopulated and, hence, overrepresented districts. A very partial reapportionment law enacted in July 1964 added five new electoral districts and 19 new seats to five of the most underrepresented metropolitan districts. The 4 July 1975 reapportionment under Prime Minister Miki added 20 new seats to the existing 491 and distributed them among a total of eleven election districts (six of these new) in such crowded areas as Tokyo, Osaka, Kanagawa, Chiba, and Saitama. Nevertheless, many inequities and discrepancies remain.

An electoral system of this sort poses formidable problems for the individual candidates as well as for the parties. These differ somewhat according to party, personality, and sociopolitical setting, but they may be summarized as follows. Candidates of the Liberal Democratic Party normally run as incumbents or, at least, as former members out of office for a term or two. In the 1972 general election, for example, the average successful Liberal Democratic candidate had served more than five terms. As serving members of the party's delegation in the House of Representatives, they normally receive the status of an officially approved party candidate without serious difficulty. If they were candidates running for the first time or former members trying to regain a lost seat, securing this status of an approved Liberal Democratic candidate would be their initial problem. This is usually a highly contentious matter, pitting faction against faction within the party, each seeking approval for its own candidate. Since the Liberal Democratic Party normally runs two or more candidates in most election districts, it is taken for granted that a Liberal Democratic candidate's most menacing rivals are as apt to be other LDP candidates running in the same district as the candidates of other political parties. Seldom, however, are these intraparty rivals from the same faction of the Liberal Democratic Party. They generally come from other factions, and this adds bitter fraternal competition to the contest.

Having secured approved status, the candidate's problem then becomes how to secure adequate financing—campaign costs, although legally fixed at a nominal level, are in actual fact very high in Japan—and how to organize a winning campaign. Campaign finance is, of course, a murky area in which rumors abound but proven facts are scarce. During a recent upper house election, however, the Japanese press made a good deal of the slogan, *Go-to —yon-raku* (literally ¥500 million [$1.6 million] wins—¥400 million [$1.3 million] loses). These are post-inflation and post-devaluation of the yen figures, but they are doubtless still somewhat exaggerated. A considerably more moderate estimate made in connection with the 1967 general election placed the average campaign costs of Liberal Democratic candidates somewhere between forty and eighty thousand dollars. However, this estimate applies only to actual expenditures in the legal campaign period of the thirty days immediately preceding the election and thus seriously understates the real costs.

Where do these very sizable funds come from? In general, it varies with parties. Liberal Democratic candidates draw upon their own and family resources and upon those of whatever wealthy connections they may have in the area or elsewhere. Some financial support for all approved candidates comes directly from party headquarters in Tokyo, while a very important portion comes from the leader of the Liberal Democratic faction with which the candidate is affiliated. Major businesses do not normally give directly to individual candidates because of the invidious choices and possibly adverse consequences involved in picking some and rejecting others. They give rather to the party headquarters and to selected factional leaders within the party. Socialist candidates rely heavily upon the labor unions, especially those associated with the labor union confederation known as *Sohyo*, for both funds and volunteer labor. They also receive some business funding. Democratic Socialists depend upon the *Domei* unions in similar fashion. The Clean Government Party's candidates call upon their parent organization, the Buddhist sect called *Sokagakkai* and its members, while the finances of the Japan Communist Party come from party publications, dues, and so on.

The organization and conduct of election campaigns—which are technically limited to the thirty days immediately preceding an election day but in fact involve many months of strenuous effort—also differ somewhat by party and individual style. All of the candidates in general elections cultivate what are now called *koenkai* or support groups. These are often, especially in rural areas, particular areas where the candidate for reasons of local residence, family connections, or career service is well known and enjoys strong support. Such geographically defined bailiwicks are traditionally referred to by the Japanese as *jiban*. *Koenkai* may also be constituted—and today usually are—from aggregations of interest groups that lack the degree of geographic specificity and unity associated with *jiban* and to which the candidate is able to make some special appeal. *Koenkai* of this sort are more typical of urban jurisdictions, and once put together, they are assiduously "nursed" by the candidate at great and continuing expense. The costs involved are not so much outright bribes in our sense of the term as they are entertainment, contributions to the causes and interests involved, and expected gifts on ritual occasions. Support groups of this sort are the secret of success in Japanese elections. On the progressive side, they tend to involve unions and their members substantially; on the conservative side, they are more diffuse but often better organized and more effective. They are, however, a universal phenomenon; once established, the constancy of the electoral support they provide for their patron is a potent reason for the low turnover rate in Japanese politics at the national level.

Thus, electoral campaigns in Japan are highly professional, very costly, and elaborately structured contests that in reality go on three hundred sixty-five days—and nights—of the year. They involve fierce competition across party lines and, in the case of the Liberal Democratic Party and less frequently the Socialist Party, bitter rivalries between the candidates of different factions within the party as well. Professional politicians in Japan live a strenuous life.

Electoral Participation

Among nations in which voting is not compulsory, Japan has a very high rate of electoral participation. The great majority of those who are eligible ordinarily vote. The latest available compilation of the national list of qualified electors shows that a total of 78,244,787 Japanese were entitled to vote in the general election of 1976 (see table 8–1). This represented 70 percent of the total population of Japan. In the 1976 general election, 56,612,755 of those then eligible to do so (or 73.5 percent of the qualified voters) cast valid ballots. This was the fifth lowest turnout for such an election since 1947. It still compares very favorably with the 55–56 percent of the American adult population who have voted in recent presidential elections.

By American standards, it is also interesting to note in table 8–1 that rural voting turnouts in Japan are uniformly and appreciably higher than urban and that electoral participation increases as one goes down the scale from national through prefectural to local elections. In both cities and countryside, a local assembly election has usually brought out anywhere from 77 to 95 percent of the eligible voters. Both of these phenomena reverse the usual American experience. The higher voting rate in the countryside is primarily explained by the greater political docility and mobilizability of farm as opposed to city voters. Also, failure to vote, which is socially disapproved, is hard to conceal from one's friends and neighbors in the countryside, whereas urban residence provides a measure of anonymity in this respect. The survival of traditional views of one's village, town, fief, or other local unit as the arena of most meaningful political interests and loyalties further accounts for the greater appeal of local elections. These

TABLE 8-1
PERCENTAGE OF QUALIFIED VOTERS PARTICIPATING IN POSTWAR ELECTIONS

	HOUSE OF REPRESENTATIVES Percentage voting				HOUSE OF COUNCILORS Percentage voting		PREFECTURAL ASSEMBLIES Percentage voting				LOCAL ASSEMBLIES Percentage voting	
Election	Total	Urban	Rural	Number of qualified voters	National constituency	Local constituencies	Total	Urban	Rural	Assemblies of the five great cities	City assemblies	Town and village assemblies
1947	67.95			40,907,493	60.93	61.12	81.65			—[a]	—[a]	81.17
1949	74.04			42,105,300								
1950				43,461,371	72.19	72.19						
1951				44,230,610			82.99			72.92	90.56	95.92
1952	76.43			46,772,584								
1953	74.22	66.06	80.23	47,090,167	63.18	63.18						
1955	75.84	71.90	80.60	49,235,375			77.24			62.26	85.00	92.33
1956				50,177,888	62.10	62.11						
1958	76.99	74.19	81.18	52,013,529								
1959				53,516,473	58.74	58.75	79.48	76.41	84.75	65.09	85.81	92.50
1960	73.51			54,312,993								
1962				56,137,295	68.21	68.22						
1963	71.14			58,281,678			76.85	73.63	83.72	65.60	82.32	91.50
1965				59,542,585	67.01	67.01						
1967	73.99			62,992,906			71.31	67.46	80.78	57.65[b]	77.90	91.53
1968				65,886,745	68.93	68.93						
1969	68.51			69,260,424								
1971				71,177,667	59.23	59.24	72.93			61.37[b]	78.18	92.42
1972	71.76			73,769,636								
1974				75,356,068	73.20	73.20						
1975				77,051,384			74.13			64.43[b]	77.54	92.66
1976	73.45			78,244,787								
1977				78,321,715	68.49	68.49						

[a] These figures are included in the town and village figure for 1947.
[b] For the six largest cities in the 1967 elections and the eight largest in the 1971 and 1975 elections.

older identifications have not yet been effectively superseded by a more modern focus on the nation as the prime claimant of popular political interest and allegiance. Such a transfer is gradually in process, however, in recognition of the increasingly obvious fact that most of the policy decisions that seriously affect the well-being of the countryside are made by the national government in Tokyo, not by local governments.

Women were enfranchised in Japan in December 1945. Since the end of World War II, they have also consistently outnumbered the male population —by 56.8 to 55.0 million, for example, in the latest census of 1975. It is important to note, therefore, that they actually make use of this enfranchisement. Normally a slightly higher proportion of eligible females vote than do males. The figures for the turnout at a recent general election, for example, were 72.4 percent for women and 71.0 percent for men.

The Electoral Record: General Elections

Against this background, let us examine the results of twelve of the general elections for members of the House of Representatives held in Japan since the enactment of the new Constitution in 1947 (see table 8–2). There have, of course, been a number of political parties involved during this period and, as a result of splits and amalgamations, some of these no longer exist as independent units. For introductory purposes, therefore, it may be more satisfactory to talk first in terms of "conservative" versus "progressive," or left-wing, parties, to consider these as units, and then to define the parties more precisely.

The most notable fact about the Japanese electoral record is the continuous predominance of the "conservative" vote. Since 1945 and the end of the war, there has been one brief nine-month period in 1947–48 when a Socialist, Katayama Tetsu, was prime minister. He was, however, the leader of a coalition government involving the Socialist Party and a dissident conservative party. It is difficult to regard his record in office as in any way socialistic. With this single exception, all of Japan's postwar governments have been led by conservative politicians, and all but the first two of these were members of the Liberal Democratic Party or its immediate forebears. Their electoral record is interesting and may be viewed in terms either of the proportion of the total popular vote polled in general elections for the House of Representatives or of the percentage of the seats in that house controlled by their party; both are significant.

In terms of their proportion of the popular vote, the conservatives' share did not—with the exception of the 1947 election—fall below 63 percent of the total until 1958. In that year it declined to 57.8 percent, and in the course of the 1960 and 1963 elections fell gradually to 54.7 percent. In the general election of 1967, it went below 50 percent for the first time, declining to 48.8 percent. In the 1969, 1972, and 1976 elections, it dropped to 47.6, 46.8, and 41.8 percent respectively. These proportions require qualification in one important respect, however. A large majority of the candidates who run as independents in general elections are in fact conservatives who

TABLE 8-2

RESULTS OF POSTWAR GENERAL ELECTIONS FOR JAPAN'S HOUSE OF REPRESENTATIVES

Party	23RD GENERAL ELECTION (1947)[a]				24TH GENERAL ELECTION (1949)				25TH GENERAL ELECTION (1952)				26TH GENERAL ELECTION (1953)			
	Valid votes	Per-cent-age of votes	Seats	Per-cent-age of seats	Valid votes	Per-cent-age of votes	Seats	Per-cent-age of seats	Valid votes	Per-cent-age of votes	Seats	Per-cent-age of seats	Valid votes	Per-cent-age of votes	Seats	Per-cent-age of seats
Conservatives (subtotal)	16,111,914	58.9	281	60.3	19,260,500	63.0	347	74.5	23,367,671	66.1	325	69.6	22,717,348	65.7	310	66.5
Liberal Party (Jiyuto)	7,356,321	26.9	131	28.1					16,938,221	47.9	240	51.4				
Democratic Party (Minshuto)	6,839,646	25.0	121	26.0	4,798,352	15.7	69	14.8								
People's Cooperative Party (Kokumin Kyodoto)	1,915,947	7.0	29	6.2	1,041,879	3.4	14	3.0								
Democratic Liberal Party (Minshu Jiyuto)					13,420,269	43.9	264	56.7								
Progressive Party (Kaishinto)									6,429,450	18.2	85	18.2	6,186,232	17.9	76	16.3
Hatoyama Liberal Party (Hatoyama Jiyuto)													3,054,688	8.8	35	7.5
Yoshida Liberal Party (Yoshida Jiyuto)													13,476,428	39.0	199	42.7

TABLE 8-2 (continued)

Party	23RD GENERAL ELECTION (1947)[a]				24TH GENERAL ELECTION (1949)				25TH GENERAL ELECTION (1952)				26TH GENERAL ELECTION (1953)			
	Valid votes	Percentage of votes	Seats	Percentage of seats	Valid votes	Percentage of votes	Seats	Percentage of seats	Valid votes	Percentage of votes	Seats	Percentage of seats	Valid votes	Percentage of votes	Seats	Percentage of seats
Progressives (subtotal)	8,178,842	29.9	147	31.5	7,721,414	25.2	90	19.3	8,664,826	24.5	115	24.7	10,209,311	29.5	144	30.9
Socialist Party (*Shakaito*)	7,175,939	26.2	143	30.7	4,129,794	13.5	48	10.3								
Left-Wing Socialist Party (*Saha Shakaito*)									3,398,597	9.6	54	11.6	4,516,715	13.1	72	15.4
Right-Wing Socialist Party (*Uha Shakaito*)									4,108,274	11.6	57	12.2	4,677,833	13.5	66	14.2
Labor-Farmer Party (*Ronoto*)					606,840	2.0	7	1.5	261,190	0.7	4	0.9	358,773	1.0	5	1.1
Democratic Socialist Party (*Minshu Shakaito*)																
Communist Party (*Kyosanto*)	1,002,903	3.7	4	0.8	2,984,780	9.7	35	7.5	896,765	2.6	—	—	655,990	1.9	1	0.2
Minor parties	1,490,057	5.4	25	5.4	1,602,496	5.2	17	3.6	949,036	2.7	7	1.5	152,050	0.4	1	0.2
Independents	1,580,844	5.8	13	2.8	2,008,109	6.6	12	2.6	2,355,172	6.7	19	4.1	1,523,736	4.4	11	2.4
Totals	27,361,657	100.0	466	100.0	30,592,519	100.0	466	100.0	35,336,705	100.0	466	100.0	34,602,445	100.0	466	100.0

[a] Japanese general elections are numbered consecutively from the first, which was held on 1 July 1890.

TABLE 8-2b

RESULTS OF POSTWAR GENERAL ELECTIONS FOR JAPAN'S HOUSE OF REPRESENTATIVES

Party	27TH GENERAL ELECTION (1955)				28TH GENERAL ELECTION (1958)				29TH GENERAL ELECTION (1960)			
	Valid votes	Per-cent-age of votes	Seats	Per-cent-age of seats	Valid votes	Per-cent-age of votes	Seats	Per-cent-age of seats	Valid votes	Per-cent-age of votes	Seats	Per-cent-age of seats
Conservatives (subtotal)	23,385,502	63.2	297	63.6	22,976,846	57.8	287	61.5	22,740,272	57.5	296	63.3
Liberal Party (*Jiyuto*)	9,849,457	26.6	112	24.0								
Democratic Party (*Minshuto*)	13,536,044	36.6	185	39.6								
Liberal Democratic Party (*Jiyu Minshuto*)					22,976,846	57.8	287	61.5	22,740,272	57.5	296	63.3
Progressives (subtotal)	11,903,639	32.2	162	34.7	14,106,028	35.5	167	35.7	15,508,005	39.2	165	35.2
Socialist Party (*Shakaito*)					13,093,993	32.9	166	35.5	10,887,134	27.5	145	31.0
Left-Wing Socialist Party (*Saha Shakaito*)	5,683,312	15.3	89	19.1								
Right-Wing Socialist Party (*Uha Shakaito*)	5,129,594	13.9	67	14.3								
Labor-Farmer Party (*Ronoto*)	357,611	1.0	4	0.9								
Democratic Socialist Party (*Minshu Shakaito*)									3,464,148	8.7	17	3.6
Communist Party (*Kyosanto*)	733,121	2.0	2	0.4	1,012,035	2.6	1	0.6	1,156,723	2.9	3	0.6
Minor parties	496,614	1.3	2	0.4	287,991	0.7	1	0.2	141,941	0.3	1	0.2
Independents	1,229,081	3.3	6	1.3	2,380,795	6.0	12	2.6	1,118,905	2.8	5	1.0
Totals	37,014,837	100.0	467	100.0	39,751,661	100.0	467	100.0	39,509,123	100.0	467	100.0

TABLE 8-2c

RESULTS OF POSTWAR GENERAL ELECTIONS FOR JAPAN'S HOUSE OF REPRESENTATIVES

Party	30TH GENERAL ELECTION (1963)				31ST GENERAL ELECTION (1967)				32ND GENERAL ELECTION (1969)			
	Valid votes	Per-cent-age of votes	Seats	Per-cent-age of seats	Valid votes	Per-cent-age of votes	Seats	Per-cent-age of seats	Valid votes	Per-cent-age of votes	Seats	Per-cent-age of seats
Conservatives (subtotal)	22,423,915	54.7	283	60.6	22,447,834	48.8	277	57.0	22,381,566	47.6	288	59.2
Liberal Democratic Party (*Jiyu Minshuto*)	22,423,915	54.7	283	60.6	22,447,834	48.8	277	57.0	22,381,566	47.6	288	59.2
Progressives (subtotal)	16,576,545	40.4	172	36.7	18,421,124	40.1	175	36.0	16,909,720	35.9	136	28.0
Socialist Party (*Shakaito*)	11,906,766	29.0	144	30.8	12,826,099	27.9	140	28.8	10,074,099	21.4	90	18.5
Democratic Socialist Party (*Minshu Shakaito*)	3,023,302	7.4	23	4.9	3,404,462	7.4	30	6.2	3,636,590	7.7	31	6.4
Communist Party (*Kyosanto*)	1,646,477	4.0	5	1.0	2,190,563	4.8	5	1.0	3,199,031	6.8	14	2.9
Clean Government Party (*Komeito*)					2,472,371	5.4	25	5.1	5,124,666	10.9	47	9.7
Minor parties	59,765	0.2	0	0.0	101,244	0.2	0	0.0	81,373	0.2	0	0.0
Independents	1,956,313	4.8	12	2.5	2,553,988	5.5	9	1.9	2,492,559	5.3	16	3.3
Totals	41,016,540	100.0	467	100.0	45,996,561	100.0	486	100.0	46,989,884	100.0	486	100.0

TABLE 8-2d

	33RD GENERAL ELECTION (1972)				34TH GENERAL ELECTION (1976)			
	Valid votes	Percentage of votes	Seats	Percentage of seats	Valid votes	Percentage of votes	Seats	Percentage of seats
Conservatives (subtotal)	24,563,199	46.8	271	55.1	26,017,608	45.9	266	52.0
Liberal Democratic Party (*Jiyu Minshuto*)	24,563,199	46.8	271	55.1	23,653,624	41.8	249	48.7
New Liberal Club (*Shin Jiyu Club*)					2,363,984	4.1	17	3.3
Progressives (subtotal)	20,636,522	39.3	175	35.7	21,145,272	37.4	169	33.0
Socialist Party (*Shakaito*)	11,478,742	21.9	118	24.0	11,713,005	20.7	123	24.0
Democratic Socialist Party (*Minshu Shakaito*)	3,660,953	6.9	19	3.9	3,554,075	6.3	29	5.7
Communist Party (*Kyosanto*)	5,496,827	10.5	38	7.8	5,878,192	10.4	17	3.3
Clean Government Party (*Komeito*)	4,436,755	8.5	29	5.9	6,177,300	10.9	55	10.8
Minor parties	143,019	0.3	2	0.4	45,113	0.1	0	0.0
Independents	2,645,582	5.0	14	2.8	3,227,462	5.7	21	4.1
Totals	52,425,077	100.0	491	100.0	56,612,755	100.0	511	100.0

failed for one reason or another to receive party approval to run as officially recognized candidates of the Liberal Democratic Party. Consequently, they run as independents and, if they win, return to the party and serve in the Diet or Parliament as regular members of the party. Obviously such candidates' votes should be counted in addition to the total explicitly conservative vote. If this is done, it seems probable that the Liberal Democratic Party's share of the total popular vote did not really fall below the 50 percent mark until the 1976 election. Taking into consideration the popular vote for candidates of the conservative New Liberal Club, it was still the case that in 1976 the conservative camp as a whole—that is, the Liberal Democrats, the New Liberals, and those independents who were in fact conservatives—probably accounted for more than half the popular vote.

Looking at the electoral record from the standpoint of the proportion of seats in the lower house or House of Representatives, the conservative superiority is even more pronounced. Their explicit majority has varied from a high point of 74.5 percent of the seats in the 1949 election when the conservative group was split into three elements to a low of 52 percent in 1976 for the Liberal Democrats and the New Liberals combined. Correcting for the ostensibly independent seats these figures change to 77.1 percent in 1949 and 54.6 percent in 1976.

The circumstances of the Liberal Democratic Party following the 1976 general election call for a bit more explication. It captured only 249 of the 511 seats on that occasion, 7 less than a majority. After the election, 11 victorious independent candidates promptly rejoined the Liberal Democratic Party, thus producing a total of 260 seats for the Liberal Democratic Party—a slim majority of 5 seats. To this must be added two other victorious independents (former Prime Minister Tanaka Kakuei and former Transportation Minister Hashimoto Tomisaburo) who, because they were under indictment for their alleged role in the Lockheed scandal found it politic—for the time being at least—to refrain from formally rejoining the Liberal Democratic Party. However, they consistently voted with their former party, thus giving the Liberal Democrats a scant working majority of 262 seats.

The question naturally arises as to how, while actually polling only about 43.5 percent (including independents) of the vote in 1976, the Liberal Democratic Party was able to control 51.3 percent of the seats in the all-important lower house. The answer is that the unique Japanese electoral system with its multimember districts combined with a single entry ballot (each voter is able to vote for only one candidate) places a high premium on effective campaign strategy. The secret of success lies in achieving an optimal relationship between the number of candidates a party runs in a given election district and the number of votes it controls in that area, given a fairly equable distribution of those votes among the party's total number of candidates. For example, assume the following circumstances. There are five seats assigned the Second Election District of Okayama Prefecture, and it takes a minimum of about sixty thousand votes to win a seat. The Liberal Democratic Party estimates that it should receive a total of about two hundred thousand to two hundred thirty thousand votes. How many candidates should it run? Obviously not five, but should it try for four, or play it safe with three (which is what it actually did in 1976)? The art lies in distributing the available vote with maximum efficiency. In this case, if the party decides to run four candidates—a risky decision— it would try to insure that each would receive slightly more than sixty thousand votes. Any significant deviation from this target is apt to cost them a seat because candidates polling much more than sixty thousand votes would draw this excess from other weaker Liberal Democratic candidates. Obviously in such a system the variables are numerous, and the chances of disaster plentiful. In practice, the Liberal Democrats have usually proven to be more skillful campaign managers than their collective opposition. Adding to this the fact that the Japanese system of electoral districts extensively overrepresents rural areas at the expense of urban ones to the Liberal Democratic Party's advantage, the reasons for the seemingly unearned increment of seats the Liberal Democrats enjoy in the House of Representatives become clear.

A rough measure of a party's skill in securing the maximum number of seats for their total vote may be obtained by dividing the overall number of seats won by that party in a given election by the number of candidates it ran nationwide. This yields a percentage of successful candidates that in turn represents a crude measure of that party's electoral and campaign efficiency. If, for example, this is done for the 1976 general election, the following results: Liberal Democratic Party, 78 percent; Socialist Party, 76 percent; Democratic Socialist Party, 57 percent; Communist Party, 13 percent; Clean Government Party, 65 percent; and New Liberal Club, 68 percent.

The electoral record of Japan's other political parties is, of course, a reciprocal of that of the Liberal Democratic Party. Table 8–2 sets forth the relevant electoral statistics for all major parties in twelve of the general elections (the twenty-third to the thirty-fourth) that have taken place since World War II. The table also makes clear that a substantial number of such parties—nine "conservative," six "progressive," and three others—have been active during this period. Figure 7–1 portrays the lineages and interrelationships involved. For present purposes, however, we are concerned with only the six major parties that currently exist: Liberal Democratic, Socialist, Democratic Socialist, Communist, and Clean Government parties, and New Liberal Club.

Since its reunification in 1955, the Japan Socialist Party has been the largest and most important member of the opposition. Following a disastrous performance in the 1949 general election, when it polled only 13.5 percent of the vote and won only 48 seats, support for the Socialist Party peaked in 1958 with 32.9 percent of the vote and 166 seats. Since then it has steadily declined until by the early 1970s it hovered around 21 percent of the vote and 90 to 123 seats (18 to 24 percent of the total number). This represents an average decline in holdings from roughly one-third to one-fifth of both the vote and the total number of seats.

The electoral fortunes of the Japan Communist Party have in general been a reciprocal of Socialist performance. Discounting the 1949 election that was quite exceptional, the Communist Party until 1963 normally polled less than 3 percent of the vote and controlled three or fewer seats in the lower house of the Diet. Beginning with the 1963 general election, however, its fortunes began to improve. In both the 1963 and 1967 elections, it received from 4 to 5 percent of the popular vote (1.6 to 2.1 million) and secured five seats. In the 1969 and 1972 elections, its percentages of the vote rose to 6.8 and 10.5 (3.1 and 5.4 million), and its seats to fourteen and thirty-eight respectively. It seems probable, therefore, that the Communists have in some measure benefited from the decline in popular support for the Socialist Party. In the 1976 general election, their share of the vote remained stable at 10.4 percent, but their share of the seats declined disastrously to seventeen. In this case it seems to have been the Clean Government Party that benefited by the Communists' losses. Poor campaign management was also a factor.

The Democratic Socialist Party originated in 1960 as a result of a defection of right-wing elements from the Japan Socialist Party. It competed as a separate entity for the first time in the general election of that year. In one sense the party's fortunes have declined ever since. They controlled forty seats in the lower house just before the 1960 election. The closest they have come to that since then has been thirty-one seats in the 1969 election. In 1976 they captured 6.3 percent of the votes and twenty-nine seats. Their portion of the vote in the 1969, 1972, and 1976 elections held steady at about 7 percent, while the number of seats they controlled fluctuated between thirty-one and nineteen. The difference between a steady vote and a decline in seats was largely accounted for by poor campaign management.

The Clean Government Party was established as an official national party in 1964 and participated in its first general election only in 1967. For a new party its initial success was spectacular—5.4 percent of the vote and twenty-five seats at the outset, increasing to 10.9 percent of the vote and forty-seven seats in the very next election (1969). The 1972 election brought sharp reverses, and these figures shrank to 8.5 percent and twenty-nine seats. In 1976, however, they more than made up for this setback; they polled 10.9 percent of the vote and got a total of fifty-five seats to make them once more the third largest party in the lower house.

A new party, the New Liberal Club, entered candidates for the first time in the 1976 general election. The party originated in June 1976 when five Liberal Democrats of the lower house and one from the upper house resigned from the Liberal Democratic Party to form a small party of their own. In December, when the election was held, they ran twenty-five candidates with a remarkable degree of success. They polled a total of 2.3 million votes (4 percent of the total) and elected seventeen members (3.3 percent of the seats) to the new Diet. They obviously benefited at the polls from a sizable number of Liberal Democratic supporters who were disillusioned with the party's chronic internal warfare, its involvement in scandals, and its alleged corruption.

The balance of the electoral record can be treated very briefly. There are a few minor parties of a local sort that normally run a few candidates—from fifteen to thirty-seven in recent elections—for seats in the lower house. One or two at the most have been successful under normal circumstances.

Independent candidates have already received incidental attention since most of them are in fact Liberal Democrats who for one reason or another —usually interfactional politics and competition within the party—have failed to gain recognition as "official" party candidates. Therefore, they run as independents and, if successful, normally make a deal and rejoin the Liberal Democratic Diet contingent as full-fledged party members. Usually independent candidates are quite numerous. There have, for example, been an average of about one hundred twenty of them in the three general elections between 1969 and 1976. The odds are heavily against their success, however, for in those same elections only fourteen to twenty-one of them won. In addition to frustrated Liberal Democrats running under this banner, there are also a few true independents who occasionally win a seat. Their numbers and influence are, however, insignificant.

An overall electoral record of this sort poses an obvious question. Is the Liberal Democratic control over the House of Representatives—and hence control of the prime ministership and the governance of Japan—apt to continue? The question is given point and urgency by the steady decline in the electoral fortunes of the Liberal Democratic Party since organization in its present guise in 1955. At that time its two component elements (the separate Liberal and Democratic parties) received jointly 63.2 percent of the vote and controlled 297 of the 467 seats (63.6 percent) in the lower house. Since then the party's support has steadily dwindled; in the 1976 general election it received only 41.8 percent of the vote and 249 seats (48.7 percent). Even adding the appropriate independent quota to this, it still yields less than 50 percent of the vote and 262 seats (51.3 percent). There is a great deal of speculation as to whether this trend will continue and, if so, what will be the consequences.

Three rather tentative observations would seem to be in order. First, given the demonstrated superiority of the Liberal Democratic Party's skills in campaign management, it is quite conceivable that its share of the popular vote could decline still further, but that it would retain a slim majority of the seats. Second, if the Liberal Democrats should lose their majority in the lower house, this is no warrant that some opposition party or coalition would then take over power. The differences of principle and policy among the several opposition parties are so profound and bitter as to make it extremely difficult for them to form a governing coalition for majority control in the lower house. Finally, this last circumstance would seem to argue for the probability either of the Liberal Democrats continuing to rule as a minority government with open or tacit support from some opposition elements or of a coalition government in which the Liberal Democrats would be the predominant party.

One further point is worth noting with respect to the relative strengths of the Liberal Democratic and opposition parties in Japan. Since 1955 the opposition parties have collectively controlled more than one-third of the votes in the lower house of the Diet. This gives them the power to prevent any attempts to amend the present Constitution, since such proposals require the concurrence of two-thirds or more of all members of both houses of the Diet.

The Electoral Record: House of Councilors Elections

As will be made clear later, the position and powers of the House of Councilors, or the upper house, in the Japanese political system are substantially inferior to those of the House of Representatives, or lower house. As a consequence, elections for the upper house are less dramatic and do not give rise to quite the same intensity of public and political involvement. They are of serious consequence, however, and are so regarded by the parties, the press, and the public. Elections for the House of Councilors are organized differently from those for the lower house. Members are returned from two different constituencies. Of the 252 seats, 100 represent a "national constituency." This consists of the entire country; candidates for these seats run as national candidates and, in theory, solicit votes from all over Japan. The other 152 seats are collectively referred to as the "local constituency." They are apportioned among the forty-seven prefectures in rough proportion to population so that the voters of each prefecture elect candidates to represent them in the House of Councilors. The number of seats involved range from two for the less populous prefectures to as many as eight for Tokyo and Hokkaido. One-half the membership for both constituencies is replaced by elections held every three years. Because of this dual system, each qualified voter is entitled to cast two votes, one for a candidate running in the national constituency and one for a candidate running in the voter's own prefecture (the local constituency).

This somewhat unusual electoral system is historically attributable to a compromise reached between Japanese and American views in the early years of the Allied Occupation of Japan. The American occupation authorities originally favored a unicameral national legislature for Japan. The Japanese government argued strongly for a bicameral legislature of a corporative sort that would provide specific representation for major segments of the population such as business and labor. In the ensuing negotiations, the Americans agreed to a bicameral legislature but insisted on the direct popular election of all members of both houses on the basis of geographically defined districts. The ultimate result for the upper house was this dual constituency system. The local constituency was supposed to insure the inclusion of locally knowledgeable and popular candidates, while the national constituency would provide for the choice of candidates of truly national stature, attainments, and popularity.

In practice these have proven to be elusive goals. The local constituency does in fact return the anticipated sort of candidate with reasonable efficiency, but the national constituency has not worked out as well. The system is biased in favor of either national celebrities such as television stars, best-selling novelists, and highly publicized athletes or, more frequently, individuals capable of mobilizing sizable electoral support in a number of localities throughout Japan. This usually means candidates enjoying the support of major businesses, labor unions, or interest groups with widely dispersed branches and influence.

The results of recent elections for the House of Councilors are set forth in table 8–3. Obviously, the Liberal Democratic Party has been losing strength. Since only one-half the membership stands for election on any one

TABLE 8-3

RESULTS OF ELECTIONS FOR THE HOUSE OF COUNCILORS, 1968–77

Election	Number of candidates	Number elected	RESULTS BY PARTIES (NUMBER OF SEATS WON)						
			Liberal Democratic	Socialist	Democratic Socialist	Communist	Clean Government	Minor parties	Independents
July 1968									
National constituency	93	51	21	12	4	3	9	0	2
Local constituency	212	75	48	16	3	1	4	0	3
Total		126	69	28	7	4	13	0	5
June 1971									
National constituency	106	50	21	11	4	5	8	0	1
Local constituency	199	75	41	28	2	1	2	0	1
Total		125	62	39	6	6	10	0	2
July 1974									
National constituency	112	54	19	10	4	8	9	0	4
Local constituency	237	76c	43	18	1	5	5	1	3
Total		130	62	28	5	13	14	1	7
July 1977									
National constituency	102	50	18	10	4	3	9	3	3
Local constituency	218	76	45	17	2	2	5	3	2
Total		126	63	27	6	5	14	6d	5e

Source: *Nihon Tokei Nenkan, 1975*, pp. 597, 600–601.

aThe normal number of seats in the national constituency would be fifty. When it exceeds fifty as in this case, it signifies that additional seats in that half of the upper house whose terms still have three years to run have fallen vacant by reason of death or resignation and are consequently being filled by this election.

bNote that only half the total membership of the upper house, that is, formerly 125 and now 126 (plus adventitious vacancies), is replaced at any given election.

cFollowing the return of Okinawa to Japanese control in 1972, two seats were added to the local constituency quota to represent that prefecture, thus raising the total membership of the House of Councilors from 250 to 252 and the total number of seats in the local constituency to be filled at any one election from 75 to 76.

dOf the minor parties, the New Liberal Club won three of the six seats involved.

eShortly after the election, two of the independents joined the Liberal Democratic Party.

occasion, the table does not show overall party strengths in the upper house. Since the enactment of the new Constitution in 1947, however, the conservative forces—the Liberal Democratic Party in recent years—have invariably enjoyed a secure margin of control. Lately this has begun to erode. Prior to the 1974 election, for example, they held 134 of the 252 seats, 7 more than the 127 seats required for a majority. Since they lost a total of 8 seats in the election, the Liberal Democratic holdings were technically reduced to 126, or precisely half the total membership of the house. The party's actual margin of control rested, therefore, with about 6 independents who were supporters of the Liberal Democratic Party.

The 1977 election did not really change these circumstances. The Liberal Democratic Party won 63 seats and increased their seats to 65 when two independents joined the party shortly after the election. This once more gave the Liberal Democrats a total of 126 seats or precisely half the membership. Thus, their control depended on the support of a handful of friendly independent members. This tenuous margin of control was, however, somewhat offset by the highly fragmented nature of the opposition that was split into five parties and that collectively controlled only 114 seats.

A very small gain in the collective strength of the opposition parties would, therefore, destroy the Liberal Democrats' majority in the House of Councilors. While such a development would not in itself cause them to fall from power, it would represent a very serious setback to the party's political fortunes. It would necessitate either the formation of a continuing coalition —or a series of ad hoc coalitions on important bills—involving concomitant concessions to some element of the opposition or adjustment to more delay and deadlock on important legislation in the upper house than is already the case. For the Liberal Democrats neither alternative is at all attractive.

The Electoral Record: Local Elections

The great majority of elections in Japan take place at the local level. All forty-seven prefectures elect—normally at four-year intervals—governors and some 2,787 members of unicameral prefectural assemblies. Similarly, the electorates of 643 cities choose mayors and upwards of twenty-one thousand five hundred city or special ward assemblymen. At the lowest level, about 2,613 towns and villages vote for mayors and almost fifty thousand members of local assemblies. Election districts are coterminous with the political jurisdictions involved, and voter interest and turnout is very high (see table 8–1). In 1976, for example, 77.5 percent voted in the city mayoral assembly elections, and more than 92 percent voted in both the mayoral and assembly elections at the town and village levels.

Table 8–4 describes the situation at the beginning of 1975, and illustrates a typical partisan outcome of these local elections. The data indicate that 76 percent of local offices are held by individuals describing themselves as independents, 9 percent by Liberal Democrats, 5 percent by Socialists, 4 percent by Communists, 3 percent by members of the Clean Government Party, 1 percent by Democratic Socialists, and less than 1 percent by adher-

TABLE 8–4

PARTISAN DISTRIBUTION OF LOCAL GOVERNMENTAL OFFICES (1975)

Office	Number	Liberal Democratic	Socialist	Democratic Socialist	Communist	Clean Government	Minor parties	Independents
Prefectural governors	47	18	1	0	0	0	2	26[b]
Prefectural assemblymen	2,787	1,663	477	97	135	118	61	122
City mayors	643	65	17	0	0	0	10	550
City assemblymen	21,530[a]	3,395	2,161	627	1,379	1,574	147	11,730
Town and village mayors	2,620	109	8	0	0	0	4	2,491
Town and village assemblymen	49,299	1,522	1,018	95	1,303	879	70	43,182
Totals	76,926	6,772	3,682	819	2,817	2,571	294	58,101

Source: *Nihon Tokei Nenkan, 1975*, p. 596.

[a]This category includes 1,091 special ward assemblymen in the city of Tokyo.

[b]While most "independents" are in fact conservative, some are "progressives."

ents of minor parties. These official figures very substantially distort the true picture, however. In fact, most of the independents are conservatives who for local reasons prefer to run under the independent label.

Despite this preponderance of Liberal Democratic strength at the local level, "progressive candidates" (those from the left-wing parties) have made steady and imposing inroads into what were once bastions of conservative strength. For example, of the forty-seven prefectural governorships in 1976 nine were held by "progressives," and included among the nine were Tokyo, Kanagawa, Osaka, and Kyoto—four of the most populous and important prefectures in Japan. In 1976, a similar situation existed for big-city mayors; seven of Japan's ten largest cities (Tokyo, Osaka, Yokohama, Kyoto, Nagoya, Kobe, and Kawasaki) had "progressive" mayors. Developments such as these and similar ones in a number of city assemblies are most unsettling for the Liberal Democrats. The systematic policy of the Socialist and Communist parties of focusing their resources and energies on winning the governorships and mayorships of Japan's greatest metropolitan areas seems to be remarkably successful. This is strongly reminiscent of recent left-wing strategy in Italy.

It should be noted, however, that there is a "step-effect" to this phenomenon. In local elections, left-wing candidates prosper most at the higher levels and posts (prefectural governorships and big city mayorships). Even here, however, the conservatives controlled in 1976 thirty-four of the forty-seven prefectures; while in the mayoral elections in 165 cities, conservative candidates were victorious in 121 contests—73 percent of the total.

There are other types of local elections occasioned by the exercise of what the Japanese call "direct popular demands." The electoral aspects of this system resemble, and are inspired by, the American system of recall elections. Provision is made by the Local Autonomy Law for the circulation of petitions requesting the recall of assemblymen, mayors, and prefectural governors as well as the dissolution of local assemblies. If these petitions are signed by one-third of the registered voters in the jurisdiction concerned, an election is held to determine whether a majority of the electorate approves such a move. If they do, recall or dissolution is mandated. Elections of this sort have not been uncommon in postwar Japan.

In addition to local elections and elections for the House of Representatives and House of Councilors, the Japanese Constitution also provides for popular referenda on the records of Supreme Court judges at ten-year intervals. These are routinely held but attract very little public attention or concern. Without exception, the records of all judges have been approved on such occasions.

BIBLIOGRAPHY

BLAKER, MICHAEL K., ed., *Japan at the Polls: The House of Councilors Election of 1974*. Washington, D.C.: American Enterprise Institute, 1976, 157 pp.

CURTIS, GERALD L., *Election Campaigning:*

Japanese Style. New York: Columbia University Press, 1971, 275 pp.

FLANAGAN, SCOTT C., *Japanese Electoral Behavior: Social Changes, Social Networks and Partisanship*. Beverly Hills, Calif.: Sage Publications, 1977.

Chapter *9*

Political Dynamics

LEADERSHIP

The characteristics and quality of political leadership in postwar Japan are particularly difficult to assess. Both Japanese tradition and practice place far less emphasis on individual "leaders" and "leadership" than does American culture. This tendency is reinforced by the multifactional nature of political party organization and the prevalence of committee and consensual techniques of decision making. Under such circumstances, it becomes peculiarly difficult to assign meaningful responsibility for particular political policies or actions and thus to determine what any given "leader" may have contributed to a particular decision. Despite such problems, certain persons who occupy positions of leadership in the Japanese political system can be identified. The members of the Liberal Democratic and opposition contingents in the National Diet have already been mentioned. The Cabinet, a more selective and important leadership group, represents the top level of governmental leadership.

An examination of appointments to the postwar Cabinets demonstrates the impact of war, defeat, and the Allied Occupation on Japan's political leadership. The military figures and the representatives of court circles and the aristocracy so prominent before the war are no longer encountered. Among the prewar elites, only the party politicians, the bureaucrats, and the representatives of business have survived. The onus of defeat, the American-enforced purge of military and ultranationalist elements from public office, and the provisions of the new Constitution combined to drive the traditional leaders from office; in the resulting vacuum of leadership, new faces—or at least new looks—appeared in the higher ranks of the conservative parties and for the most part remain there today.

The standing of these leaders is not based on their appeal to the masses. Just as Japan's political parties are largely associations of professional politicians rather than mass membership organizations, so too are the ranks of its leaders filled by private and closeted means rather than by any sort of popularity contest. In conservative circles, it makes very little difference whether a given person is an accomplished public speaker or possessed of a personality with wide popular appeal. The meaningful criteria are more apt to be length of political service, abilities as a fund raiser, skill as a tactician, administrative ability, possession of useful connections, and a personal reputation for loyalty and sincerity. Such a system tends to bring to the fore men of experience, caution, and a generally conservative approach to political problems rather than more brilliant or venturesome types. Almost all the conservative leaders have had long experience in government. Article 68 of the Constitution requires that a majority of the ministers of state, that is, the Cabinet, must be chosen from among the members of the Diet, and custom decrees that a large majority hold seats in the lower house during their Cabinet service. In practice about 80 percent are normally chosen from the House of Representatives and practically all of the rest from the House of Councilors, with only an occasional Cabinet post given to individuals who are not elected members of the National Diet.

Since the prime ministership is the highest and most powerful political office in postwar Japan, it may be helpful to look briefly at some of the more salient sociopolitical characteristics of the thirteen men who have held that office between 1945 and 1977 (see table 10–1). All but the last three were born in the nineteenth century. Their average age on assuming the prime ministerial office was sixty-three. Individual cases ranged from Tanaka Kakuei who was only fifty-four when he took office in 1972 to Ishibashi Tanzan who was briefly prime minister in 1956–57 at the age of seventy-two. The average tenure of office has been about one year, but this really distorts the picture. Of the twelve whose terms had ended in 1977, four served for a year or less; the terms of Higashikuni Naruhiko, slightly less than two months, and Ishibashi, just over two months, were the shortest. Four of the others held office for more than three years apiece, with the record for longevity (for prewar as well as postwar times) going to Sato Eisaku who served for seven years and nine months, followed by Yoshida Shigeru, six years and nine months.

The background of the prime ministers is mixed. The first two postwar prime ministers—Higashikuni, an imperial prince, and Shidehara Kijuro, an aristocrat and prewar foreign minister—are exceptional and represent a transition to the new Constitution. Yoshida and Ashida Hitoshi were professional diplomats, though Ashida resigned and served for many years in the House of Representatives before becoming prime minister. Katayama Tetsu was a lawyer and Ishibashi a journalist, but both had also long been Diet members. Hatoyama Ichiro and Miki Takeo were really professional politicians; at the time they became prime ministers, Hatoyama had served twenty-five years in the lower house and Miki had served thirty-seven. Kishi

Nobusuke (Ministry of International Trade and Industry), Ikeda Hayato and Fukuda Takeo (Ministry of Finance) and Sato (Ministry of Transportation) were all career bureaucrats who in the latter stages of their service were elected to the postwar Diet and had extensive legislative and Cabinet-level experience before becoming prime ministers. Only Tanaka came from a business background. With the exception of Tanaka, all were university graduates; eight of the thirteen were from Tokyo University's Law Department. All seem to have come from prosperous families. Two were brothers —Kishi and Sato (Sato was adopted, left his own family, and changed his name).

A recent study suggests the following generalizations about Cabinet members.[1] Practically all postwar Japanese Cabinet members have been male. In the 1946–73 period, 275 men and 2 women attained Cabinet rank. On the average, they first attained this high office between the ages of fifty-one and fifty-five, but the modal figures are probably more representative. When first appointed, 58 percent were fifty-six or older, and only 11 percent were under forty. They held Cabinet office for an average of two years in the course of their entire political career—not necessarily, or even normally, in continuous sequence. About 57 percent served for less than one year and 77 percent less than two years—a testimonial to the postwar practice of rapid rotation of the Cabinet to reward as many deserving party members as possible. These brief terms are, however, somewhat offset by the relatively few (about 10 percent) major figures who have held Cabinet rank for periods of four to more than seven years.

This generally high rate of turnover in the Cabinet is, of course, calculated. The factionalized nature of the ruling parties in postwar Japan requires a prime minister to maintain a majority coalition of factions within his party—the mainstream group—if he hopes to stay in office. Therefore, factional leaders belonging to the mainstream group—and, to a limited extent, others as well—must be continuously rewarded and kept in line. In order to retain the allegiance of their followers in the Diet and to attract new members, these factional leaders must also dispense rewards for loyal service. In addition to campaign and operational funds, the major prize for factional leaders and their followers is access to Cabinet positions, especially the most important and prestigious ones such as finance, international trade and industry, or agriculture and forestry. These are prizes that only the prime minister can bestow. Obviously, the higher the turnover rate in Cabinet office, the more often he can reward the virtuous and punish or mollify his intraparty opponents. Major reorganizations of postwar Cabinets have occurred frequently (see table 10–1). Starting with the fourth reorganization of Yoshida's Cabinet in October 1952 when the postwar pattern really established itself and ending with the last Tanaka Cabinet of 1974, the average ministerial term was only about nine months. Thus, although the normal Japanese Cabinet member may be a person of high intelligence and ability, the probability is that he or she will hold office too briefly to acquire

[1] Peter P. Cheng, "The Japanese Cabinets, 1885–1973: An Elite Analysis," *Asian Survey*, vol. XIV, no. 12 (December 1974), 1055–71.

a real feel for the job or to formulate and enact any sort of program. These are circumstances calculated to enhance the importance of bureaucratic at the cost of political leadership. This is not equally true of prime ministers, however. In recent years they have served for much longer terms. In some degree, this brevity of tenure for the Cabinet ministers may be compensated for by experience gained in the course of multiple terms in the Cabinet. About one-third of the Cabinet members have over the years held more than one Cabinet post; one has actually served at the ministerial level in seven different posts.

Postwar Japanese Cabinet ministers have generally been well educated. Most (88 percent) have been university graduates, usually from law departments. Almost 47 percent of these have graduated from the same university, Tokyo, followed by Kyoto (8 percent) and Waseda (7.6 percent). A few have attended universities in Western Europe (3.6 percent) or the United States (2.2 percent). Another 17 percent have had significant experience abroad. There is no notable pattern of geographic areas from which postwar Cabinet ministers originally derive.

Finally, it is of some interest to note the professional backgrounds of Cabinet ministers. Over the 1946–73 period, about 46 percent have been career politicians, usually with prior service in prefectural assemblies as well as the National Diet. About 18 percent have been former bureaucrats in the national service who, after retirement or resignation, have run successfully for the Diet. Another 19 percent come from careers in business, while about 15 percent were professionals from fields such as education, law, or journalism. Unlike the United States, relatively few lawyers achieve Cabinet status or, for that matter, figure prominently in politics at any level. The military are totally unrepresented because Article 66 of the postwar Constitution requires all ministers to be civilians.

The number of ex-bureaucrats in the Cabinet has been a subject of prolonged and bitter controversy in Japan. Almost without exception, former bureaucrats who run for the Diet do so on the Liberal Democratic ticket. This is even more applicable to the forty-odd who have achieved Cabinet office. This combined with a fairly widespread tendency to regard ex-bureaucrats as an elite and anti-democratic force in Japanese politics has made bureaucrats as a group a frequent target for abuse, suspicion, and condemnation by opposition elements and the press. There is little evidence to document a blanket accusation of this sort, but it has figured prominently in the political discourse of postwar Japan.

We come finally, therefore, to a deeper truth about the nature of political leadership in postwar Japan. Obviously, Cabinet ministers are in no position to exercise effective or continuing control over national policies. The prime minister, by experience, tenure, and authority, is better equipped to do so, and in fact, he is without doubt the single greatest source of ultimate direction and control. To assert this, however, is not to claim or to clarify a great deal. The prime minister is limited by and dependent upon the support of the factional leaders in the mainstream group. He is continuously and vitally dependent upon the higher reaches of the professional bureaucracy for technical and policy advice and for action of any sort. His own and his party's essential financial support derives largely from big business sources that are only partly subject to his influence. He is even somewhat dependent upon the leadership of the opposition parties to maintain that degree of civility in the Diet without which a parliamentary system cannot function or long survive. Beyond all this lies the great, unmobilized but potent force of Japanese public opinion. For all these reasons and more it would be a serious error to regard a prime minister as an independent force of great and autonomous authority in Japanese politics. Neither his autonomy nor authority rival that of an American president, although the president is also subject to similar external influences.

Who then rules Japan? Some years ago Japanese commentators occasionally employed an analogy based on an old children's game called *Jon-kem-po*. ("scissors-paper-rock"—scissors cut paper, paper covers rock, and rock breaks scissors). These commentators so portray the complex interactions of the party in power, which can allegedly control the bureaucracy, which can in turn through its regulatory powers make or break big business, which has the capacity to nourish or starve the party in power by granting or withholding financial support. This imagery dramatizes in simple terms the interactions and interdependencies of three major elements in the Japanese pantheon of political power: the party in power (particularly the prime minister), the higher civil servants, and big business. It is, however, far too simple to be either accurate or very useful. It imputes a wholly spurious unity to the major elements involved and tempts the incautious or the credulous to assume that any or all of these three elements share common interests and goals, concert common policies for their realization, or act as a unit in striving to effectuate such policies. None of these theses are even remotely true. There are actually very few issues of practical importance on which there is anything approximating general agreement within the ranks of the party in power, the bureaucracy, or big business. Much more common —indeed, normal—are varying degrees of internal suspicion, rivalry, competition, and outright strife. Furthermore, any significant issue in which this normal dissension prevails automatically creates an occasion and incentive to improvise ad hoc alliances, first, among like-minded elements within each of these three camps and, second, with potential allies in the other two camps. The possible combinations and permutations are numerous and are regulated only by the nature and importance of the policy issue or action at stake and by the ranges of loyalty or obligation that can be invoked by the several parties in their search for allies. Some very improbable bedfellows are apt to emerge from so complicated a process.

The complexity of the distribution of political power and influence is important in any modern political system, but it is especially true of Japan. There is no single or satisfactory answer to the question, Who rules Japan? It varies with time, with issues, with specific circumstances, and with personalities. It is always more complex and more obscure than it seems to be. Throughout Japanese history political power has seldom, if ever, really been wielded by those whose official position apparently entitled them to do so. In this sense the degree of real, albeit qualified, authority inherent in the postwar prime ministership probably represents something of a departure from tradition. In systems in which authority and decision-making power are diffuse, it is extraordinarily difficult to assign responsibility for particular governmental policies and actions. This is certainly true in Japan, as in all modern political systems. To some extent, however, the legal fiction that holds the party in power and its leadership formally and legally accountable for all governmental acts provides a viable substitute for another more accurate means of assigning responsibility.

BIBLIOGRAPHY

KUBOTA, AKIRA, *Higher Civil Servants in Postwar Japan.* Princeton, N.J.: Princeton University Press, 1969, 197 pp.

MANNARI, HIROSHI, *The Japanese Business Leaders.* Tokyo: University of Tokyo Press, 1975, 296 pp.

NAJITA, TETSUO, *Hara Kei in the Politics of Compromise, 1905–1915.* Cambridge, Mass.: Harvard University Press, 1967, 314 pp.

SILBERMAN, BERNARD S., *Ministers of Modernization: Elite Mobility in the Meiji Restoration, 1868–1873.* Tucson: University of Arizona Press, 1964, 135 pp.

SILBERMAN, BERNARD S., AND H. D. HAROOTUNIAN, eds., *Modern Japanese Leadership: Transition and Change.* Tucson: University of Arizona Press, 1966, 433 pp.

SPAULDING, ROBERT M., JR., *Imperial Japan's Higher Civil Service Examinations.* Princeton, N.J.: Princeton University Press, 1967, 416 pp.

Chapter *10*

Decision Making

THE ORGANS
OF GOVERNMENT

The primary function of politics is to enable men to make and administer decisions in the realm of public affairs, an area that is variously defined by different societies. The machinery by which these decisions are formally made and administered is government. Government provides both a mechanism for determining and administering public policies and a process for bestowing legitimacy on the decisions and products of this mechanism. In practice it does more than this. By providing a context and a structure for the making of official decisions, it also comes to influence the types of questions that are posed and decisions that are made. Government—the formal political institutions of a society—thus interacts continuously with the broader and less formalized "political system" or "political process" of a given society.

The political system includes government but also encompasses such unofficial components of a society's decision-making apparatus as interest groups, the leadership structure, value systems, and political style. Since the government and the political system are intimately linked and vitally affect each other, there is a constant struggle among interests and groups for control of some or all of the mechanisms of government. Whoever controls government controls the official apparatus for promulgating views and promoting interests and thus has a distinct advantage over his or her competitors. Control of the machinery of government is the immediate issue in the political struggle in Japan. This machinery is the normal instrument of political achievement.

141

The Constitution of Japan

Politics involves struggle and competition, and to keep these within tolerable limits, societies agree on certain rules to regulate the game of politics. Some of these rules are adjudged to be more fundamental than others and are usually formulated into separate bodies of law known as constitutions. Constitutional provisions command greater status and veneration, are presumed to have more permanency, and are deliberately made harder to change than the normal body of laws and ordinances.

In modern times Japan has had two constitutions. The first of these, the Meiji Constitution, was promulgated in 1889 and took effect in 1890. The second, the Constitution of Japan, was promulgated on 3 November 1946 and took effect six months later on 3 May 1947. Its origins were most unusual. In the early days of the Allied Occupation, General MacArthur, the Supreme Commander for the Allied Powers (SCAP), was charged with the democratization of Japan. The higher American officials in Washington and those involved in the occupation generally agreed that the achievement of this goal would necessitate some rather substantial changes in the Meiji Constitution. The Japanese government was so informed, and during the early months of the occupation, the initiative was left in its hands. When by February 1946 the committee established by the Japanese Cabinet to propose revisions in the Meiji Constitution showed no signs of recommending the types of democratic changes judged necessary by General MacArthur and his aides, the entire matter was secretly turned over to SCAP's Government Section, which was ordered to produce a model constitution incorporating the types of political changes General MacArthur considered necessary.

The decision to intervene directly and decisively at this time in the rewriting of the Japanese Constitution was partly due to the fact that the Far Eastern Commission, an international agency responsible for setting basic policies for the Allied Occupation of Japan, was scheduled to commence its activities in Washington on 26 February 1946. If the United States, or any of its agents such as SCAP, was interested in having a controlling voice in the contents of a new Japanese constitution, it was essential that it act before 26 February. In fact, the decision to intervene at this particular time seemed to be taken solely on General MacArthur's own authority in Tokyo, and the authorities in Washington probably knew nothing about it until the first draft of the new Constitution was published in Japan on 6 March 1946.

In six days, between 4 and 10 February, the Government Section produced, in English, the original draft of the present Japanese Constitution. This draft was first submitted to the Japanese at a small private meeting on 13 February. During the nine days that followed, the draft was translated into Japanese and sufficient pressure was brought upon the Japanese Cabinet to insure its reluctant adoption of the draft as its own. Thereafter, the Cabinet Draft—as it was now known—went through several revisions that resulted in some changes, largely minor, after which it was submitted to the Imperial Diet as a proposal for the total amendment of the Meiji Constitution. After extensive debate, especially in the House of Peers, the bill of amendment was adopted by overwhelming majorities in both houses and subsequently promulgated by the emperor. The circumstances were such that any other form of action by the Japanese was almost inconceivable. Thus, the present Constitution was drafted and put into effect.

How voluntary was the adoption of the present Constitution by the Japanese government and people? The question continues to be a subject of controversy in Japan. In fact, the Cabinet in 1957 appointed a Commission on the Constitution to study and report on precisely this issue. The commission failed to agree after seven years of elaborate investigation and debate. A majority found that it was "an imposed constitution"; a minority of seven held on somewhat varying grounds that there had been sufficient consultation with the Japanese people at several stages of the drafting and ratifying process to make such a finding excessive and inaccurate. There is some merit in this minority viewpoint. In drafting the constitution, the Government Section did pay some attention to and did draw to some extent upon several drafts of a new constitution proposed by a number of Japanese political parties and private groups. Also, a few significant concessions were made to Japanese preferences before the actual publication of the SCAP draft on 6 March 1946, including the shift from a unicameral to a bicameral National Diet. Thereafter, a larger number of changes were accepted at Japanese urging in the course of the ensuing spring and the parliamentary debates. Despite these concessions, however, the present Constitution of Japan is essentially of American, not Japanese, provenance, and officials of SCAP and the general domestic and international circumstances in which Japan found itself in 1946–47 combined to bring pressures that made it very difficult for the Japanese government to consider seriously any policy but one of fairly total acquiescence in this American initiative. The Japanese people were not directly or effectively consulted on this issue at any time.

Nevertheless, the most important consideration of all may well be that over the ensuing years the Japanese people—and, somewhat more reluctantly, the Japanese government—have come to accept and in general feel comfortable with the document, despite its alien authorship, and have shown no really significant disposition to change it. The few active agents for constitutional change have usually been members of the ruling party. Their specific proposals generally call for rather minor changes, and they have in practice been unable to obtain sufficient agreement on these issues even within their own party to permit any effective action. Consequently, some thirty years after the "imposed adoption" of this new constitution, there has neither been a formal motion for amendment introduced into the National Diet, nor has the Diet considered or adopted legislation prescribing the manner in which the process of constitutional amendment should be effectuated should such a bill ever be offered.

The new Constitution, although almost twice as long as the Meiji Constitution, is reasonably brief as modern constitutions go, consisting of a preamble, 11 chapters, and 103 articles (see appendix 5). The Constitution provides a system of government based essentially on a unique amalgam of

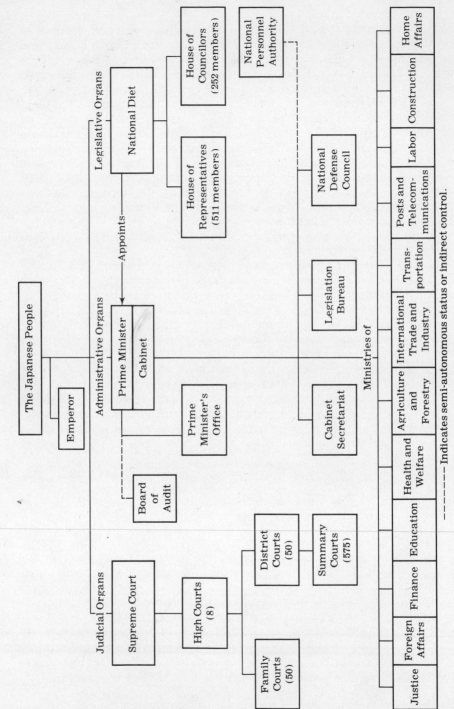

FIGURE 10-1 THE ORGANIZATION OF JAPAN'S NATIONAL GOVERNMENT

British and American institutions (see figure 10–1). It preserves the monarchy but strips the emperor of any semblance of political authority. It also retains a bicameral legislature but completely reconstitutes the relationship and powers of the prewar upper and lower houses. Superior legislative and financial powers are entrusted to the lower house. At the national level, executive and administrative authority is concentrated in a responsible Cabinet, and an independent American-style judiciary is vested with the power of judicial review. The Constitution places great stress on civil rights and includes what is probably one of the world's most detailed and ambitious constitutional statements of the rights and duties of the people. It introduces into Japanese law for the first time the principle of local autonomy, involving decentralization of national power and a reciprocal increase in the rights and independence of local governments to a degree quite foreign to earlier Japanese practice.

One of the best-known and most controversial provisions of the Constitution appears in Chapter II, Article 9. In this famous "renunciation of war" clause, Japan renounces war as a sovereign right of the nation and the threat or use of force as a means of settling international disputes. Indeed, the Constitution seems to obligate Japan never to maintain land, sea, or air forces. This is the only known instance in which a major modern state constitutionally renounces war. The Constitution also specifically provides that it is the supreme law of the land and that no act contrary to its provisions shall have legal force or validity. Amendments to the Constitution require initiation by a two-thirds concurring vote of all members of both houses of the National Diet and ratification by the people through an affirmative vote by a majority of those participating in a referendum on the proposed amendment.

The Constitution of Japan is admirably democratic. It introduces rights, institutions, and practices into Japanese politics that undoubtedly go far beyond anything the Japanese themselves might realistically have been expected to establish. In fact, on the basis of text alone, it is a considerably more democratic document than is the Constitution of the United States. It is also a workable document, although it has flaws and does create problems. For example, any pronounced degree of local autonomy is probably impractical in Japan; judicial review has not yet proven meaningful in practice; and some of the more ambitious civil and human rights and freedoms envisaged in Chapter III of the Constitution will probably long remain pious hopes rather than social or legal facts. Also, the functioning of the National Diet has left a great deal to be desired, especially in parliamentary relationships between the opposition and the party in power. Despite such problems, however, the system as a whole has by any realistic standard of comparison functioned well and has done this along the general lines anticipated in the Constitution. The current circumstances of the Japanese people, particularly when compared to those of 1946–47, testify abundantly to this.

To revert briefly to a matter mentioned earlier in another context, the fact that the 1947 Constitution stands unchanged today, given its antecedents and the enormous political changes it imposed on a reluctant Japanese leadership, is perhaps the most remarkable phenomenon of all. The Japanese have adopted a new and largely foreign set of political institutions with surprising ease and speed and have so far displayed a considerable reluctance to exchange them for something more familiar and more Japanese. This does not mean, however, that there has been a total absence of desire for constitutional change. Some leaders of the Liberal Democratic Party, especially its older elements, have strongly been in favor of revision and have argued that the present Constitution does not really represent the "freely expressed will of the Japanese people," that it was imposed by foreigners, that it is un-Japanese in both spirit and language, that it is poorly drafted, and that it needs changes in a number of particulars. Specifically, many of those who favor constitutional revision advocate such matters as a redefinition of the status of the emperor, constitutional recognition of Japan's right of self-defense, some greater measure of limitation on individual rights when they conflict with the public interest, reforms in the composition and powers of the House of Councilors, the establishment of a special court to judge questions of constitutionality, an increase in the authority of the central government over the localities, and an easier system of constitutional amendment. None of these proposals tampers with the principle of popular sovereignty, and none of them advocates—openly at least—any sort of across-the-board return to prewar conditions. Most of the proposals are for fairly moderate reforms. In the official report of the Commission on the Constitution (1964), a large majority of its members recommended some measure of constitutional revision. Despite this, no actual amendments have yet been formally proposed, and it seems unlikely that the government will seriously attempt to press this issue in the near future.

The absence of amendments plus the fact that the Supreme Court of Japan—although possessed of the power of judicial review—does very little creative or innovative interpretation of the Constitution of Japan does not imply that Japan is saddled with a completely inflexible system of government incapable of adjusting to changed circumstances or shifts in elite or popular views. There are serious problems, but there have also been at least two ways of getting around them. First, "administrative interpretation" of the intent of the Constitution has on occasion been very liberal—amounting, its critics would claim, to subversion by the executive branch of what they hold to be the clear intent of the Constitution. Second, not all the fundamental rules of Japanese politics are incorporated in the Constitution. In practice this document is supplemented by a considerable number of basic laws. These put flesh onto the rather bare bones of the Constitution and prescribe the actual nature and operations of the country's primary political institutions. Examples of such laws are the Imperial House Law, the National Diet Law, the Law of the Courts, the Cabinet Law, the Finance Law, the Public Office Election Law, and the Local Autonomy Law. Since these can be changed by normal statutes rather than by constitutional amendments, they add a desirable quality of flexibility to the structure of the Japanese political system.

The Emperor

In postwar Japan the emperor has only a symbolic role in the Japanese political system. He does not have any specifically political or executive functions of more than ritual or ceremonial importance. Article 1 of the Constitution states the following:

> The Emperor shall be the symbol of the state and of the unity of the people, deriving his position from the will of the people with whom resides sovereign power.

The effect of this and the remaining articles of Chapter I is to deny the emperor any "powers related to government" and to confine his official acts to such ceremonial functions as appointing the prime minister and chief judge of the Supreme Court (after they are designated by the Cabinet); promulgating laws, Cabinet orders, treaties, and amendments to the Constitution; convoking the Diet and dissolving the House of Representatives; attesting certain official appointments; awarding honors; receiving ambassadors and ministers; and performing certain other ceremonial functions. None of these involves any initiative, discretion, or influence on his part; he acts only at the behest of responsible governmental officials and in accordance with their decisions.

The emperor is systematically informed about affairs of state and official policies, but his opinion about them is not formally solicited. Conceivably, on a few issues affecting the imperial family or in a moment of national crisis such as that in August 1945 over the question of Japan's surrender—in which he did play a positive and critical role—the emperor could exert influence, but this would be purely a function of his personal and institutional prestige. He has no legal or theoretical right to do so, and thus his official position is far weaker than that of the British monarch. Technically, he is not even "chief of state" but merely a "symbol of the state," a phrase that the conservative advocates of constitutional revision would like to change. Under these circumstances, the danger that the emperor will once again become an effective screen for or political instrument of a revived militant or ultranationalist faction seems remote.

The Japanese imperial family is by far the oldest reigning family in the world. The traditional date of its founding—660 B.C.—is, of course, mythological rather than factual, but there is reliable evidence that it existed by at least the early sixth century A.D. and has been continuous since then. Today the composition of the imperial family is rigidly and narrowly defined by law. It is limited to the legitimate and direct descendants of an emperor, and adoption is not permitted within the imperial family. Succession to the throne is by the eldest son of the emperor, followed by the eldest son of the eldest son. Matters of succession and regency are regulated by an Imperial House Council, which is completely controlled by ex officio members representing popularly responsible representatives of the legislature, the Cabinet, and the Supreme Court. Curiously by both Japanese and Western standards, the imperial family has no last name. Japanese emperors at their enthronement take regnal titles, a different one for each emperor. The regnal title of the present emperor is, somewhat ironically given the intervention of World War II, *Showa* (Enlightened Peace). Japanese dates are adjusted to these titles. Thus the first year of the present emperor's reign (1925) was the first year of *Showa;* the year 1977 is then *Showa* 52, the fifty-second year of the present emperor's rule. Emperors also have personal names that they sign—or rather stamp with their official seal—on state documents. The present emperor's is Hirohito, but no one ever calls him that. He is usually referred to impersonally as "His Majesty" or "the Present Emperor."

The present imperial family consists only of the emperor, the empress (Nagako), their two sons and the children of these sons, and the families of the emperor's three brothers—the princes Chichibu (who died in 1953), Takamatsu, and Mikasa. Six of the emperor's seven children are still living (one daughter died): four daughters (all of whom have married and thus lost their imperial status), Crown Prince Akihito (born in 1933), and his younger brother, Prince Hitachi. The emperor and empress reside in the former castle of the Tokugawa Shoguns, an enormous enclosure with spectacular battlements and moats located in the heart of downtown Tokyo—thus adding a further and most formidable obstacle to the flow of traffic in streets that are already hopelessly clogged. The prewar palace buildings proper within this compound were destroyed by American bombing during World War II, and it was not until 1969 that a magnificent new palace for state occasions was completed. The emperor and empress actually live elsewhere, and far more modestly, within the grounds. The crown prince and princess live separately, also in downtown Tokyo.

Before the war the imperial family was extremely wealthy in its own right. So extensive were its holdings, in fact, that its critics sometimes referred to it as the greatest of the *Zaibatsu* (cartels). The occupation authorities required that it be stripped of most of its holdings, except for personal property, and that these become public property. This was done, but it is generally believed that the family is still quite wealthy. Its normal expenses, however, are met by sums voted annually by the National Diet. In recent years these appropriations have usually amounted to about seven million dollars annually to cover the expenses of the privy purse, the imperial family, and the imperial household. The official functions and activities of the imperial family are administered by a division of the Prime Minister's Office known as the Imperial Household Agency with a staff of more than one thousand officers and employees.

The emperor's official and ceremonial functions are numerous and time consuming. They are conducted on a plane of extreme formality; there is absolutely none of the fairly casual social or semiofficial mixing with either subjects or foreigners that characterizes most contemporary European royalty. Public appearances of any sort are planned in minute detail and carried out in stiff and ritualistic fashion. While attributable in part to the shy and reclusive character of the present emperor, it is probably even more the result of the extremely traditional and conservative preferences of the higher officials of the Imperial Household Agency who in practice control these matters. It is perhaps of some interest in this connection that the present emperor is the first of his line ever to have traveled abroad. As a young man and crown prince in 1921, he traveled in Europe for several months. In 1971 he and the empress made a brief state visit to six European countries, and in 1975 they spent two weeks in the United States. His son, Crown Prince Akihito, has, however, traveled much more extensively. Such visits are, of course, only ceremonial, although they do have political significance and implications.

It would be a serious mistake, however, to conclude that because of his purely ceremonial position and negligible governmental powers the emperor does not play a very important role in the Japanese political system. A nation historically needs powerful, loyalty-begetting symbols about which to forge its national unity. The absence of such a nationally shared emotional rallying point is one of the greatest problems confronting many of the new states of Asia and Africa. For Japan such a focus is provided preeminently by the imperial family. It symbolizes two thousand years of "Japaneseness," of the unity of the people and their culture. Under present circumstances, there is nothing that can readily or effectively take its place. Its role is not to be discounted or lightly discarded, and many thoughtful Japanese are, therefore, understandably troubled by the low regard in which the imperial institution is held by some segments of Japanese youth. Others feel that a somewhat more humanized or popularized imperial family would be more effective.

The National Legislature

The Constitution describes the Diet, or Parliament, of Japan as "the highest organ of state power" and the "the sole lawmaking organ of the State." It further states that the Diet shall consist of two houses, a House of Representatives (or lower house) and a House of Councilors (or upper house). These provisions are basic, and their significance becomes most apparent when compared with comparable clauses of the Meiji Constitution. Under the terms of that document, the emperor was more than the highest organ of state power; in a mystical way, he embodied the state and wielded its sovereign powers. Although laws were formally the product of the Imperial Diet, both the emperor and the Cabinet had the power to issue decrees that had the force of law. The present Constitution vests sovereignty in the people and makes the Diet both the highest organ of the people's sovereignty and the sole source of law. These changes are basic to both the legal and the power structure of the Japanese state. The government has thus been technically transformed from an emperor-centered to a parliament-centered system, and the elected representatives of the people have, in theory at least, become vastly more powerful.

The organization and powers of the two houses of the Diet differ considerably. The House of Representatives is a body of 511 members who are returned from 130 districts by an electoral system that has already been described. Its members are elected for four-year terms, but only one post-war Diet has survived that long without dissolution by the Cabinet. Actual terms between general elections have ranged from six and one-half months to four years. The tenure of members is thus indeterminate and depends in practice on the relationship between the lower house and the Cabinet as well as on the internal political situation of the lower house and on party politics in general.

The organization of the House of Representatives is quite simple. A speaker, chosen from the ranks of the majority party, presides over its deliberations and maintains order. There is also a vice-speaker, who is normally selected from the membership of the majority party. For delibera-tive purposes, the house functions either in plenary session or in commit-tees. Under American influence, the latter have become the more important mode of operation. There are at present about sixteen standing committees, with functions largely paralleling the principal divisions of the government's administrative organization, for example, foreign affairs, finance, justice, education, agriculture, local administration, budget, and audit. A Commit-tee on House Management (steering committee) and a Committee on Disci-pline deal with problems of internal housekeeping. Members are assigned to these committees, and their chairmanships are usually allocated in accord-ance with relative party strengths in the house. Normally, therefore, all chairmen are from the majority party. Assignments to specific committees are actually made by the parties. Special committees also exist on a tempo-rary basis to deal with particular problems. Examples would be the special committees on the election system, Okinawa and the northern islands, price policies, or traffic safety. Although by definition temporary, a number of these special committees are practically permanent, and all committees have their own staffs. Their chairmen are in some cases drawn from the opposi-tion parties. The members of the lower house each have two private secre-taries, provided at public expense, and the house as a whole is serviced by an administrative and custodial staff numbering slightly under two thousand people. The majority of these are organized into a Secretariat and a Bureau of Legislation. The National Diet Library supplies reference and legislative services to the members of both houses.

The scheduling and flow of legislative business is controlled by the Com-mittee on House Management, composed of senior and experienced repre-sentatives of each political party in numbers proportional to that party's strength in the lower house. Under normal circumstances—a term that applies to a large majority of the bills coming before the house—this system works quite effectively. On noncontroversial matters, the members of the Committee on House Management are briefed in advance by their parties' Diet Strategy Committees and are able to calendar bills and assign time quotas to each party for speaking on the issues involved. On controversial matters, however, the system sometimes breaks down completely, and the committee is unable to agree. In such cases the matter is usually referred to the secretaries-general of all the parties for negotiation and settlement. Protracted negotiations can ensue during which the normal functioning of the house may come to a complete halt.

In general the most meaningful discussions and decisions within the legislative sphere take place in the committees. In this respect alone the Japanese parliamentary system more closely resembles its American than its British prototype. Actually, however, since the Liberal Democratic Party has constantly maintained a working and normally substantial majority in both houses, it would be a serious error to overestimate the importance of what takes place either in the committees or on the floor of the Diet. The Liberal Democratic Party has the legal authority and the parliamentary strength to enact any legislation it cares to. The real issue involved is tactical. Is the enactment of a seriously controversial bill worth the price in terms of the delay, parliamentary disturbances, and adverse public and media reactions that will surely ensue if the Liberal Democrats decide to use their majority to railroad the legislation through the Diet? In practice, the party is usually very reluctant to pay this price. Although in general and with the preceding qualifications, activities in the committees are more important than those on the floor of the Diet at plenary sessions, one exception to this rule should be mentioned. In the British fashion, Cabinet ministers, including the prime minister, normally appear before both houses of the Diet to make policy speeches at the opening sessions and, more routinely, to answer formal questions from the floor called interpellations. Interpellations are the favorite and most effective means at the disposal of the opposition parties to get their views on controversial issues before the Japanese people. The press and media pay close attention to these interpellations and publicize extensively the opposition's criticisms of government policy.

The upper house, or House of Councilors, is constituted along somewhat different lines. Originally, the American occupation authorities favored a unicameral legislature, and this was written into the first draft of the Constitution. The Japanese leadership objected strenuously to this proposal, however, and favored an appointive upper house or a corporative one representing the professions and selected portions of the electorate. The present House of Councilors represents a somewhat unsatisfactory compromise between these two viewpoints. It consists of 252 members popularly elected from two different types of constituencies. One hundred fifty-two are chosen from forty-seven electoral districts—collectively called local constituencies—that are conterminous with the prefectures. The number of seats controlled by any one prefecture is roughly proportional to its population and varies from two for the smallest to eight each for Tokyo and Hokkaido. The remaining one hundred members are chosen from the national constituency; all Japan is regarded as a single electoral district for these members.

The terms of members are set at six years; since the upper house cannot be dissolved, its members usually serve the full period. Terms are staggered, however, and one-half the membership in the two categories is chosen in elections held at regular three-year intervals. In such elections, each elector votes twice, once for a candidate running in his local constituency and once for a candidate running in the national constituency. The justification advanced for this unusual and complicated system is that it combines the advantages of informed local representation with those of a panel of nationally eminent candidates. It has not actually worked out in this fashion, however. Although some men of truly national stature are elected from the national constituency, most of those chosen represent organizations having branches or influence in several heavily populated areas of Japan—for example, labor unions, big business, and nationally organized interest groups —or are well-known figures from sports, the arts, or the media. Under these circumstances, it is hardly surprising to find that the upper house has become practically as partisan a body as the lower house. Few independents are elected to either body; the great majority of the successful candidates run as party nominees. The party composition of the upper house closely resembles that of the lower; the Liberal Democrats and independent conservatives uniformly control a majority of the seats, although in recent years this has dwindled to an uncomfortably narrow margin. The internal organization of the upper house parallels that of the lower house, although its administrative and custodial staff is somewhat smaller.

The relations between the upper and lower houses of the Diet are prescribed by both the law and Constitution, which combine to make the House of Representatives far stronger than the House of Councilors. For example, the lower house may enact a law against the opposition of the upper house by passing it a second time by a majority of two-thirds or more of the members present. Normally, however, legislative differences between the two houses are resolved by an interhouse conference committee. Again, on such important matters as the enactment of the budget, the selection of the prime minister, or the ratification of treaties, the House of Representatives can, against the Councilors' opposition, decide the issue by a simple majority vote. As a consequence, the legislative and political roles of the upper house have been distinctly subordinate to those of the lower house in both law and practice. Serious disagreements between the two houses do not often occur, however, and bills are normally processed by both without recourse to the previously mentioned expedients. Under these circumstances, some Japanese feel that the upper house, as presently constituted, makes little if any positive contribution to the political process. This has led in recent years to arguments for its reform or reconstitution, particularly along corporative lines—that is, composed of representatives of the professions and other elements of the electorate.

Diet sessions are prescribed by law and are of three kinds. "Ordinary" sessions must be convened at least once a year. They uniformly begin in mid-December and last for one hundred fifty days, unless extended by vote of the Diet. Only one extension is permitted, and the question of whether or not to grant this permission is often controversial and apt to be resisted by the opposition parties as a means of impeding the accomplishment of Liberal Democratic policies. "Extraordinary" sessions can be called at any time by the Cabinet or upon petition by one-fourth of the members of either house. "Special" sessions are mandated by the Constitution and must be convoked within thirty days following a general election. As is the case in most modern democracies, the Japanese Diet is now normally in session for the greater part of the year.

The terms of members of the lower house and thus, in a larger sense, Diet sessions are brought to an end through the prime minister's dissolution of the House of Representatives or by the resignation of the Cabinet en masse. Cabinets are constitutionally required (Article 70) to resign en masse after every general election of members of the House of Representatives—whether they win or lose—or when the post of prime minister falls vacant. Article 69 requires an en masse resignation of the Cabinet if the House of Representatives passes a nonconfidence resolution in the Cabinet or rejects a resolution of confidence, unless the house is dissolved within ten days. Dissolution is also possible under the terms of Article 7. The prime minister is theoretically free to dissolve the lower house at any time. In 1952–53, Yoshida Shigeru did so twice in a six-month period, thus forcing two general elections in this short space of time. In practice, of course, the prime minister times his dissolutions of the house within its four-year term to coincide as optimally as possible with his own and his party's political needs, fortunes, and putative electoral strength. Barring a motion of nonconfidence, which given the parliamentary strength and discipline of the Liberal Democratic Party is unlikely, the critical factor in bringing about a dissolution is the prime minister. He determines when and why a general election will be held. Dissolutions, and hence elections, occur for a variety of reasons: the prospects for electoral success are good; changes take place in the presidency of the Liberal Democratic Party; the prime minister's ill health entails resignation; or scandals drive a government from office.

Dissolution affects only the House of Representatives. The House of Councilors, having a fixed term, cannot be dissolved. Its sessions are, however, suspended when the lower house has been dissolved and resume only with the convocation of the postelection Diet. Should a national emergency occur, however, the Cabinet may—but very seldom does—convoke the upper house in emergency session.

The operations of this bicameral legislature are too complicated for this to be more than summary treatment. Its principal function is, in theory, the making of laws; it is, the Constitution states, the sole law-making organ of the state. In practice, however, few laws of any significance originate in either house of the Diet. The vast majority are initiated and drafted in bill form by bureaucrats serving in the ministries and other administrative branches of the government. Some originate with the Cabinet, and some are initiated by the policy research committees of the political parties, which often work in collaboration with civil servants experienced in the field concerned. A survey by Professor T. J. Pempel of the 5,501 bills enacted by the National Diet between its first session in 1947 and its seventy-sixth in 1975 demonstrated that 85 percent were public bills, that is, they were introduced into the Diet and officially sponsored by the Cabinet. Only 15 percent were private, or members', bills, and of these many were actually initiated and drafted by bureaucrats or party sources and turned over to a Diet member for sponsorship and formal introduction.

In fact, therefore, the Diet and its members do not actually make many laws. They take projects of law originating elsewhere and then examine, debate, and publicize them; sometimes they amend them, and eventually they enact many of them into law. This is not much different from what other major legislative bodies actually do in most Western democracies. In this system, the most important legislative deliberations and decisions take place in the standing committees; plenary sessions usually just ratify such prior committee decisions. Party discipline is exceedingly strict on legislative matters, and the members of any given party almost always vote as a solid bloc in committee and in the Diet. Given the "one-and-one-half-parties system" with its Liberal Democratic majorities in both houses, there is seldom any doubt as to the fate of a bill once it has been brought to a vote. The opposition is very skillful in the use of obstructionist techniques, however, and the real problem is often how to bring a proposal to a decisive vote without completely disrupting normal parliamentary procedures and relationships.

The Diet has other important functions in addition to legislation. Japan has a parliamentary system of government in most respects, and the prime minister must be selected from among the members of the Diet—in practice, from the lower house—by a formal resolution of the Diet. The House of Representatives alone has the right to vote lack of confidence in the Cabinet and thus to bring about either its resignation or a dissolution of the house and a general election. The Constitution also entrusts the ultimate and sole authority to raise and spend money for public purposes to the Diet. All taxes that are levied and all payments from public funds must be authorized by law. Both of these activities are provided for annually in the national budget bill and its several supplements. These constitute the government's overall income and expenditure plan for the year. Budget bills must be submitted first to the House of Representatives, where they receive the most extensive and careful of scrutinies. Probably no regular activity of the Diet is considered to be of more importance than its approval of the budget. Strangely enough by American standards, the houses usually attempt to raise rather than cut the estimated expenditures approved by the Cabinet. The Diet is also responsible for approving the government's settled accounts. An independent Board of Audit examines these for accuracy and legality, and its report must finally be examined and accepted by the Diet. Finally, both houses of the Diet have been given investigative functions by the new Constitution. They are empowered to appoint special committees that can call and hear witnesses and demand records on matters relating to the efficiency or honesty of government. The Diet in this way is supposed to exercise a continuing supervisory function over the quality of governmental performance.

This legal and organizational description of the National Diet does not, however, convey an adequate picture of its actual operations and its role in the larger political system. It has several other characteristics that should be noted. First, its internal political alignments reflect, of course, the relative strengths of the various political parties. The government party, currently the Liberal Democrats, controls a majority of the seats in both houses through the unremitting application of a rigorous system of party discipline over the committee and floor voting of its Diet members. As a consequence, it can dominate proceedings both in committees and on the floor whenever it is willing to pay the price of doing so. The opposition parties are thus relegated to the difficult and trying position of a seemingly permanent minority. This creates very serious strains on normal parliamentary procedure. The dilemma for members of the opposition is what to do when the government party attempts to enact a piece of legislation that runs directly counter to what they consider to be the vital interests of their party or the Japanese people. Their chance of coming to power by normal electoral means seems small in the foreseeable future. Should they then abide by normal parliamentary practice and allow the Liberal Democratic majority to pass the legislation in question, or should they have recourse to filibustering and obstructionist tactics, climaxed perhaps by unruly demonstrations and the use of violence both on the floor of the Diet and in the streets?

When the stakes seemed important enough, the opposition parties have chosen violence and the nonparliamentary path. For a number of years now, they have engaged in systematically planned campaigns involving the use of violence on the floor and in the corridors of the Diet in desperate attempts to prevent the enactment of legislation affecting such matters as the powers of the police, the composition of local boards of education, the revision of the security treaty between the United States and Japan, the enactment of a treaty with South Korea, and the passage of a law regulating violence on university campuses. These are merely the most dramatic instances of minority obstructionism. Despite occasional periods of moderate reconciliation—such as that resulting from Prime Minister Ikeda's "low posture" strategy— the "confrontation," as it is called, of opposition against Liberal Democratic policies in the Diet has been recurrent and bitter in the extreme. This is one of the most conspicuous and worrisome characteristics of the Japanese Diet. A sizable segment of its members seem not to be reliably committed to the use of the parliamentary process. Despite dramatic instances of hostility and conflict between the party in power and the opposition parties, however, such episodes are not the norm. More frequently, the government and opposition work out quiet and mutually acceptable compromises. Such arrangements result in the adoption without opposition in the Diet of more than 75 percent of all national legislation.

A second characteristic is the rather close relationship that exists between the permanent committees of the Diet—which perform its most important legislative functions—and the ministries and agencies charged with corresponding interests, for example, the Committee on Agriculture and Forestry and the Ministry of Agriculture and Forestry, and the Committee on Commerce and Industry and the Ministry of International Trade and Industry. It is widely claimed that "clientele relationships" have been established that tend to be controlled by the bureaucrats. This troubles those who believe that the professional bureaucracy in Japan is an antidemocratic force and who conceive of the people's representatives in the Diet as providing an effective means of supervision and control over the civil service. This is, however, perhaps only another way of saying that in Japan, as in most modern states, the government is not in fact "parliament centered," regardless of what the Constitution and basic laws may stipulate. The concerns and needs of a political system today have grown too vast, too complex, and too specialized for any body of elected popular representatives to provide effective control over anything but the broadest outlines of policy. We live in the day of the administrative state, and this is as true in Japan as it is in England, the Soviet Union, and the United States.

The Cabinet

The Constitution vests executive power in the Cabinet. This is a group of political leaders, including the prime minister and about twenty ministers or ministers without portfolio. It is headed by the prime minister. The Constitution requires that all members of the Cabinet be civilians and that a majority of their number, including the prime minister, be members of the Diet. In practice this has meant that the overwhelming majority of the members of all Cabinets under the 1947 Constitution, invariably including the prime minister, have been chosen from the membership of the House of Representatives. A few—seldom more than three or four—may also be drawn from the upper house or from circles outside the Diet. The prime minister is selected by a formal resolution of the Diet. On such occasions, it is customary for the several parties represented in the Diet to place the names of their respective leaders in nomination for the post. A majority of those present and voting is required for selection, and thus, the post goes to the leader of the majority party or majority coalition in the lower house. The vote in the lower house is controlling and overrides any contrary decision that might be made in the upper house.

The prime minister selects, and may discharge at will, the other members of the Cabinet. The number of Cabinet members varies somewhat and has ranged in recent years from seventeen to twenty. All are technically of equal rank, but actually only twelve have "portfolios," that is, they preside over ministries: the ministers of justice, foreign affairs, finance, education, health and welfare, agriculture and forestry, international trade and industry, transportation, posts and telecommunications, labor, construction, and home affairs. The other Cabinet members who lack "portfolios" are ministers of state. Jobs parceled out among them include the deputy prime ministership; the chairmanship of the Atomic Energy Commission; the director-generalships of the Prime Minister's Office, the Administrative Management Agency, the Defense Agency, the Economic Planning Agency, the Science and Technology Agency, and the Environment Agency; the chief secretaryship of the Cabinet; and the directorship of the Cabinet Bureau of Legislation. Although largely free to choose whom he wants to serve in his Cabinet, a prime minister is politically obligated to apportion these posts so as to maximize the support behind his own position. A very delicate weighing and balancing operation is involved. Once having selected his colleagues, the prime minister is also free to remove them from office at his discretion, provided, of course, that his political position is firm enough to survive the consequences. Strong prime ministers like Yoshida Shigeru or Sato Eisaku have appointed and removed large numbers of ministers.

Since 1947 prime ministers have been much more durable than Cabinets

TABLE 10-1

CHRONOLOGY OF POSTWAR JAPANESE CABINETS

Dates	Prime minister[a]	Major reorganizations[b]
17 Aug. 1945–9 Oct. 1945	Higashikuni Naruhiko	
9 Oct. 1945–22 May 1946	Shidehara Kijuro	
22 May 1946–24 May 1947	Yoshida Shigeru	First
24 May 1947–10 Mar. 1948	Katayama Tetsu	
10 Mar. 1948–15 Oct. 1948	Ashida Hitoshi	
15 Oct. 1948–16 Feb. 1949	Yoshida Shigeru	Second
16 Feb. 1949–30 Oct. 1952	Yoshida Shigeru	Third
30 Oct. 1952–21 May 1953	Yoshida Shigeru	Fourth
21 May 1953–10 Dec. 1954	Yoshida Shigeru	Fifth
10 Dec. 1954–19 Mar. 1955	Hatoyama Ichiro	First
19 Mar. 1955–22 Nov. 1955	Hatoyama Ichiro	Second
22 Nov. 1955–23 Dec. 1956	Hatoyama Ichiro	Third
23 Dec. 1956–25 Feb. 1957	Ishibashi Tanzan	
25 Feb. 1957–10 July 1957	Kishi Nobusuke	First
10 July 1957–12 June 1958	Kishi Nobusuke	Second
12 June 1958–18 June 1959	Kishi Nobusuke	Third
18 June 1959–19 July 1960	Kishi Nobusuke	Fourth
19 July 1960–8 Dec. 1960	Ikeda Hayato	First
8 Dec. 1960–18 July 1961	Ikeda Hayato	Second
18 July 1961–18 July 1962	Ikeda Hayato	Third
18 July 1962–18 July 1963	Ikeda Hayato	Fourth
18 July 1963–9 Dec. 1963	Ikeda Hayato	Fifth
9 Dec. 1963–18 July 1964	Ikeda Hayato	Sixth
18 July 1964–11 Nov. 1964	Ikeda Hayato	Seventh
11 Nov. 1964–3 June 1965	Sato Eisaku	First
3 June 1965–31 July 1966	Sato Eisaku	Second
31 July 1966–3 Dec. 1966	Sato Eisaku	Third
3 Dec. 1966–25 Nov. 1967	Sato Eisaku	Fourth
25 Nov. 1967–30 Nov. 1968	Sato Eisaku	Fifth
30 Nov. 1968–14 Jan. 1970	Sato Eisaku	Sixth
14 Jan. 1970–5 July 1971	Sato Eisaku	Seventh
5 July 1971–6 July 1972	Sato Eisaku	Eighth
6 July 1972–22 Dec. 1972	Tanaka Kakuei	First
22 Dec. 1972–25 Nov. 1973	Tanaka Kakuei	Second
25 Nov. 1973–11 Nov. 1974	Tanaka Kakuei	Third
11 Nov. 1974–9 Dec. 1974	Tanaka Kakuei	Fourth
9 Dec. 1974–15 Sept. 1976	Miki Takeo	First
15 Sept. 1976–24 Dec. 1976	Miki Takeo	Second
24 Dec. 1976	Fukuda Takeo	First

[a] All prime ministers except Katayama Tetsu have represented conservative parties.

[b] This table lists and numbers major reorganizations of the Cabinet, that is, occasions when the prime minister replaces one-half or more of the Cabinet's membership. The numbering of Cabinets does not change with quite this frequency. Legally a prime minister's first Cabinet dates from his assumption of office and subsequent Cabinets occur only after general elections held and won during his term in office. Thus, Prime Minister Ikeda headed only three rather than seven Cabinets: the first from 19 July to 8 December 1960; the second from the Cabinet reorganization of 8 December 1960, following upon the general election in November, to 9 December 1963; and the third from the reorganization of 9 December 1963, occasioned by the general election in November of that year, until Ikeda's resignation from office on 11 November 1964 because of ill health.

(see table 10–1). For example, Yoshida Shigeru reorganized the Cabinet five times; Hatoyama Ichiro, three; Kishi Nobusuke, four; Ikeda Hayato, seven; Sato Eisaku, eight; and Tanaka Kakuei, four. The average life of a Cabinet since 1952 was nine months, but the average term in office of the prime ministers from 1948 through 1976 was forty-three months, ranging from two months for Ishibashi Tanzan to more than seven years for Sato Eisaku. During the entire postwar period, there has only been one Cabinet headed by a Socialist—the Katayama government, a weak Socialist-conservative coalition that lasted for nine and one-half months in 1947–48. All the rest have been led by conservative politicians.

Cabinets fall and new Cabinets arise for complex reasons. Since the conservative dominance has been so complete, parliamentary successes by the opposition party or formal votes of lack of confidence in the lower house have seldom brought down a Cabinet. More often, intraparty and interfactional differences on policy or personal matters within the conservative camp make some reconstitution of the Cabinet advisable. Public dissatisfaction over government policy or scandals involving high party or governmental officials—nourished and exploited by the opposition and the media—have also been common causes of the dissolution of Cabinets. There is also constant factional and intraparty pressure on all Cabinets to step aside in favor of other deserving colleagues. This pressure is so strong on any prime minister that frequent Cabinet changes are almost the necessary political price for his own continuance in power. This lack of stability in the Cabinet does not, however, mean that there is a comparable instability in major national policies. The offices are rotated within the same party or at least within the general conservative camp. The prime ministership does not change with the same frequency, although in the future it seems improbable that any conservative prime minister will be able to serve for more than six years. This is due to the fact that all recent prime ministers have achieved office by virtue of their prior election to the presidency of the Liberal Democratic Party. A change in that party's rules during the prime ministership of Sato Eisaku limited any party president to two three-year terms in office. In addition to the relatively long terms served by prime ministers, the administrative vice-ministers, who for the most part actually run the ministries and agencies, are always career civil servants with much experience. These factors make for a considerable amount of policy stability in what otherwise might seem a highly unstable situation.

The Cabinet's functions are both formal and informal. Some of the latter have already been mentioned. Under the guidance of the prime minister, for example, it exercises leadership for the political party or coalition of parties upon whose support its position depends. Again, Cabinets provide a vehicle for the recognition and reward of loyal or able party service. These are important functions, although less frequently noted than are its formal legal responsibilities. Chief among these is its role as the highest executive authority in Japan. It is the Cabinet that is by law responsible for such major executive tasks as preparing and submitting the annual budget—which means, essentially, planning the overall activities of the state for the coming year—managing the nation's foreign and domestic affairs, administering the civil service, controlling the administrative branches of the government, submitting bills to the Diet, executing the laws, and regularly informing the Diet and the people of the state of the nation. It is thus a form of collective chief executive. Since the Diet is actually incapable of providing policy guidance, its authority also extends to the formulation, or at least advance approval, of practically all major policies of state. Beyond this, it performs a number of other functions. It issues Cabinet orders in pursuance of law, convokes extraordinary sessions of the Diet, advises the emperor about the dissolution of the Diet and the proclamation of general elections, and appoints the justices of the Supreme Court. The Cabinet, therefore, possesses practically all the major leadership or executive powers of state at the national level.

Under the present Constitution, Japanese Cabinets exercise their formidable powers through a system of collective responsibility; that is, all members of the Cabinet are jointly responsible for any policy or decision officially taken by the Cabinet. This means that the Cabinet acts by consensus, or unanimous decision—the traditionally approved way of making group decisions in Japan. Formal votes are rarely, if ever, taken. Issues are discussed until some general agreement is reached, and this then becomes the decision of the Cabinet. Any member seriously dissenting from this decision is expected to resign or face dismissal by the prime minister.

The Cabinet's relationship with the Diet is, of course, one of the most important aspects of any Cabinet's activities, especially since the Constitution has deliberately made them mutually interdependent. The relations between the House of Representatives and the Cabinet are particularly close. The House of Councilors, since it cannot be dissolved and has but secondary and inferior powers, stands in somewhat different circumstances. The Cabinet is, to begin with, the creature of the Diet—ultimately of the lower house—through the Diet's power to select the prime minister. Cabinet members are further made responsible to the Diet through their duty to attend sessions of both houses and their committees and to reply to questions about their policies when officially requested to do so by Diet members. Again, the Diet is legally free to accept, amend, or reject bills submitted by the Cabinet—in practice they accept most of them—or to grant or refuse the funds that are necessary for the implementation of the Cabinet's programs.

Either house of the Diet is also free to level resolutions of impeachment against individual Cabinet members. The lower house may adopt a resolution of no confidence or reject a resolution of confidence in the Cabinet as a whole, or refuse to support some major piece of legislation sponsored by the Cabinet—which amounts to a vote of lack of confidence. A vote of no confidence or the refusal to pass major Cabinet-backed bills are the most drastic means at the disposal of the lower house for the enforcement of ministerial responsibility to the will of the house. A formal expression of lack of confidence automatically presents the Cabinet with two choices: it must, within a ten-day period, resign en masse, or it must dissolve the House of Representatives and call for a general election to select the members of a new house. If it does the latter, the Cabinet must still resign upon the first convocation of the new Diet after the election, leaving the members of this new Diet free to reinstate or replace the former prime minister. These are all devices for insuring the responsibility of Cabinets to the Diet. In practice, however, votes of nonconfidence by the lower house are almost meaningless. It has been done only twice—in 1948 and in 1953—in the entire postwar period, both times against Prime Minister Yoshida. In normal circumstances, the prime minister has always been able to rely upon party discipline to insure an automatic majority against any opposition attempt to adopt a resolution of nonconfidence in the Cabinet.

Responsibility runs both ways in this relationship, however. Since the members of the Cabinet are high party officials and dispensers of patronage through both legislative and administrative channels, they have substantial influence over the actions of at least their own majority party or coalition in the Diet. They can usually advance or hamper the political careers of individual members. In practice, too, party discipline is rigorously enforced against their delegations holding seats in the Diet, although occasionally individuals or small groups have resigned from their parties to take up independent status. Serious backbench insurrections against Cabinet leadership—as distinguished from interfactional squabbles—are almost unknown in the Japanese Diet. The ultimate weapon of the Cabinet against a refractory lower house, however, is the power of dissolution, which has the consequence of forcing all members to stand for reelection. Election campaigns are very costly in Japan, and the outcome is by no means always certain. Members of the House of Representatives do not lightly court the expense and uncertainty following upon dissolution and a new general election. It is a cost and risk shared by the majority of the Cabinet, who are members of the lower house, but their financial connections are apt to be superior and their seats safer than the average member's. Considerations of this sort tend to make Diet members follow the Cabinet's leadership and loyally support its programs both in committee and on the floor of the house. What problems occur in the ranks of the majority party are almost always the result of factional intrigues and maneuvering.

In executive-legislative relationships, therefore, the Cabinet is dominant. This does not imply, however, that the Cabinet by itself provides the ultimate leadership of the Japanese state, for the Cabinet's legal or formal role is qualified in several ways. One of the most important checks against unbridled Cabinet power is the existence of dissident factions within the majority party. To succeed, a Liberal Democratic Cabinet must maintain a delicate balance among mainstream factions composed of party members who support the prime minister. In setting policy or making decisions, the Cabinet must always take into account the interests of these groups as well as those of the antimainstream factions composed of members who, although belonging to the Liberal Democratic Party's delegation in the Diet, are opposed to its present leadership and are promoting their own candidate for the prime ministership. The Cabinet is thus subject to continuous influence and partial controls from elements within its own party. For quite different reasons, the Cabinet is also constantly influenced by the "advice" of the professional bureaucracy. The major ministries of state are headed by career civil servants who are administrative vice-ministers. This group meets regularly and frequently with the director of the Cabinet Secretariat and the director of the Cabinet Bureau of Legislation as a sort of "little cabinet"—and it is far better informed about most matters of policy and administration than are the members of the Cabinet.

As technicians operating in highly technical fields, these bureaucrats decide a great many matters, which are then sent up for fairly routine approval by the Cabinet proper. In this manner, the professional bureaucracy, through its own leaders, exercises a very considerable influence on many Cabinet actions. To some extent, this influence is counterbalanced by the extensive professional and technical staff that is attached directly to the prime minister. Known as the Office of the Prime Minister, this staff contains more than thirty thousand employees, exclusive of the National Defense Agency. It serves as a professional staff for the Cabinet and somewhat reduces the Cabinet's dependence on the bureaucracy in the regular ministries and agencies. In sum, primary political power in contemporary Japan rests with the Cabinet, and in particular with the prime minister; they probably perform more decision making of major importance than any other formal unit of government. They are, however, subject to constant interaction with and substantial influence from several other official and unofficial groups. There is no simple answer to this question of political primacy.

In performing its executive and coordinating functions, the Cabinet has the assistance of a Cabinet Secretariat, the Cabinet Bureau of Legislation, the National Personnel Authority, and the National Defense Council. The chief of the Cabinet Secretariat now normally holds cabinet rank either as a state minister or minister without portfolio. He is invariably a close and trusted associate of the prime minister, and he performs a variety of important political functions and administers and staffs the collective activities of the Cabinet. The Cabinet Bureau of Legislation coordinates the drafting and enactment of all legislative bills throughout the executive branch of the government. The National Personnel Authority attempts, with varying success, to standardize and rationalize recruitment, promotion, transfer, grievance, and retirement procedures for the entire national civil service. One of its most important functions is to recommend pay scales and adjustments for all governmental employees. It enjoys a semiautonomous status within the government. The National Defense Council was established in 1954 primarily as a means of insuring civilian control of the military. Its membership is totally civilian, headed by the prime minister, and it is supposed to approve all important defense-related policies.

In addition to these staff and coordinating agencies attached to the Cabinet, the Prime Minister's Office *(Sorifu)* is both sizable and very important. The Cabinet contains no ministry of defense or of the army, navy, or air force. The equivalent exists in Japan, but it is called the National Defense Agency *(Boeicho)*. It has a total staff of some two hundred ninety-four thousand including two hundred sixty-four thousand in the armed forces proper and a civilian staff of about thirty thousand. Because of Article 9 of the Constitution, which ostensibly forbids Japan to maintain land, sea, or air forces, and because of the political sensitivity attaching to this entire issue of the legality, necessity, and desirability of the present "self-defense forces," the agency that controls them has never been given the status of a full-fledged ministry. Its director-general has Cabinet rank and the status of state minister, but the agency is formally a part of the Prime Minister's Office. Excluding the National Defense Agency, the staff of the Prime Minister's Office still numbers more than thirty thousand and includes a variety of important agencies such as the Imperial Household Agency, the Administrative Management Agency, the Economic Planning Agency, the Science and Technology Agency, the Fair Trade Commission, the National Public Safety Commission, and the Environment Agency. These perform many of the most important planning, developmental, security, and coordinating functions for the central government, including, for example, overall economic planning and direction of the national police force.

Although legally equal in status and authority, the twelve Cabinet ministries differ a great deal in actual importance and prestige. By general consent the Ministry of Finance—and, hence, the post of Minister of Finance—is the most important ministerial position in the Japanese government after the prime minister. In fact, it is often regarded as a stepping stone to the prime ministership. Essentially, however, its salience derives from the fact that it plans, and in substantial part controls or influences, the revenues and expenditures of the entire national government of Japan. This is true not only of its own intradepartmental operations but also of the budgets—and hence the operations—of all other national governmental agencies, since their annual budgets must all be approved by the Ministry of Finance before they become operational. Next in importance and influence is probably the Ministry of International Trade and Industry because of its extensive licensing and regulatory powers over all major Japanese industries. The Ministry of Foreign Affairs is a special case. It lacks completely any domestic authority and regulatory power and thus has no significant clientele among Japanese public or business circles. Still the position of Minister of Foreign Affairs is viewed as one of great national importance and conveys much status and prestige upon its holder. The Ministry of Agriculture and Forestry and the Ministry of Transportation regulate economic interests of enormous size and domestic importance, and both these posts are eagerly sought as a consequence. On the other hand, the ministries of justice, education, and labor are known for the professional headaches and embarrassments attendant upon their leadership. They are still sought, since to have served as a Cabinet minister, however briefly and in whatever post, is still the capstone of any political career in Japan, but their desirability and political status are substantially less than that of the more prestigious posts. In general, the status of minister of state without portfolio ranks below that of any of the ministers who head the twelve formal ministries. However, these posts are frequently occupied by the heads of major mainstream factions or other very prominent political figures who, for one reason or another, find it expedient to serve in the Cabinet but prefer a capacity that does not entail onerous and time-consuming administrative responsibilities. Also, a nonportfolio Cabinet post such as the chief of the Cabinet Secretariat is of central political importance.

Within this hierarchy, the present Ministry of Home Affairs has had a somewhat unusual history. Before World War II, it ranked with the Ministry of Finance as the most powerful and prestigious of the domestic ministries. It was then abolished in 1947 by the authorities of the Allied Occupation in the course of their attempt to decentralize the Japanese governmental system and return authority to the local level. Restored to ministerial status as the Ministry of Local Autonomy in 1960 and later renamed the Ministry of Home Affairs, it possessed far less power and prestige. It remains today a small agency with less than six hundred employees and very limited authority over the prefectures, cities, towns, and villages of Japan.

The Bureaucracy

Ever since the Meiji Restoration of 1867–68—which might itself be described as a sort of bureaucratic coup d'état—the bureaucracy has been very important in the Japanese political system. The founders of modern Japan were not themselves democrats, and they were not particularly concerned to establish a "civil service," that is, a politically neutral, professionalized service dedicated to the achievement of democratically set goals by means determined and supervised by the representatives of the people. The conception of a bureaucrat as a "public servant" was almost totally absent from both Japanese political theory and practice until it was inserted in Article 15 of the new Constitution by Americans in 1946. Before 1946, a Japanese bureaucrat was officially viewed as a chosen servant of the emperor, a politically and socially superior being who derived status and privileges from his imperial connection. The old Tokugawa adage, *kanson mimpi* ("officials honored, the people despised"), well describes the prewar bureaucrat's attitude toward the public. A tradition of this depth and intensity dies hard. Despite a number of postwar reform attempts, there is a good deal yet to be done before the average bureaucrat successfully negotiates the transition to the status of "public servant," a circumstance not peculiar to Japan.

As in many other countries, postwar times brought to Japan an enormous inflation in the size of its bureaucracy. Just before the war in 1940, for example, the Japanese national government had 231,898 employees, excluding the military and certain temporary employees. In 1975 the comparable figure was 1,993,008 employees, a more than eightfold increase (see table 10–2). In 1975 the bureaucracy in Japan—including the civilian employees of both national and local governments and the military—totaled about 4.8 million persons; thus, roughly one out of every eleven members of the labor force worked for the government. This is a very sizable number. For our purposes, however, it is the higher civil service that is most important. These higher civil servants may be loosely defined as those individuals who attain the first, second, or third grades (out of eight total grades) in the administrative service. In 1974 there were only 15,885 such positions in the entire national government (1,070 first grade, 4,277 second grade, and 10,539 third grade positions), and less than half were really important.

TABLE 10-2
JAPANESE GOVERNMENTAL EMPLOYEES

National government employees (1975)

On General Account Budget	
National Diet	4,028
Judiciary	24,391
Board of Audit	1,216
Cabinet	932
Office of Prime Minister	30,303
Ministry of Justice	49,613
Ministry of Foreign Affairs	3,053
Ministry of Finance	67,607
Ministry of Education	3,230
Ministry of Health and Welfare	7,955
Ministry of Agriculture and Forestry	29,037
Ministry of International Trade and Industry	12,234
Ministry of Transportation	25,200
Ministry of Posts and Telecommunications	2,852
Ministry of Labor	15,463
Ministry of Construction	5,951
Ministry of Home Affairs	532
National Defense Agency	294,653
Subtotal	578,250
On Special Account Budgets[a]	613,185
Employees of Government Corporations[b]	801,573
Total	1,993,008

Local government employees (1974)

Prefectures[c]	1,588,613
Cities, towns, villages, and cooperatives	1,268,723
Total	2,857,336
Grand Total	4,850,344

Source: Nihon Tokei Nenkan, 1975, pp. 594–95.

[a] For the ministries of finance, education, health and welfare, agriculture and forestry, international trade and industry, transportation, post and telecommunications, labor, and construction.

[b] Largely for the Japan National Railways (431,024) and the Japan Telegraph and Telephone Public Corporation (318,379).

[c] Of which teachers account for 810,238 and police 189,280.

Access to these positions is usually restricted to persons who pass the higher civil service examinations. The higher bureaucracy is not a very large group, numbering about five or six thousand people, and it replenishes itself at a rate of three to four hundred members at the bottom per year. Its training and preparation are rigorous.

Government service has always been regarded as one of the most desirable careers open to young Japanese. Access to its higher levels is achieved through an outstanding academic record. In elementary school, the brighter students are constantly faced with the necessity of getting the highest possible grades in an endless series of difficult examinations. Brilliant performances in these provide entrance to the best high schools and ultimately to the best universities. The equivalent of an honors degree from a good university is particularly essential to anyone hoping to take and pass the higher civil service examinations. A few universities in prewar times acquired a practical monopoly over access to these higher positions. The elite of the prewar administrative service, for example, consisted of those who took and passed the higher civil service examination while still students, then graduated from imperial universities, and went on to achieve the first or second grades of the civil service. Among these, 92 percent were graduates of Tokyo Imperial University's Law Department and 4 percent of Kyoto Imperial's Law Department.

The tests were largely set and graded by members of the law faculties of these schools, and their graduates, once in the higher services, were given preferential status and advancement by their fellow alumni of earlier classes and higher rank. This situation has improved since the war. There are now many more graduates of Kyoto, Waseda, Keio, Hitotsubashi, Nihon, and other colleges, but a pronounced "old-school tie" prejudice, fostered by a Tokyo University clique, is still evident. In the 1949–59 period, for example, 69 percent of all Japanese higher civil servants were graduates of Tokyo University; at the level of vice-ministers and bureau chiefs, the proportion exceeded 80 percent. The courses of study and tests leading to a civil service career have been somewhat broadened in comparison with their excessively narrow and legalistic prewar counterparts. A heavy emphasis is still placed, however, on the applicant's ability to recall legal and technical details.

A college graduate who has passed the higher civil service examinations normally enters the service as a sixth-grade employee. If possible, the graduate chooses one of the more important ministries that has promotional paths leading to the heart of political and administrative power in the Japanese system and that may lead, after retirement, to a lucrative post in private business or perhaps to an elective political career. Since retirement comes early in most ministries—in the early fifties on the average—and pensions are markedly inadequate, such postretirement considerations are important. The most promising careers before the war lay in the Ministry of Home Affairs. Today, they are to be found primarily in the Ministry of Finance and secondarily in the Ministry of International Trade and Industry or the Ministry of Agriculture and Forestry. To some, the Ministry of Foreign Affairs is also attractive as a sort of special case.

Once having been accepted by a particular ministry, the new civil servant's career is apt to lie primarily within that ministry. A survey of interministerial mobility demonstrated that in the 1949–59 period, a third of the major civil servants had served in only a single ministry, another third had served in more than one ministry but had returned ultimately to the ministry of their first assignment, and only the remaining third had been permanently transferred to other ministries or agencies. Interministerial rivalry and suspicion are acute, and administrative cooperation across ministerial boundaries is difficult to achieve. Displays of individual initiative or brilliance on the part of junior employees are not highly valued. Loyalty and obedience to superiors, tact, anonymity, patience, and a capacity for the endless details and rituals of administration are the normal virtues. Personal and job security is complete; accountability to the public is practically nil. Yet, since the initial recruiting process is so rigorous and highly selective, very intelligent and able men are obtained, and they normally move rapidly up toward the pinnacle of bureaucratic achievement, a vice-ministership.

The higher bureaucracy in Japan is deeply involved in politics for several reasons. First, such involvement is a solidly entrenched part of the Japanese tradition. Politics, even of the party variety, has been a prominent and constant concern of the higher administrators ever since the Restoration. Second, the fact that the national legislature is weak and ill-equipped to deal with the complex problems of a modern society has left a vacuum that bureaucratic expertise and enterprise have gladly filled. Third, in modern times political decisions have become so inextricably mingled with problems of administration and technology that it is unrealistic to think separately of bureaucracy and politics. The bureaucrats and specialists of Japan, for example, have a great deal to say about the incidence of taxation, the granting of licenses and permits, the determination of bank rates, the availability and allocation of credit and public subsidies, and the location and construction of public works. All of these are decisions that vitally affect the interests of important and organized sectors of the Japanese population—business, finance, labor, agriculture, and so forth. Under these circumstances, it is scarcely remarkable that these interests seek to influence critically placed bureaucrats.

Since the war, a fourth aspect of bureaucratic involvement in politics has received a good deal of attention. Upon retirement from the higher bureaucracy—usually in their early fifties—substantial numbers of former civil servants have been running successfully for elective political office, a practice far less common in prewar days. Estimates of the scale on which this occurs vary somewhat, but in recent years about 25 percent of Liberal Democratic members of the House of Representatives have been former bureaucrats; in the House of Councilors, the average is perhaps 35 to 40 percent. Such cases are encountered almost exclusively in the ranks of the Liberal Democratic Party. Few former bureaucrats have joined any of the opposition parties. Once elected, particularly to the lower house, the knowledge, skills, and connections that these former bureaucrats bring to their jobs stand them in very good stead. A high proportion of them in time attain Cabinet rank. One study, for example, found that fully 35 percent of the membership of Cabinets between 1954 and 1961 were former bureaucrats, while another study for the 1946–1973 period put the figure at 18 percent. Similarly, excluding the unusual case of Prince Higashikuni, seven of the twelve postwar prime ministers have been former bureaucrats: Shidehara Kijuro, Yoshida Shigeru, and Ashida Hitoshi from the Ministry of Foreign Affairs; Kishi Nobusuke from the Ministry of International Trade and Industry; Ikeda Hayato and Fukuda Takeo from the Ministry of Finance; and Sato Eisaku from the Ministry of Transportation.

Because of this prevalence of ex-bureaucrats in high political office, questions have frequently been raised about both the means by which they have achieved these offices and the consequences for the quality of governance in Japan. The ensuing controversies have generated more heat than light.

There is little doubt that as a group the connections and skills these men acquired in the course of twenty-five to thirty years of service in the higher bureaucracy have been very valuable assets when they ran for elective office. These have usually been the prime source of both their financial and political support. The question of whether, once in elective office, they have constituted a sort of bloc with widely shared interests and goals that are antidemocratic has been a far more controversial issue. The opposition parties and media in Japan generally take it for granted that this is the case and denounce with vehemence and enthusiasm both the individuals concerned and the Liberal Democratic Party. In some cases there is undoubtedly truth in the charges involved. In general, however, this seems an overly simple view of a complex matter. It fails, for example, to take into account such factors as the following. The general reputation of the Japanese higher bureaucracy for individual and collective honesty and integrity in office is very good. As individuals they represent a quite broad spectrum of political views and interests. As former bureaucrats they derive from particular ministerial backgrounds noted for their mutual exclusiveness and lack of cross-ministerial association or communication. As party members, while practically all affiliated with the Liberal Democratic Party, they operate as members of particular factions that are in constant and strenuous competition with each other. These are scarcely the circumstances out of which cabals are born or conspiracies hatched. It is not excessive to conclude that their political views and convictions can be collectively described as ranging from conservative to liberal, that they are not in sympathy with most of the causes espoused by the opposition parties, and that their influence is usually exercised in support of programs that are moderate or conservative. It is probably also the case that a substantial part of the explanation for their success in politics—as formerly in the bureaucracy—is attributable to the fact that they represent one of the most highly trained, most carefully selected, and on the record, most capable elements of the Japanese population.

Local Government

Prior to the effectuation of the new Constitution in 1947, Japan had an extremely centralized form of government in two different senses. First, all political power was legally and theoretically concentrated in the person of the emperor. Second, all political power was legally and actually concentrated at the national level; local governments enjoyed no autonomous rights and were created and controlled by the national government in Tokyo. The American authorities who controlled the Allied Occupation of Japan objected strenuously to the continuance of this system. Their political goal was the democratization of Japan, and they felt that democratic institutions and practices flourish in direct proportion to their closeness to the people. The Japanese system of government required drastic decentralization through the granting of extensive rights of local self-government to the prefectures, cities, towns, and villages of Japan.

In this way, local government could be made directly responsive to local desires and conditions, and its democratic potential greatly enhanced.

Relatively little thought was given to any deleterious effects that such a decentralization of authority might have on the strength or efficiency of the national government. In fact, such consequences were probably regarded as desirable. The result of such views on the part of the occupation authorities was, first, the enshrinement of the principle of local autonomy in Article 92 of the new Constitution and, second, the enactment of the Local Autonomy Law on 17 April 1947. The combination of these with other related legislation provides the legal basis for the present system of local government in Japan. Judged by earlier Japanese standards, this is a highly decentralized system, although it is, of course, not as decentralized as the federally organized system that exists in the United States. Japan still technically has a unified system of government.

At its highest level below the nation, local government in Japan is organized into forty-seven prefectures (see figure 10–2). The prefectures are governed, subject to national laws, by a popularly elected governor and a single-house legislature. The total territory of each prefecture is then further subdivided into cities, towns, and villages. These are the lowest units of self-government in Japan—with the exception of Tokyo's twenty-three special wards *(Ku)* that have a unique form of local government and thus comprise a special case. There is nothing corresponding to unincorporated territories in Japan. Each city, town, or village directly elects its own mayor and single-house assembly. All these local governments, from the prefecture down, are parliamentary systems in which the chief executives and their assemblies are rendered mutually interdependent through their respective powers of dissolution and votes of nonconfidence. The law also extends very considerable powers of local self-government to all these levels and units and, thereby, denies the exercise of such powers to agencies of the national government.

This is a brief description of the legal position of local governmental units in Japan. Their actual position deviates from this in several important respects. They are not really autonomous to the degree anticipated by the law. In practice, local officials spend most of their time administering the policies and business of the national ministries. The laws and ordinances that they adopt are frequently exact copies of model statutes developed initially in Tokyo. Furthermore, few, if any, local governments are financially self-supporting. In recent years about 47 percent of their essential revenues have normally been derived from subsidies and grants-in-aid received from the national government. This pronounced degree of fiscal dependency plus the long-ingrained bureaucratic habit of looking to Tokyo and the national government for guidance detracts greatly from the actual degree of autonomy enjoyed by the prefectures, cities, towns, and villages of Japan.

A structural and legal description of this sort falls far short of providing an adequate picture of the present state of local government and politics in Japan. The current scene is a lively one, unprecedentedly so in fact. Two aspects in particular stand out: the citizens' or residents' movements and the incursions by the opposition parties into what has normally been a conservative political stronghold.

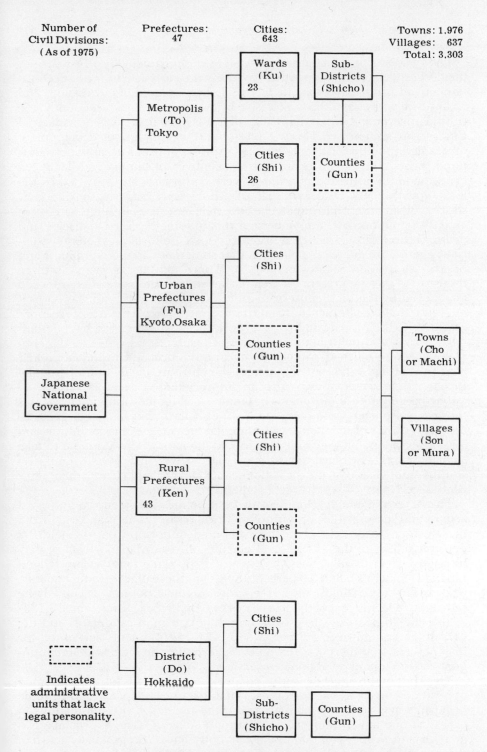

FIGURE 10–2 THE STRUCTURE OF JAPANESE LOCAL GOVERNMENT

The residents' movements *(jumin undo)* are fundamentally a response to the decentralization of industry in Japan. By the early 1960s, the concentration of industrial development in the Tokyo, Nagoya, Osaka-Kobe, and Kitakyushu areas was already excessive by any standards. Consequently, the central government enacted in 1962 what was known as the New Industrial Cities Construction Act. This was intended to encourage the development of sizable new industrial complexes in a variety of urban areas widely scattered throughout Japan. Quite lavish incentives, including free land, tax breaks, and the provision of utilities, were enthusiastically provided by the local governments concerned, all of whom were eagerly seeking new sources of revenue. Unfortunately, these new industries brought with them extensive pollution of the air and water that in some cases led to disease and death. In time this engendered organized local political movements, especially against air and water pollution, that sometimes adopted dramatic and occasionally violent modes of protest. There may be as many as three thousand of these at present. In their earlier stages, they were often opposed or ignored by the local conservative political authorities, and they consequently tended to ally themselves with the opposition parties that were more receptive to their causes and tactics. More recently, impressed by the number, success, and political potentialities of residents' movements, the conservatives have taken up the banner of antipollution and conservation and have thus reduced, but not eliminated, the partisan quality of the struggle. Residents' movements have been an unprecedented exemplar of a truly public-based political movement in Japan. In a significant number of cases they have also been quite successful. Not only have they moved large numbers of local governments to take remedial measure against pollution and for conservation, but they have also forced the national government to take similar actions. The beneficial results are clear. Even in Tokyo, certainly the world's smoggiest city, the air is noticeably cleaner and clearer than a few years ago. However, a great deal remains to be done.

The other notable development in local politics has been the increased activity and success of the opposition political parties. This is apparent from the electoral record. In 1966 the combined opposition parties held 8.2 percent (6,697) of the 81,019 local elective offices in Japan—from prefectural governors to village assemblymen. At the same time, acknowledged Liberal Democrats held 10.9 percent (8,901) of these offices. Independents, who in fact were almost all conservative in their politics, occupied the remaining 80.9 percent of the seats (65,421). By 1975, 13.2 percent (10,183) of the 76,926 posts involved were held by opposition candidates and the LDP share was down to 8.8 percent (6,772). Independents accounted for 75.5 percent, and there was reason to believe that the independent contingent was no longer so solidly conservative.

This shift in the figures constituted an appreciable gain for the combined opposition parties. It has been most notable and most spectacular in some of Japan's major metropolitan areas. Of the ten cities with populations in excess of one million, for example, seven (Tokyo, Osaka, Yokohama, Nagoya, Kyoto, Kobe, and Kawasaki) currently have "progressive" mayors, that is, mayors elected primarily by varying coalitions of the opposition parties, most commonly the Japan Socialist and Communist parties. The same is true of several of the governorships in several of the more important prefectures, for example, Tokyo, Osaka, Kyoto, Okayama, and Saitama.

This increase in local office-holding has been especially marked for Communist candidates. In 1966 they held—openly at least—only 1,214 local elective offices in all Japan, and all except 29 of these were in city or village assemblies. By 1975 they had increased this quota by 132 percent to 2,817. This is a remarkable performance and, at the same time, a tactic reminiscent of a similar shift of attention and resources from the national to the local scene by the Italian and French Communist parties.

These are significant gains for the opposition, especially in the metropolitan areas, and they may foreshadow similar progress at the level of national elections. The latter outcome, however, is far from certain. Several other factors must be taken into account. We have been speaking largely of gains by a "combined opposition." In fact at the local as at the national level, the opposition is anything but combined. The local opposition parties feud and fight just as bitterly and continuously as do their national counterparts. Occasionally, however, and usually on a distinctly ad hoc basis, they manage to patch together a shaky coalition in support of a shared mayoral or gubernatorial candidate. Sometimes they win, more often they lose. Despite their gains, the local political arena in Japan is still overwhelmingly conservative in its political preferences. Even in those spectacular cases in which "progressive" candidates have won major mayoral and gubernatorial posts, the probability is that they will face assemblies with either a majority or a plurality of conservative members and that these, plus the power of the national bureaucracy over local actions, will very seriously qualify the ability of such local leaders to effectuate "progressive" programs.

The opposition hopes that their gains in local elections foreshadow victories at the national level, but perhaps the greatest electoral mystery in Japan is the extent to which much of the vote for the opposition is cast for reasons of protest rather than conversion. It is an article of faith in many conservative quarters that fundamentally the Japanese voters collectively mistrust the opposition to an extent that makes it improbable that they will ever really vote them into power. The degree to which this faith is justified or misplaced is simply not known.

The Judicial System

The judicial system, like so many of the other institutions of prewar Japan, was greatly changed by the occupation. Anglo-American common law principles were widely introduced into a system that had been largely European in derivation. The legal, civil, and political rights of Japanese citizens were greatly expanded; the government and its servants were made far more accountable for their actions; and in general, a serious attempt was made to introduce into Japanese society the almost completely foreign principle of the rule of law. A series of basic reforms in the judicial system lay at the root of these attempts.

In prewar Japan, the courts had been an arm of the national government administered by the Ministry of Justice. Under the Constitution of 1947, this was completely changed. Article 76 vests "the whole judicial power" in a Supreme Court and in such inferior courts as may be established by law. This provision creates a judicial branch of the government with an independent status that is substantially equal to that enjoyed by the legislative or executive branches. The Supreme Court is given complete administrative control over all inferior courts and is further explicitly given the right of judicial review, that is, the power to determine the constitutionality of any law, order, regulation, or official act. The fifteen judges of the Supreme Court are appointed by the Cabinet, except for the chief judge who is appointed by the emperor upon nomination by the Cabinet. The judges serve for life, subject to decennial referenda by the voters upon their records. Beneath the Supreme Court is a hierarchy of inferior courts ranging from eight high courts (plus six branches) through fifty district courts (with attached family courts) to five hundred seventy-five summary courts at the base of the pyramid. Together with a large number of civil and family conciliation commissions, each composed of one judge and two intelligent and experienced laymen and intended to provide facilities for the out-of-court settlement of disputes, these are the principal components of the present Japanese judicial system.

The courts, although they seem to be functioning reasonably well, do not play as important a role as might be expected. The Japanese are a rather remarkably nonlitigious people. They are traditionally suspicious of the courts and of formal legal processes and have a pronounced preference for settling disputes by informal methods of conciliation and mediation. These methods are highly developed, especially in the countryside, and normally recourse is had to the courts only when the issue is very serious and older techniques of mediated settlement have failed. The number of civil suits per capita brought before the courts in Japan is only between one-tenth and one-twentieth of that in England or the United States. Thus, there are a smaller number of attorneys—actually 1 per 10,800 of population as opposed to 1 per 587 of population in the United States or 1 per 1,700 in the United Kingdom.

From a political standpoint, few judicial issues have aroused more comment and controversy than the Supreme Court's American-inspired power of judicial review. This is completely foreign to the Japanese legal tradition, and many have watched with interest to see whether or not the Supreme Court would actually make use of this power and occasionally declare an act of the Diet, of a ministry, or of a local government unconstitutional, thus asserting its right to play a positive role in national politics in the way that the United States Supreme Court does. Since 1947 there have only been a few cases—mostly of no particular importance—in which the Supreme Court has held laws to be unconstitutional. In fact, the Court ruled in 1960 that "an official act that is of a highly political nature directly affecting the basis of the government is beyond the reach of judicial review." A 1976 decision in which the Court ruled that the existing apportionment of seats in the House of Representatives among the 130 election districts was unconstitutional may, however, mark a new departure in the Court's attitude toward "political issues." The overall record to date though documents great reluctance on the Court's part to intervene in such matters. It would seem highly improbable, under present circumstances at least, that the Supreme Court will soon make significant use of the power of judicial review.

This abstention by the Supreme Court from involvement in determining issues of constitutionality has not always been reflected in the judgments of inferior courts. These are usually staffed by younger judges whose professional and political views sometimes differ markedly from those of their seniors on the Supreme Court bench. This has on a number of occasions given rise to judicial decisions on constitutional issues at the district court level that were highly political and controversial. Probably the best known of these was a 1959 decision by the Tokyo District Court that the United States–Japan Security Treaty was a violation of Article 9 of the Japanese Constitution ("The Sunakawa Case"). In due course this judgment was overruled by the Supreme Court. This is a pattern that has repeated itself in a growing number of cases involving highly controversial political issues such as freedom of expression, especially by means of organized mass demonstrations, versus the right of the police to regulate this in the public interest. In almost all cases, the Supreme Court has ruled in favor of public rather than private rights.

BIBLIOGRAPHY

Entries marked with an asterisk are general texts on Japanese politics containing broad treatments of many aspects of the political system in addition to the structure of government.

BAERWALD, HANS H., *Japan's Parliament: An Introduction.* New York: Columbia University Press, 1974, 155 pp.

BEER, LAWRENCE W. *The Constitutional Case Law of Japan: Selected Supreme Court Decisions, 1961–1970,* Seattle: University of Washington Press, 1977.

*IKE, NOBUTAKA, *Japanese Politics: Patron-Client Democracy.* New York: Knopf, 1972, 149 pp.

ITOH, HIROSHI, ed., *Japanese Politics: An Inside View, Readings from Japan.* Ithaca, N.Y.: Cornell University Press, 1973, 248 pp.

MAKI, JOHN M., *Court and Constitution in Japan: Selected Supreme Court Deci-*sions, 1948–60. Seattle: University of Washington Press, 1964, 445 pp.

*McNELLY, THEODORE, *Politics and Government in Japan,* 2nd ed. Boston: Houghton Mifflin, 1972, 276 pp.

MILLER, FRANK O., *Minobe Tatsukichi: Interpreter of Constitutionalism in Japan.* Berkeley, Calif.: University of California Press, 1965.

*QUIGLEY, HAROLD S., *Japanese Government and Politics.* New York: Appleton-Century-Crofts, 1932.

*QUIGLEY, HAROLD S., AND JOHN E. TURNER, *The New Japan: Government and Politics.* Minneapolis: University of Minnesota Press, 1956, 456 pp.

*REISCHAUER, R. K., *Japan: Government-Politics.* New York: Nelson, 1939.

STEINER, KURT, *Local Government in Japan.* Stanford, Calif.: Stanford University Press, 1965, 564 pp.

*STOCKWIN, JAMES, *Japan: Divided Politics in a Growth Economy.* New York: Norton, 1975, 296 pp.

TANAKA, HIDEO, ed., *The Japanese Legal System: Introductory Cases and Materials.* Tokyo: University of Tokyo Press, 1976, 954 pp.

*TSUNEISHI, WARREN M., *Japanese Political Style: An Introduction to the Government and Politics of Modern Japan.* New York: Harper and Row, 1966, 226 pp.

*TSURUTANI, TAKETSUGU, *Political Change in Japan: Response to Postindustrial Challenge.* New York: David McKay, 1977.

VON MEHREN, ARTHUR T., ed., *Law in Japan: The Legal Order in a Changing Society.* Cambridge, Mass.: Harvard University Press, 1963, 706 pp.

WHITE, JAMES W., AND FRANK MUNGER, eds., *Social Change and Local Politics in Urban Japan.* Chapel Hill, N.C.: Institute for Research in Social Sciences, 1976.

Chapter *11*

Governmental Performance
DOMESTIC AFFAIRS

Thus far what might be termed the "input" phase of Japan's governmental operations has been discussed: the environmental, historical, and social factors that condition the functioning of the government, the process by which those who influence or control its operations are selected, and the nature of the machinery by which decisions are made, administered, and adjudicated. Yet, as with any productive process, the product, the "output," is as important as the "input" phase of its operations. How effectively do the "products" of government meet the needs of the society's time and circumstances? How well do they satisfy the various demands that government must consider in its decisions? How do they affect the equilibrium of the political process itself? These are the tests by which a political system is ultimately judged both by its own members and by foreign observers.

In examining the output aspects of Japan's political system, what standards of evaluation should be applied? No very precise or satisfactory measure of governmental accomplishment has yet been devised, and consequently, comparative political judgments are usually rendered in terms that are more resonant and impressionistic than they are accurate or informative. The problem is difficult, and there is no promising new formula to submit, although current research in the field of social indicators is promising. One thing definitely to guard against is the facile tendency of many Westerners, and Japanese as well, to judge Japan's political performance against traditional British or American standards of accomplishment

—and even these are often not realistically stated but set forth in the idealized terms of the democratic theorist. Japan's modern political heritage and circumstances bear very faint resemblance to those of Great Britain or the United States.

If a society's cultural background, political history, and political forces are this different from those of the major democratic states of the West, its political views and behavior should not be expected to parallel closely those of such states. Yet this is precisely the assumption that is too often made by both foreigners and Japanese sitting in judgment on Japan's recent political record. Japan has an Asian culture and a primarily Asian heritage. Its significant political associations with the West date back only a little more than one hundred years. It is too much to expect that a century of largely authoritarian political experience will produce in Japan the same type of democratic system that has been more than four hundred years in the making in Great Britain or two hundred years in the making in the United States. It is far more fruitful and constructive to look at the Japanese political record as an example of what can happen under appropriate conditions to non-Western societies and polities undergoing the process of modernization.

In describing the performance of a foreign political system, we tend to concentrate on the degree to which that system achieves certain fundamental values embodied in basic democratic theory. The phrase "popular and responsible government" sums up many of these values. In Japan, great pains have been taken since 1945 to establish optimal conditions for the development of such a "popular and responsible government." To what extent has this been accomplished? Inevitably, the answer is complicated. An examination first of the "popular" element and then of the "responsible" element is helpful, although the overlap between the two is extensive.

Few modern states can equal the scope of opportunities legally available to the Japanese people to vote for those who occupy the leading positions in both national and local governments. The major political offices at all levels are elective; elections are held regularly; and the right to participate is as free and untrammeled by sex, age, residential, or other restrictions as anywhere. Beyond this, a number of special methods of popular participation are provided, including popular plebiscites on constitutional amendments, regular referendums on Supreme Court judges, and rights of initiative and recall at the local level. Also, such informal types of political organizations as interest groups have increased rapidly in numbers and importance and acquired the forms and influence similar to those in the West.

Japanese citizens have, therefore, numerous opportunities to participate in their political system, and they ordinarily make good use of them. The Japanese voting rates, for example, are extraordinarily high, judged by either Asian or Western standards. How well informed and how democratically meaningful is this high level of political participation? The answer has in some respects been disappointing. Factual studies indicate that the average voter is frequently ill-informed about both issues and personalities, that apathy and nonvoting are increasing among the electorate, and that political allegiance and voting behavior are more often determined by emotional factors, group loyalties, or a sense of personal obligation than by reason, principle, or issues. These circumstances, incidentally, are found in the ranks of both the conservative and the socialist electorates. While undoubtedly true, they constitute a commentary more on the human than on the Japanese condition. Much the same judgment can be made—with allowance for cultural variations —about American, British, French, or Italian voters.

All the normal structural and procedural safeguards to insure that government is really responsible to the people have been elaborately built into the Japanese political system at all levels. These safeguards include elections, recall, referendums, initiative, votes of no confidence, rights of interpellation, governmental fiscal accountability, and judicial recourse. Their introduction into what had been a distinctly oligarchical political system has enormously increased the responsibility and accountability of Japan's elected political leaders to the public. Elected officials have become far more powerful in Japanese politics than they were before the war, and the importance of elections has risen correspondingly. To become prime minister, the governor of a prefecture, or mayor of a town, a Japanese politician must usually run several successful election campaigns, and he obviously cannot flout or ignore public opinion as the prewar leadership did. This increased need to win elections and to court public favor does not tell the whole story, however. In practice, elected leaders share political power with both the bureaucracy and the representatives of a variety of influential private interests. These two groups are not as effectively responsible to public control in Japan as are elected officials—although to be fair, there are few, if any, political systems in which they are. In Japan, however, the relative newness and weakness of the "public service" concept, the traditional ascendancy of group over individual interests, and the traditional authority of the bureaucracy somewhat magnify these shortcomings in the degree of the government's responsibility to the people.

There are other and more precisely measurable aspects of governmental performance. Since World War II, the Japanese government has displayed distinctly more interest in the economic than in the political aspects of its performance. There can be no doubt that its highest priority has been the economic rehabilitation and development of Japan. Postwar Japanese governments inherited a country devastated by bombing and blockade, an economy in shambles, a people in desperate need of food and jobs, and a world economic position and prospect that looked dire indeed. The enormity of the challenge was obvious. Therefore, successive governments, at first with occupation prodding and assistance and, since roughly 1950, on their own initiative, have concentrated on improving the country's economic circumstances, and it is in this area that they have achieved their most spectacular successes.

One has only to look back to the situation in Japan at the end of the war to comprehend how dazzling the improvement in its economic conditions has been. In August 1945, at least a quarter of the national wealth and a third of the nation's industrial machinery and equipment had been destroyed; production figures stood at about one-tenth the 1935–36 average. Inflation was rampant, and within a year prices for food and clothing on the free market rose from seventy to one hundred forty times the prewar averages. Expenditures for food comprised about 80 percent of the total family budget, and the average city worker got only about 1,600 calories of food a day instead of the 2,150 calories needed for strength and good health. People were still living in air raid shelters, and necessities of every sort were in acutely short supply. The gross national product in 1947 was about $3.6 billion, a per capita rate of about $34.

In 1975, thirty years after the end of the war, the Japanese people were enjoying a degree of affluence and physical comfort and well-being that was completely unprecedented in their national experience. The economy was the third largest in the world, after the United States and Soviet Union. The gross national product was approximately $488 billion, or $4,432 on a per capita basis. Over the twenty-year period, 1950–1970, the economy had grown at an average rate of 10.2 percent—a record unprecedented in recent economic history. Between 1971 and 1975, this slowed to an average rate of about 4.4 percent but promised to pick up again to 6 or 7 percent in the latter 1970s. The gap that separates the circumstances in 1945 and 1975 is enormous. Never in modern times has a major economy grown so explosively in so brief a time. The result is a general standard of living that is now higher in most respects than that in Italy or Great Britain. The day of the consumer has dawned in Japan, and television sets, refrigerators, electric washing machines, vacuums, family automobiles, vacation travel both at home and abroad, quality clothing, and high protein diets have become commonplace. Beyond this, the populace has become habituated to "progress" measured in these terms and expects and politically demands that it continue with sizable annual increments. Until recently, for example, the real wages of unionized labor in Japan had been increasing at an annual rate of about 12 percent. Because of the degree to which the Japanese economy is guided and regulated by the government, a good deal of the credit for what has been called the Japanese "miracle" (spectacular postwar economic growth) is undoubtedly attributable to the political system working in remarkably effective and cooperative fashion with an enterprise economy.

All of these economic changes constitute basic and very important improvements in the way of life of the average Japanese. There are, of course, shortcomings. Some parts of the population do better than others. In general, the rural sectors lag behind the urban in the incidence and scale of prosperity. Nevertheless, real poverty, either urban or rural, is relatively uncommon in Japan. Employees of larger firms normally fare better than those of smaller firms or family businesses. Since the late 1960s, however, the salary gap separating these groups has narrowed very appreciably, initially because of the labor shortage that developed at that time and a consequent rise in the price of formerly cheap labor. It is still true though that the "permanent" employees of Japanese firms have superior salaries and security to the very sizable group of more casual employees. Another economic dissatisfaction arises from the traditional Japanese practice of linking pay scales primarily to seniority rather than to skill. This gives rise to a sort of automatic discrimination against the more youthful members of any labor force and is currently causing increasing protest by youth no longer willing to accept such traditions without complaint. Despite the remarkable progress of the economy in general, therefore, there are still a number of groups that consider themselves relatively disadvantaged or inequitably treated by the system. Beyond this, since the fall of 1973 the financial problems of all Japanese have been multiplied and intensified by a very serious inflation touched off by the energy crisis. Prices that had been rising at a rate of 10 percent a year at the most suddenly rose by 20 or even 25 percent. This rate of increase has now been substantially moderated, but concern about inflation and the high cost of living continues to be very widespread in Japan as elsewhere. By any realistic standard of achievement or comparison, however, it is the successes of the postwar Japanese economy and the degree to which these have brought an unprecedented prosperity to all classes of the population, rather than the remaining shortfalls of performance, that merit notice and emphasis.

Public health is also a sphere in which governments have important responsibilities. Here again the Japanese record is excellent. Life expectancy rates in Japan are among the very highest in the world, exceeded only by Sweden in all probability. The same is true of the Japanese death and morbidity rates. Average caloric intake of food, while somewhat lower than in the major Western states, is still very high by international standards. It now includes sizable quantities of meat and dairy products, and its nutritional value is such that there have been quite marked changes in the Japanese physique since 1945. The average child today is considerably taller and more robust than his or her parents and has an appreciably greater life expectancy.

Public safety and security is another major governmental responsibility—more so than health in fact. Here the Japanese record is truly remarkable. The following are a few examples from a recent article by Professor David H. Bayley. The number of crimes committed annually in Japan in recent years is actually lower than twenty-five years ago, and the incidence of crime per unit of population is declining. Compared to the United States, an individual is ten times less likely to be murdered, thirteen times less likely to be raped, six times less likely to be burglarized, and two hundred eight times less likely to be robbed in Japan. There are almost as many homocides committed each year in New York City alone as in all Japan—sixteen hundred versus nineteen hundred—and New York City has only about one-fourteenth of the population of Japan. Drug offenses are a relatively trivial problem. The result is that "law and order" in a criminal sense is more or less taken for granted in Japan, and the keen anxieties that so many Americans feel for their safety are largely absent in Japan.

Since the war, the Japanese government has also recognized an entirely new range of obligations in the field of social security. Before the war, the government took on very limited obligations in this area. It was primarily the duty of the family to support any of its members who became incapacitated because of injury, illness, old age, or adverse economic circumstances. In fact, much of the strength of the traditional family system derived from its role as a welfare agency. The new Constitution changed this situation.

Article 25 states that "all people shall have the right to maintain the minimum standards of wholesome and cultured living" and that "in all spheres of life, the State shall use its endeavors for the promotion and extension of social welfare and security, and of public health." These are, of course, vague statements, but they have served to make welfare and social security explicit responsibilites of the state. The Japanese government has established a complex network of assistance programs that includes unemployment, health, old-age, survivors', seamen's, and industrial accident insurance plans. These are supplemented by government-supported vocational, guidance and training centers, employment exchanges, a child welfare program, and aid for the physically handicapped. The sum of all these services scarcely amounts to a cradle-to-grave security program. Some of the programs, for example, are applicable only to the regular employees of establishments employing five or more workers, thus excluding the portion of the labor force engaged in agriculture, forestry, fisheries, and service or family industries. Also, the financial benefits involved remain markedly inadequate for the needs of those concerned. Still, in 1975 the national budget provided more than ¥5 trillion ($17 billion) in support of various social security and welfare programs, a very appreciable sum particularly when linked with the contributions of employees and individual beneficiaries. However, Japan spends a lower percentage of its gross national product for welfare purposes than any other major industrialized state.

Education is another area in which the government has a primary responsibility. Again, in statistical terms, the Japanese record is exemplary. Almost 100 percent of six- to fifteen-year-olds are enrolled in the nine-year compulsory curriculum. About 82 percent of the graduates of this elementary course take some schooling beyond the compulsory level. About 23 percent of those eighteen to twenty-one years old are enrolled in a college or university; this figure is exceeded only by the United States' 31 percent. As a result, Japan has one of the world's most literate, highly educated, and skilled populations in the world today.

These accomplishments that are in significant part attributable to a high degree of governmental performance or "output" should not convey the impression that the Japanese record is without blemish. Figures for gross national products are statistical artifacts that reflect the actual quality of life of a people only in very general terms. A high gross national product figure does not necessarily connote a high standard of living. The Soviet Union, for example, has the second highest gross national product in the world. Obviously its populace does not enjoy commensurate living standards. The same is true of Japan to some extent and in particular regards.

There are, for example, appreciable differences in the quality of urban and rural life, and urban families in general tend to do better—or at least think that they do better—than their counterparts in the countryside. As a consequence of this and the relative rigors and hardships of farming for a living, the rural areas of Japan are steadily being drained of their population by migration to more urbanized settings. Today only about 14 percent of the labor force is in agriculture, while 34 percent is engaged in mining, construction, and manufacturing and a massive 52 percent in the service trades. Considering that as recently as 1955 39 percent of the labor force was engaged in agriculture or forestry, the rapidity of this surge to the cities becomes manifest. Despite such differences, however, one encounters relatively little real poverty anyplace in Japan, even by Western standards.

Many important aspects of daily life are inadequate, however. For example, housing is a major problem. About one-third of the inhabitants of Tokyo live in apartments that are an average size of one hundred twenty-four square feet—about eleven feet square. Perhaps one-half have their own bathrooms; the rest share toilets in the building and go to public baths in the neighborhood. Modern sewage facilities are still unusual in Japan; in 1970 only 22 percent of Tokyo's residents had flush toilets. The preceding figures for the size of dwellings do not represent the norm for Japan. Actually the average floor space in a Japanese residence is about eight hundred square feet, the equivalent of twenty by forty feet. Still, Japan's homes and apartments are by general consent uncomfortably small and crowded, especially for the citizens of a country with the third largest gross national product in the world.

Many Japanese regard more adequate housing as the country's single greatest need, especially in the urban areas where most Japanese now live. About 60 percent of all families own their own homes, but in Tokyo and Osaka less than one-third do. Becoming a home owner is a traditional aspiration shared by most Japanese, but today the problems involved seem almost insuperable. A 1972 bank survey, for example, indicated that the average Tokyo or Osaka worker taking out a mortgage loan had an annual income of seventy-four hundred dollars. With the loan he was able to buy eleven hundred square feet of land and build a house of six hundred seventy square feet. It was located in the suburbs, forcing an extended commute to his job, and it cost twenty-four thousand dollars. Today the same house would probably cost between forty and fifty thousand dollars. Even in 1971 —with 1955 as the base year—the index of consumer prices in Japan was 209, while the index of city land prices was 2338. Both indices are higher today, especially the latter. Some Japanese employees—actually only about 7 percent—are fortunate enough to evade this problem by living in houses provided by their employers or in public housing with low rents, sometimes only five to twenty-five dollars a month. These people are fortunate, however, and their numbers are not as yet great. The total demand for new houses and apartments is estimated to be about twenty-four million units in the next few years, practically as many as the twenty-six million existing units. The government and private construction industry have major programs under way that in time should alleviate this problem, but they still have a long way to go.

In Japan as elsewhere inflation and the associated high cost of living are major problems. Double-digit inflation was late in coming to Japan. It was not until 1973 and the energy crisis that the average Japanese was seriously affected. The relevant statistical indexes tell something about the problem. With 1970 as a base at 100, the consumer price index and the index of real wages changed between 1970 and 1975 as shown in table 11–1. Like laborers elsewhere, the average Japanese laborer has been losing some purchas-

TABLE 11-1
CONSUMER PRICE INDEX AND INDEX OF REAL WAGES, 1970-75

Year	CPI	Real wages
1970	100.0	100.0
1971	106.1	108.0
1972	110.9	119.9
1973	123.9	130.3
1974	154.2	132.7
1975	172.4	133.6

Source: *Nihon Tokei Nenkan, 1976,* pp. 362, 383; and *Nihon Kokusei Zue,* 1976, p. 102.

ing power in recent years as a result of the failure of real wages to keep pace with the inflationary surge in the economy. The rate of inflation had tapered off in 1976, however, and conditions seemed to be improving.

Transportation is also a major and growing problem in Japan. The system of public and private rail systems—and, in the major cities, of subways—is one of the world's most extensive, modern, and impressive. By any but American standards, the same is now true of domestic airlines. However, the burden placed upon the rail system is almost incredible. For example, within a fifty-kilometer range of the central Tokyo station, the national and private railway systems plus the subway system carried a daily average of 19.7 million passengers in 1973. Literally millions of people commute five or six days a week into Tokyo, with the average trip taking more than one hour in each direction. Anyone who has ever traveled in a Japanese commuter train or subway at rush hour will readily understand the cumulative frustration and discontent harbored by many Japanese. As land prices increase in direct proportion to one's proximity to downtown Tokyo or other major cities, the average would-be homeowner is driven farther and farther from the city, and the time and distance he or she must travel to work increase accordingly.

The situation for automobile traffic is even worse. In 1974, there were 27.8 million motor vehicles of all kinds in Japan, and 13.2 million of these were passenger cars. Manufacturers are adding to this number at a rate of about 4 million cars per year, though many are exported. These are figures second only to the United States. For these millions of vehicles, Japan has a total of about 656,000 miles of roads. Only 13 percent (85,280 miles) of these are paved. Japan ranks about fifty-seventh internationally in its ratio of paved roads to total roads. The situation is particularly bad in the major cities. In Washington, D.C., and New York, for example, the ratios of road space to total space are 43 and 35 percent respectively. In Tokyo and Osaka they are 12 and 9 percent. Japanese roads were designed for men and horses, not automobiles. They are narrow, and except for major arteries, there are no sidewalks. The government is spending huge amounts of money on new construction, but the task is immense and the problems obvious. Purchase of the land necessary to extend or widen roads is inordinately expensive, parking facilities are grossly inadequate, the accident rate is very high, and traffic jams are such as to make crosstown Manhattan traffic at rush hour resemble a freeway.

Most Japanese still work six days a week. The actual figures for 1975 were 48.8 hours a week for males and 41.6 hours for females—a weighted average of 46.1 hours. A number of the larger companies have for several years been giving their workers some Saturdays off each month, but most still routinely work for six days. This is changing, but its continued prevalence is still surprising by American standards.

In the light of these anachronisms, there is a good deal of concern in Japan about the lack of social infrastructure. Observations contrast the dazzling accomplishments of the postwar Japanese economy as a whole with the grievous shortcomings in housing, in sewage, in transportation, in paved roads, or in public recreational facilities. For example, Tokyo has 13 square feet per capita of park space compared with 206 square feet in New York or 245 square feet in London. These items may be frills lacking in an otherwise impressive standard of living, but in terms of human comfort, well-being, and aspirations, they are of substantial and increasing importance. Serious efforts are being made to cope with them by both the public and the private sectors, but it is very difficult in Japan to keep abreast of the tide of rising popular expectations. Japanese have, therefore, real reasons for particular dissatisfactions with the quality of their lives. These should not, however, be allowed to detract unduly from an overall national record of effective performance in postwar times that is without equal in the developed world. Measured in tangible terms, the gap in affluence, in living standards, or in general well-being that separates the Japan of 1945 from that of 1976 is almost astronomical. It would be very difficult to assess precisely the share of the government's credit for these accomplishments, but by any standards, it must be adjudged as substantial. It certainly compares very favorably with that of any other major government in the world.

Chapter 12

Governmental Performance
FOREIGN RELATIONS

The previous chapters dealt with the domestic aspects of politics and governance in contemporary Japan. This chapter focuses on another sphere, foreign relations and foreign policy. The implied distinction between domestic and foreign affairs is merely conventional. While historically they have been treated as separate spheres of concern and activity, this has never been true in any absolute sense and is certainly not true of our times. One of the hallmarks of the late twentieth century is the degree to which the traditional boundaries delimiting foreign from domestic politics have progressively lost their validity and significance.

In the United States, for example, foreign policy decisions are no longer the exclusive prerogative of a small group of professionals in the Department of State and the White House. Today practically all major executive departments have overseas interests or programs. Congress, the states, the media, and the public—acting through a variety of interest groups—are also heavily involved in both the formulation and implementation of foreign policy. At the same time, developments abroad such as security problems, population growth, resource distribution, crop surpluses or deficits, pollution, or monetary and economic policies have a vital, continuous, and increasing impact on the domestic fortunes and well-being of Americans. Under these circumstances, it is totally unrealistic to think of foreign affairs as somehow different and distinct from domestic affairs. The two are intimately interrelated, and the web of interests and processes that ties them together is growing rapidly in complexity and scale. This is even more true of Japan than of the United States, which is a relatively self-sufficient country.

Japan's Geopolitical Circumstances

Two sets of circumstances define Japan's basic position vis-à-vis the rest of the world. The first is geography, conditioned by history and the prevailing stage of technological development. The second is resource endowment and needs, conditioned by the effective political demands and expectations of the Japanese people.

Geographically Japan is small—about 143,700 square miles—and insular —about 130 miles from the Korean coast and 475 miles from the Chinese mainland but only about 12 miles from the Russian-occupied island of Kunashiri. For centuries the intervening seas gave Japan a degree of security from external attacks enjoyed by no other major state. Modern technology has seriously qualified this fortuitous condition. World War II demonstrated Japan's vulnerability to air and sea attacks by an opponent of superior military strength as well as to effective blockade by both air and sea power. Japan alone has experienced the horrors of atomic bombing. Since 1945, further developments in nuclear armaments and in medium- and long-range missiles for the delivery of nuclear warheads over great distances and with impressive accuracy have enormously increased Japan's vulnerability to foreign attack. This is further enhanced by the extreme compaction of the Japanese population and economy imposed by the predominantly mountainous nature of the terrain; 50.5 percent of the population and an even higher proportion of industrial productive capacity are concentrated in the megalopolitan belt stretching from Tokyo to Kobe. Japan is rendered even more defenseless against nuclear attack by the shortness of the distances intervening between potential launching points on the continent of Asia or the surrounding seas. Maximum advance warning times of nuclear attack could well be less than ten or fifteen minutes. Thus, while Japan strategically still enjoys impressive advantages over most threats of attack or invasion by conventional military means, it is unusually vulnerable to nuclear damage and to sea or air blockades and normally susceptible to attacks by air or sea.

These circumstances cause Japanese governments to reflect seriously on the possible implications of their position and on foreign relations in both regional and global terms. Japan's nearest neighbors are the Soviet Union, Korea, the People's Republic of China, and Taiwan. The Soviet Union is a superpower whose historic relations with Japan have been anything but friendly, whose military capacities are overwhelming, and whose long-term intentions are unknown. Korea is a bitterly divided state whose animosities create the constant possibility of renewed civil war on a scale capable of involving all of its neighbors and the United States. The People's Republic of China and Taiwan are two parts of another divided state whose future relationships are at this point totally unpredictable. Taiwan itself certainly offers no direct military threat to Japan, nor does the People's Republic of

China, at least for the present when its predominant concern is the possibility of hostilities with the Soviet Union. If this threat were to dissipate or if some form of Sino-Soviet cooperation for limited purposes were to be reestablished, it is difficult to foresee the potential consequences for Sino-Japanese relations. Also, Japan is centrally situated in precisely the area where two of the world's three most serious postwar hostilities have occurred. All of these dangers are, of course, conjectural, but modern East Asian history plus a geographic location that places Japan in the eye of so many potential political and military hurricanes enjoins great caution and prudence upon any Japanese government.

Viewed in global perspective, Japan's geopolitical circumstances are also unusual. Here the problem is distance rather than proximity. As a major democratic and free-enterprise society, Japan's long-term international interests are most closely identified with those of the United States and the European Community. One is five thousand miles away and the other six thousand, not to mention the great distances in history, language, and culture separating Japan from its Western associates. Japan's relations with the great Western democracies are not only distant in a physical sense, but they are also lopsided. The Japanese association with the United States since the end of the occupation in 1952 has normally been close, cordial, and mutually supportive and beneficial. On the other hand, Japan's relations with Great Britain, France, Germany, Italy, and the smaller states of the community have been fairly casual until recently, and they have often been marked by suspicion and minor unpleasantness, largely on economic grounds. Within the past several years, however, there have been serious attempts on both sides to build closer and more systematic relations and to make of Japan practically an adjunct member of the Atlantic Community, especially for economic and financial purposes. The relations between Japan and the Western democracies have also diplomatically aligned Japan on the side of the United States and its allies and against the Soviet Union and its associates. Given the geographic distance of its allies and the proximity of its potential enemies, this has been an uncomfortable and worrisome position for the Japanese—particularly so in the light of their pacificistic inclinations and practically defenseless military status. It has given rise to widespread and intense disagreement within Japan as to the wisdom and practicality of the policies involved.

The second set of circumstances that define Japan's basic position vis-à-vis the rest of the world are predominantly economic. Fundamentally, they derive from the fact that Japan is poor in resources. One dramatic example illustrates the consequences. When the oil crisis occurred in the fall of 1973, Japan was the third largest consumer of energy in the world after the United States and the Soviet Union. Of Japan's total energy supply, 94 percent was imported, and 75 percent of that supply was derived from oil. More than 99 percent of Japan's oil was imported; 80 percent of this was from the Near Eastern states that were imposing the embargo on further oil shipments to Japan, the United States, and Western Europe. Under normal circumstances, existing stockpiles of oil in Japan would have been exhausted in less than sixty days. If the embargo had been effectively maintained, less than a two-month period without solution of the problem could have brought a disastrous collapse of the entire Japanese economy. Obviously, the Japanese economy is extraordinarily vulnerable to any serious threat to its energy supply.

This vulnerability is not limited to energy. Japan is dependent every year upon imports of all of its bauxite, rubber, phosphate, nickel, uranium, cotton, and wool; 88 percent of its iron ore; 79 percent of its coking coal; 76 percent of its copper; and 60 percent of its lumber. In caloric value, the country also imports about 50 percent of its food supply. Each one of these items represents a vital contribution to the efficient functioning of the Japanese economy, to the prosperity and well-being of the Japanese people, and thus, to the political stability and prospects of the state.

The role of foreign trade, and thus external dependency, in the Japanese economy is as follows. In 1975, for example, Japan's imports amounted to about $57.9 billion and exports to $55.8 billion—a total of $113.7 billion. In the same year the gross national product was about $488 billion; imports accounted for 12 percent and exports for another 11 percent of it. The distribution of this foreign trade in recent years is as follows: about 42 percent of Japan's imports and 48 percent of exports are attributable to the "advanced" countries; about 53 percent of imports and 45 percent of exports involve the developing countries; and the remainder—some 5 percent of imports and 7 percent of exports—is attributable to the communist countries. Given such a distribution of its foreign trading interests and the overall importance of trade to the Japanese economy, it is in Japan's economic interest to remain on friendly terms with as many countries as possible. Any sizable decreases in the volume or adverse shifts in the terms or balance of trade are certain to have a damaging effect on significant portions of the domestic economy. This has been a constant concern—most would say the principal preoccupation—of all postwar Japanese governments.

In evaluating Japanese foreign policy issues, then, it is always necessary to keep in mind these two primary factors of geopolitics and national security and of resource poverty with its attendant economic consequences. By American standards, Japan's postwar foreign policy may in some respects be unusual to the point of fantasy. While it may in the long run prove unrealistic, it is not irrational, only chancy. However, what nation's foreign policy is not?

The Legacies of Defeat: Diplomatic

The postwar settlement embodied in the Treaty of San Francisco (signed on 8 September 1951 and effective on 28 April 1952) ended the Allied Occupation of Japan and technically restored Japan to the status of an independent and sovereign state. It also posed for the Japanese government a series of very difficult problems that in some measure determined the goals and policies of Japanese diplomacy for many years to come.

First, there was the territorial issue. The Treaty of San Francisco stripped Japan of its prewar empire. The lost imperial territories included Korea, Taiwan, the Pescadores Islands, the Kwantung Leased Territory, and the

Mandated Islands of the South Seas. Lost also were certain areas that were legally considered a part of domestic Japanese territory: Sakhalin, the Kurile Islands, Okinawa (also known as the Ryukyu Islands), and the Ogasawara Islands. Together this amounted to a loss of 311,158 square kilometers, or 46 percent of Japan's total prewar territory. Of these losses Japan has since recovered only the Ogasawara Islands (26 June 1968) and Okinawa (15 May 1972), a total of 2,489 square kilometers, leaving a net loss of 308,669 square kilometers or 45 percent of its prewar holdings. In general all post-war Japanese governments have acceded to these territorial losses with two exceptions: the United States' possession of Ogasawara and Okinawa and the Soviet Union's possession of the Kuriles (including two small island groups, Shikotan and Habomai, that the Japanese claim are properly part of Hokkaido rather than the Kuriles). Both the Ogasawara Islands and Okinawa (also known as the Ryukyu Islands) were recovered as a result of negotiations with the United States, although the latter negotiations were prolonged and difficult for both sides. With the return of the Ogasawaras and Okinawa, Japan has no further territorial claims against the United States. The Japanese government has, however, consistently pressed the Soviet Union for the return of the extreme southern portion of the Kurile Islands (the islands of Kunashiri and Etorofu plus Habomai and Shikotan). Historically, Japanese title to these lands was never in dispute and was even accepted by the prerevolutionary czarist government. The Soviet government has with equal consistency refused since 1956 even to discuss the matter, claiming that it was finally settled by the Yalta Agreement and the Treaty of San Francisco, which, incidentally, the Soviet Union refused to sign. As a consequence, Japan has been unwilling to negotiate a formal treaty of peace ending the World War II hostilities with the Soviet Union. So long as it remains unresolved, the issue of the Southern Kuriles constitutes a serious impediment to closer and more cordial relations between Japan and the Soviet Union.

Second, there has been the matter of reparations. In addition to providing for the confiscation of all Japanese-owned overseas property or interests, the Treaty of San Francisco stipulated Japan's obligation to pay reparations for wartime damages and suffering to those Allied Powers who wanted them and whose territories were occupied and damaged by Japanese forces. This meant the Philippines, Burma, Indonesia, South and North Vietnam, Laos, Cambodia, Thailand, Singapore, Malaysia, South Korea, and the Pacific Trust Territories. The two Chinas and Australia did not choose to enforce their claims for monetary reparations. Starting with Burma in 1955 and ending with Malaysia and Singapore in 1968 and North Vietnam in 1976, Japan negotiated a series of reparations agreements with all of these claimants. The terms varied from case to case but often included free economic and technical assistance, special yen credits against Japan, and outright cash payments. The cost to Japan was very substantial (about $1.5 billion) but so, too, were the commercial advantages. The cash payments and special credits were uniformly made in yen and were linked to purchases in the Japanese market by the countries concerned. The technical assistance had a similar effect. Thus, reparations payments were an indirect subsidy by the Japanese government to Japanese industry, commerce, and finance that had the further effect of favorably establishing Japan in these new Southeast Asian markets. The last of Japan's obligations under these reparations agreements was discharged in 1977, and this aspect of Japan's postwar diplomacy was thereby concluded with a gratifying degree of success.

A third warborn problem concerned Japan's postwar reentry into the international community. The loss of the war and the terms of the subsequent Allied Occupation had the effect of isolating Japan from normal relations with other sovereign states and from participation in international organizations. It was necessary to reestablish such connections and memberships as rapidly as possible after the Treaty of San Francisco went into effect. In many cases there were no special problems connected with the resumption of normal diplomatic and commercial relations. Others were quite difficult. For example, the negotiation of an acceptable reparations agreement was a condition precedent to the normalization of Japan's relations with all the noncommunist states of Southeast Asia. This delayed any formal relationship with South Korea, Japan's nearest neighbor, until 1965. The communist states were also a special problem since all of them had refused to be parties to the Treaty of San Francisco. Diplomatic relations with the Soviet Union were not reestablished until 1956. Even now, there is no formal peace treaty between the two countries. It was not until 1972 that normal relations were reestablished with the People's Republic of China. A formal peace treaty was still pending in 1976. Diplomatic relations have yet to be established with North Korea, while normalization of a limited sort with North Vietnam occurred only in September 1973.

International organizations posed a similar problem, and in this instance, Japan benefited substantially from American sponsorship. In late 1956, the basic step of membership in the United Nations was successfully negotiated with American assistance that was instrumental in overcoming several years of Soviet obstruction. Gradually Japan also gained acceptance by the other major international organizations of interest, for example, the Colombo Plan, the International Bank of Reconstruction and Development, the International Finance Corporation, the International Development Association, the Development Assistance Group, the General Agreement on Tariffs and Trade, the Organization for Economic Cooperation and Development, and the International Monetary Fund. By the mid-1960s, this phase of postwar Japanese diplomacy had also been successfully concluded. Japan was once more generally accepted as a normal and major member of the international community.

A fourth consequence of defeat and occupation was economic but was soluble only by a combination of diplomatic and economic initiatives. This was the disastrous state of the postwar Japanese economy. Actually, it was for a number of years the most urgent and fundamental problem confronting all postwar Japanese governments. Even today, long after the stage of crisis, it continues to be its principal preoccupation. The war destroyed about 25 percent of Japan's national wealth, about 40 percent of the built-up area of the sixty-six major cities subjected to bombing, some 30 percent of the nation's industrial capacity, 80 percent of its shipping, and 47 percent of its thermal power-generating capacity. By 1947 the gross national product was only $3.6 billion, or a per capita rate of about $34. The economy was in deep depression; people were ill-fed, ill-clothed, and ill-housed; and the country stood on the brink of a calamitous inflation. Obviously the prime concern of the government had to be the amelioration of these economic circumstances. Because of resource poverty and trade dependence, a great deal of its prospects for success in this undertaking rested on the reestablishment of satisfactory markets and sources of supply abroad, primarily with just those states that had so recently been at war with or occupied by Japan. The complexity and difficulty of the task is obvious.

The consequences for the entire course of Japan's postwar diplomacy of these domestic economic conditions in early postwar times have been momentous. It meant at first an almost complete absorption by the Japanese government with economic problems and with how to resolve these to benefit maximally the domestic economy and thus the economic well-being of the Japanese people. It is difficult to say whether at some point this involved a deliberate and conscious decision by the government to depreciate the political aspects of foreign relations in favor of the economic. The political powerlessness of postwar Japan would doubtless have made some such policy inevitable for at least some time, and practically speaking, it is very difficult for a disarmed state to exercise much political influence abroad. Finally, the government doubtless discovered early that tangible economic progress was the most effective path to success at the polls. All of these factors combined very early to set Japan on a foreign policy path that focused most of the country's energy, talent, resources, and attention upon, first, national economic recovery and, thereafter, rapid economic growth. The government was able, in pursuit of these ends, to mobilize the support of Japan's business community with great effectiveness. Given the talents, resources, energy, discipline, and persistence of government, business, and the Japanese worker, the results were perhaps in a general way predictable. By 1955—ten years after the war and three years after the end of the occupation—the official indexes of industrial activity, public utilities, and industrial production had all broken through their prewar and wartime ceilings. By 1962 the economy had entered upon a period of explosive growth. By the early 1970s—some twenty-five years after the war—Japan had the third largest economy in the world after only the United States and the Soviet Union. There is more to national well-being than economic success, but the Japanese record is unequaled as an example of rapid progress in this sphere from most unpromising beginnings.

A great deal of this success is attributable to Japan's postwar diplomacy and to the skill with which the government has reestablished and built trading relations abroad, developed its network of overseas financial and commercial intelligence and communications, represented and assisted its businessmen, and made use of the various international organizations that service foreign trade and finance. Indeed the very efficiency and success of the Japanese government in these areas has given rise to charges by disgruntled competitors that Japan's foreign trade is conducted, not by private businessmen operating on their own, but by an entity dubbed "Japan, Inc.," or "Japan, Incorporated." This allegedly consists of the close alliance of Japanese business and the great Japanese trading companies operating with and under the control of the Japanese government. While there is justification for such a claim, it has been more true in the past when Japan, while pressing for free trade elsewhere, was more stringently protecting its own domestic market than it is today. This is not to say that the relationship between the Japanese government and those firms doing business overseas is no longer close and supportive; it obviously is. However, Japanese governmental performance along these lines has improved very substantially since the 1960s, while the intensity of the competition between Japanese companies in overseas markets is obvious. It is still true, however, that contemporary Japanese diplomacy is predominantly economic in its concerns and emphases. There are few signs of substantial change in this respect.

The Legacies of Defeat: Military and Strategic

No clear line of demarcation separates a country's military and strategic resources and policies from its diplomatic policies. Normally and historically the two are closely linked in such a way as to be supplementary. It is precisely the degree to which Japan's postwar policies have differed from this norm that makes the Japanese experience notable.

The account begins with the fact of a single crushing defeat after some two thousand years of a national history that had lacked any prior experience with either effective invasion or defeat on its own terrain. The physical and psychological shock was multiplied by a general and progressive attrition in the quality of life and security attendant upon eight years of the China Incident and almost four years of World War II, by the impact of the blockade, by nine months of incessant bombing attacks on sixty-six of Japan's largest cities and industrial areas, and ultimately, by the atomic bombings of Hiroshima and Nagasaki. The end of hostilities brought no end to the problems and suffering of the Japanese people. It simply substituted unemployment, poverty, inflation, food shortages, and a foreign military occupation for more explicitly military threats. The apparent consequences of these cumulating adversities were both unexpected and puzzling. Great nations had suffered defeat before—sometimes repeatedly—but they recovered and usually proceeded to fight other wars with varying but often equally disastrous results. This was particularly the case with nations that cherished and exalted the martial traditions and virtues as Japan historically has. Thus, it is surprising that in Japan defeat seems to have bred a widespread receptivity to pacifism, disarmament, and peaceful modes of settlement. If these sentiments prove durable—and they have now persisted for more than thirty years—it may well be the first time in history that a major nation at least has learned and abided by such a lesson.

These antimilitary dispositions among the postwar Japanese populace were institutionalized in a very remarkable way. All of the Allied planning for the treatment of a defeated Japan had emphasized the need for disarmament, demilitarization, and Allied supervision for substantial periods of time. General MacArthur in ordering his Government Section to draft the document that ultimately became the new postwar constitution of Japan, required that a provision be included abolishing the sovereign right of the nation to wage war, to exercise the right of belligerency, or to maintain an army, navy, or air force. Total and perpetual disarmament embodied in the state's most fundamental and unchangeable form of law went considerably beyond anything contemplated in Washington or other Allied capitals. Despite this, it was incorporated in the Japanese Constitution of 1946–47 as Article 9. It is still unchanged and merits quotation in full:

> Aspiring sincerely to an international peace based on justice and order, the Japanese people forever renounce war as a sovereign right of the nation and the threat or use of force as means of settling international disputes.
> In order to accomplish the aim of the preceding paragraph, land, sea, and air forces, as well as other war potential, will never be maintained. The right of belligerency of the state will not be recognized.

There is some controversy as to whether the original idea for such a provision was General MacArthur's or Baron Shidehara's (then the prime minister of Japan). Most informed opinion, including General MacArthur's, attributes it to Shidehara. There is, however, no doubt that it is in the Constitution because General MacArthur ordered that it be put there—without prior authorization from Washington authorities. To the surprise of many, it caught the spirit of the times in postwar Japan, acquired widespread public support, and now seems to be a firmly established and generally accepted part of the Constitution. This is not to say that these attitudes might not change in the future, but there are at present no significant indications of such a change.

Today, Japan maintains an army, navy, and air force, even though the Constitution seems clearly to preclude them. Several explanations are possible. First, on purely legal grounds the first ten words of the second paragraph of Article 9—"In order to accomplish the aim of the preceding paragraph"—have been interpreted to mean that only offensive forces are proscribed and that armed forces maintained for purely self-defensive purposes are legitimate. In more general terms it is also held that Japan, like any sovereign state, has an inalienable right to self-defense. Second, when General MacArthur stripped Japan of American forces to meet the North Korean attack on South Korea in 1950, he ordered the Japanese government to establish a paramilitary force of some seventy-five thousand men, called a National Police Reserve, to safeguard the country against the possibility of communist-inspired subversion. This was in a physical sense the origin of Japan's present armed forces. Finally, by the time the Treaty of San Francisco was negotiated in 1950–51, the United States had ceased regarding Japan as a recent and still potentially dangerous enemy and now looked upon the country as a most important ally against the threats posed by the new Sino-Soviet Alliance. The Korean War, then in full course, added point and reality to this fear. Under these circumstances, the United States had come to regard Article 9 as a serious mistake and obviously preferred a strong and armed ally to a weak and disarmed one. The Japanese government shared the view that the country should not be completely defenseless against subversion. After considerable wrangling with the United States about the size of the forces, the government went along with the American desire and established a National Safety Force of about one hundred ten thousand men and a Maritime Safety Force of eighty-nine hundred—much smaller forces than the United States desired.

Japan has not today significantly increased the number of its armed forces. The government spends annually less than 1 percent of the gross national product and less than 7 percent of the budget for military purposes, the lowest figures for any major state in the world. While there have been major improvements in weaponry and training, the actual current size of the armed forces is about 235,000 in all branches. Total authorized strength for the self-defense forces is about 266,000 (180,000 for the ground, 41,000 for the maritime, and 45,000 for the air self-defense forces). Since military service is not regarded as a desirable career by most Japanese, there have been persistent difficulties in meeting the full recruiting quotas and in holding those recruited (they can resign at any time). It is also important to note that Japan's armed forces are from two to fifteen times smaller than those of any of the neighboring states: the Soviet Union, the People's Republic of China, North or South Korea, and the Republic of China (Taiwan).

The mission assigned these modest forces has to date been strictly defensive in nature. The prevailing interpretation of Article 9 totally precludes any overseas service or assignments involving the actual or potential use of force. This interdiction applies even to the use of Japanese forces as one element in a United Nations' peace-keeping force. The armament, training, and equipment of Japan's armed forces also reflect the defensive nature of their mission. The largest ships in the navy are destroyers intended for highly localized operations. In fact the overall tonnage of the entire Maritime Safety Force is only about 160,000 tons, substantially less than that of a single modern supertanker. The air force purchases only fighters and interceptors with rather modest cruising ranges. It has no real bombers of either a medium- or long-range class, although some of the fighters incidentally have these capacities. The same is true of the equipment and training of the ground forces.

Given the wealth and technological skills of Japan, it was inevitable that the question would arise of whether or not the armed forces either legally could or practically should be equipped with nuclear weapons. On the question of legality, the government has on several occasions indicated that the acquisition of nuclear arms would not be unconstitutional if it was solely for defensive purposes. However, all recent governments have subscribed to what are called the "Three Non-Nuclear Principles," that is, Japan will not possess, produce, or introduce nuclear weapons into the country. Despite repeated governmental assurances, the issue of nuclear weapons is periodically reviewed by the press and opposition political circles. It is a very sensitive subject for the Japanese people, in part, perhaps, because of their "nuclear allergy" acquired as a result of the Hiroshima and Nagasaki experiences. Many are uncertain that, given sufficiently stressful and threatening circumstances, Japan might not in the future opt to acquire a nuclear warfare capacity. The resources and technical skills to do so are certainly present in abundance. The popular estimate is that Japan could manufacture effective nuclear weapons—and, probably, missiles for their delivery—approximately two years after making the decision to do so. The government, however, has shown absolutely no intention of doing so, and formally obligated itself not to do so by ratifying the the Non-Proliferation Treaty in 1976.

Given military forces so small in size and limited in strength vis-à-vis those of all Japan's neighbors and potential enemies, one may well wonder what practical purpose they serve. The answer is simple, if unusual. Successive Japanese governments on a variety of grounds, both foreign and domestic, have decided the following: first, the present or foreseeable threat to Japan's security from conventional attacks by China, North or South Korea, or Taiwan is negligible; second, conventional attacks by either the Soviet Union or, hypothetically, the United States would be irresistible; and, third, nuclear attacks by the Soviet Union, the People's Republic of China, or—again hypothetically—the United States would be overwhelming. Under these circumstances, the purposes of the self-defense forces are as follows: first, to deal effectively with any large-scale subversive uprisings—presumably communist-inspired—at home; second, to provide a sufficient deterrent against the possibility of conventional sea or air attacks from any quarter except Russia or the United States—such attacks require greater naval and air strengths than any of Japan's neighbors possess; and finally, to hold out long enough against a conventional attack by the Soviet Union to enable the United States to come to Japan's rescue under the terms of the United States–Japan Security Treaty. The forces seem adequate for the first two missions. In the last event, it would be a question of timing. Most observers doubt that Japan's forces alone could fight effectively against the Soviet Union for more than two weeks, if that.

Such a strategy does not take into serious account another, and perhaps more probable, form of threat to Japan's national security. This could take the form of an interruption of vital sources of overseas supplies by blockade, harassment, or embargo. This last, of course, is actually what occurred briefly during the Arab oil embargo in late 1973 when most of the oil-producing states of the Near East cut off Japan's oil supplies by means of an embargo, leaving Japan with no effective recourse save capitulation. Similar results could be achieved by blockade or harassment, especially at such critical maritime points as the Straits of Malacca, Sunda, Lombok, or Taiwan. Japan totally lacks the naval capacity to deal with such threats at any point south of Taiwan. Again, Japan's security would depend completely on the timely intervention of the United States through the Seventh Fleet. The same is, of course, true of any threat of nuclear attack on Japan. Japan's only safeguard against military danger is the credibility of the American security guarantee.

The Security Treaty of 8 September 1951 (effective 28 April 1952) between the United States and Japan was negotiated when the Korean War was at its height, when—only shortly before—the communist forces had won the revolution in China and promptly established a Sino-Soviet alliance aimed directly at Japan and indirectly at the United States, when the cold war in Europe was at its height, and when there were numerous and persuasive signs that the cold war had been extended to East Asia. The treaty provided for the continued presence of United States military forces and bases in Japan after the end of the occupation for contributing "to the maintenance of international peace and security in the Far East and to the security of Japan against armed attack from without, including assistance given at the express request of the Japanese government to put down large-scale internal riots and disturbances in Japan, caused through instigation or intervention by an outside power or powers." The duration of the treaty was indefinite; it was to run until satisfactory provision had been made by the United Nations or otherwise for the maintenance of international peace and security in the Japan area. Under the terms of the treaty, the United States has routinely maintained forces in Japan ranging in numbers from two hundred sixty thousand in 1952 to about fifty-one thousand in 1975, the bulk of which (thirty thousand) are naval personnel attached to the repair and logistical facilities and base at Yokosuka.

From the outset, the Security Treaty—and, for that matter, the related Treaty of San Francisco—was an object of intense domestic controversy in Japan. It was strongly opposed by most of the opposition political parties that believed it would actually detract from rather than enhance the national security by aligning Japan automatically in support of the United States in a vaguely defined area known as the Far East. Most of the opposition preferred either a neutralist status for Japan or alliance with the Sino-Soviet bloc. This opposition culminated in fierce nationwide demonstrations and rioting in 1960 at a time when the Japanese government was attempting to renegotiate the Security Treaty on terms more favorable to Japan. Despite these problems, the Kishi government did bring about such changes before being forced to resign from office.

The revised treaty of 19 January 1960 (see appendix 6), which continues in effect today, states that "each Party recognizes that an armed attack against either Party in the territories under the administration of Japan would be dangerous to its own peace and safety and declares that it would act to meet the common dangers in accordance with its constitutional provisions and processes." The agreement was valid for ten years (until 1970), after which it remains in force until either party terminates it following a year's notice of intention to do so. Under the terms of this treaty, the United States has a clear obligation to defend Japan, but Japan's reciprocal obligations under the treaty are technically limited to situations involving an armed attack on American forces in Japanese territory and nowhere else. In fact, however, the Sato government in 1969 assured the United States that the security of South Korea was essential to the security of Japan and that the maintenance of peace and security in the Taiwan area was also important for the security of Japan. Prime Minister Sato went on to assure the American government that, in the case of South Korea at least, American bases in Japan would be available for use should there be an armed attack against South Korea. Despite such formal assurances, however, there remains some doubt as to whether or not it would again be possible for the United States' forces to wage a Korean-type war from air and other bases in Japan. Subject to prior consultation with Japan, however, American forces and facilities in Japan can technically be used to support American commitments elsewhere in the Far East, a very vaguely defined and extensive area.

Despite their controversial nature in domestic Japanese politics, both the self-defense forces and the security arrangements with the United States have recently gained a larger measure of popular acceptance and support. A recent poll indicated that 79 percent of the respondents upheld the existence of Japan's self-defense forces, while only 8 percent were opposed (13 percent were uncertain). In the same poll, a narrower majority, 54 percent, felt that "Japan's security should be protected by the Japan–United States Security Treaty and the Japan self-defense forces as at present," 9 percent wanted the Security Treaty abrogated and the defense forces expanded, and another 9 percent wanted the treaty canceled and the defense forces abolished (27 percent were uncertain). This was the first occasion in recent years when the Security Treaty received majority approval.

Current Issues and Prospects

Of Japan's major current and prospective diplomatic and strategic problems, the most important in terms of sheer time, concern, and energy are the country's manifold economic problems. Basically these may be formulated in terms of a single vastly oversimplified question, What combination of foreign and domestic policies will best assure the maximal degree and duration of prosperity and security for Japan?

A general problem for Japan is how to diversify the overseas sources from which it obtains its critical imports so as best to insure a continuous, reliable, and reasonably priced flow of essential resources. This problem has many aspects. For example, it is a source of very great concern to Japan that it depends for 80 percent of its oil imports upon a group of Near Eastern suppliers that has already demonstrated its willingness and ability to curtail drastically this supply for purely political reasons. Japan can take several precautions against the reoccurrence of such a crisis, but all are only ameliorative—in the short-term sense at least—and all involve complex diplomatic arrangements. These precautions include increases in the stockpiling of oil at home; efforts to discover and develop new sources of oil, for example, in Japanese, Korean, Chinese, and Southeast Asian coastal waters; efforts to substitute Japanese-owned and controlled suppliers for the major international companies, largely American, that now control most of Japan's oil imports; exploration of the politically risky matter of obtaining sizable oil supplies from the Soviet Union or the People's Republic of China through joint development schemes; and the systematic development of energy substitutes on a large scale, such as nuclear power (Japan has a major program planned but serious problems of uranium supply and enrichment) and solar or geothermal energy.

It also worries the Japanese that 20 percent of their imports are routinely supplied by the United States. This represents a very substantial degree of dependence upon the reliability, economic capacity, pricing policies, and ultimately, the political goodwill of a single supplier. If it can be avoided, no country likes to be this dependent upon—and vulnerable to pressures from—a single supplier, no matter how friendly the present relationship. The Japanese government is not apt to forget soon the Nixon administration's arbitrary and abrupt halting of the export of American soybeans or the sudden imposition in 1971 of a 10 percent surcharge on all Japanese exports to the United States. Consequently, Japan has been striving to reduce its degree of dependency on the American market through a deliberate policy of diversification of import sources. Over the years it has been quite successful. The American share of Japan's imports has fallen from about a third in the late 1950s to a fifth today. The Japanese government would probably feel safer if this could be reduced still further.

Other economic problems of major diplomatic significance relate to Japan's relations with the European Economic Community, with the Soviet Union and the People's Republic of China, and with the developing countries of the Third and Fourth worlds. About 14 percent of Japan's overall trade (9 percent of exports, 5 percent of imports) is with nations in the European Economic Community. The Japanese feel, with some justification, that some of the nations involved have unfairly discriminated against Japanese products; the Europeans in turn fear Japanese competition and charge counterdiscrimination by Japan against their exports. Negotiations among Japan, the United States, and the European Economic Community in recent years have improved these circumstances, but much remains to be done. Also involved is the extraordinarily complex and difficult problem of devising, essentially among this same group, a new international monetary and exchange system to replace the outmoded Bretton Woods agreements.

Similarly, Japan is seriously interested in expanding and improving its economic relations with the Soviet Union and the People's Republic of China. However, the current degree of hostility between these two great communist powers enjoins great caution upon any third party that must of necessity maintain good relations with both. For example, the People's Republic of China not long ago made it completely clear to Tokyo that it would look with the greatest displeasure on Japan's participation in the Tyumen Oil Project with the Soviet Union, which would have incidentally increased very substantially the oil supplies available to Soviet armed forces stationed along the Chinese border and, thus, greatly enhanced their military capabilities. Political sensitivities of this sort must be kept constantly in mind whenever the Japanese government or private industry considers participating in schemes for the development of either Siberian or Chinese natural resources.

The political aspects of dealing with the states of the Third and Fourth worlds are equally complex. Ours is apparently fated to be a time of multiple crises involving both the developed and the developing societies. Because of its highly developed status and capacities, its resource poverty, and the importance and distribution of its trade, Japan is deeply involved in what has come to be known as the North-South Problem, that is, the relationships that should prevail in a variety of areas between the developed nations (the North) and the developing nations (the South). This problem usually takes the form of negotiations over the extent and nature of the aid or other concessions that the North should extend to the South and of what, if any, obligations should be entailed for the recipients of such aid.

The Japanese record of foreign aid to developing states has been spotty. It began late—in the mid-1960s on any appreciable scale—but developed rapidly. In fiscal year 1973 it exceeded for the first time 1 percent of Japan's gross national product, totaling $5.8 billion. This was second in size to the United States' contribution. However, only about $1 billion of this was in the form of official governmental aid for development purposes granted on "soft" or noncommercial terms. The balance was largely direct private investment abroad or loans or credits extended by the Japanese private sector for essentially commercial purposes. The "aid" portion proper of these grants or loans, the $1 billion of governmental funds, went mostly to Asian countries, including the Middle Eastern oil states in Asia. Excluding those states, about 88 percent still went to developing Asian countries. Central and South America were the largest recipients of private investments, a somewhat different form of "aid." Since 1973, however, the recession in Japan has led to a drastic fall in the level of overseas aid. In 1975, for example, it totaled only $2.8 billion, of which slightly over $1 billion was given on "soft" terms.

One further aspect of Japan's economic problems that is of diplomatic significance is the long-continuing Japanese effort to negotiate international economic settlements that cause as little domestic concern and protest as possible. Ideally, the settlement would manifestly benefit the domestic prosperity or security of Japan and at the same time not damage significantly the interests of any domestic producer or other relevant interest group. In practice this is almost impossible to achieve. For years, however, the Japanese did remarkably well in obtaining international economic concessions without reciprocal and equal concessions at the expense of the domestic Japanese market, especially in terms of lower tariff barriers, adjustments in the exchange value of the yen, and nontariff means of protecting the Japanese market. Beginning in the late 1960s, Japan was gradually induced to change these policies. Thus, the yen exchanges today on much more equable, though perhaps not yet ideal, terms, and the Japanese tariffs compare very favorably with those of practically any other major trading state. Complaints about nontariff devices for the protection of the domestic Japanese market, for example, tax benefits, concealed subsidies, and licensing and regulatory discrimination, are still common. However, these are charges encountered generally against practically all major governments.

The political and strategic elements on Japan's agenda of current diplomatic problems do not figure as prominently or incessantly among day-to-day activities and concerns, but they are always present in substantial degree and in a variety of forms. The security issue is, of course, fundamental and omnipresent in all of Japan's diplomacy, as it is for any sovereign and responsible state. One important aspect of Japan's diplomatic agenda is a quest for equality and status. This is a systematic attempt by Japan to gain a status and a degree of recognition and prestige in international political and diplomatic circles that is more commensurate with the economic status that it already has. The goals involved are numerous though, in some cases, vague. Some of the more obvious would be a permanent seat on the Security Council of the United Nations; something approximating the status, perquisites, and influence of a true superpower in all nonmilitary contexts in the eyes of other governments; and regional recognition and influence in Asia as the most developed and advanced of local states and as a leading, if not the leading, force in the area. One must not forget in this context either the uniqueness of Japan's Asian antecedents or the unparalleled rapidity of Japan's rise to its present circumstances. In one sense it began in conspicuous fashion with the Meiji Restoration just over one hundred years ago, in another with the postwar takeoff or resurrection of the 1950s and 1960s. Japan's status as an advanced world power is by either criterion unique and recent. It is still not well established among other countries, and it gives rise to certain anxieties in Japan and to a search for fresh, and presumably more objective, appreciations by others of the nation's undoubted accomplishments.

Other diplomatic problems are more specialized. Although close and generally cordial, the relationship with the United States is a matter of constant concern and anxiety. Foreign nations invariably find the United States hard to understand, predict, and deal with because of the changes of administration and policies and the complexities of its domestic and foreign politics. Japan is no exception, except in the sense that its national security depends totally upon an American guarantee, and its national prosperity depends substantially on two-way trade with the United States. These are circumstances guaranteed to produce close attention and sometimes excessive worry in Tokyo over American actions or nonactions.

Japan's two great and even more unpredictable communist neighbors, the People's Republic of China and the Soviet Union, occasion lesser but essentially similar sorts of concern in Tokyo. According to an old saying, "bedding down with giants is not apt to provide either a safe or a restful night's sleep." Geography has provided Japan with just such bedfellows. Historically, Japan's recent relations with either the People's Republic of China or the Soviet Union have not been friendly. Today both are ruled by governments that are ideologically opposed to Japan's government and disposed to regard their own political systems and views as superior and as fated in time to prevail elsewhere by means that are not really clear. Adding to this the facts that both possess the military capacity to destroy Japan and that Japan conspicuously lacks any independent capacity to defend itself against serious attack by either, it is obvious that Tokyo has impressive, if presumptive, grounds for concern over Sino-Japanese and Russo-Japanese relations.

Because of their proximity, both Koreas are also a constant worry to Japanese statesmen—"Korea is a dagger pointing at the heart of Japan." Although there have been overtures, there are as yet no regular diplomatic relations between North Korea and Japan. Thus, the normal local focus of Japanese diplomatic activity and concern is South Korea. This has been a difficult problem for a variety of reasons: the Koreans resent and dislike Japan as their former imperial master, and reciprocally, the Japanese are generally not at all fond of the Koreans; the Korean minority in Japan is difficult in a variety of ways; and Japan has heavy investments and interests in the South Korean economy. These are circumstances that insure a certain amount of friction and discord between the two countries and that, consequently, give rise to a lively and contentious agenda of diplomatic issues.

Taiwan is also a problem. After "normalizing" its relations with Peking in 1972, the Japanese government "derecognized" the government of the Republic of China based in Taiwan. Following a period of estrangement, economic relations between Taiwan and Japan were reestablished. Monetarily the Taiwan trade has for some years been practically as valuable as—and more reliable than—the trade with the People's Republic of China, and Japan does not want to lose this trade. Also, it would not like to see Peking take over physical control of Taiwan and, thus, enhance its capacities to interdict that major lifeline of Japanese trade that leads southward to the states of Southeast Asia, the Indian Ocean, Indonesian and Near Eastern oil, and Europe. Thus, even though there are no longer any formal diplomatic relations between Japan and Taiwan, the situation is one that continuously engages much interest in Japan.

There are, of course, many other bilateral or regional issues of serious concern to Japanese diplomacy. Underlying all of these is the basic problem of what policies and relationships are most likely to insure durably the security and the prosperity of Japan. The problem is an excruciating one, and there are no specific answers or assured solutions. International conditions are not stable enough for that. Furthermore, the policies that promise most in terms of prosperity are not necessarily the same as, or even always compatible with, those that promise most in terms of security. For example, the communist states are, by current conviction and practice at least, as autarchic in their economic policies as circumstances will permit, that is, they seek systematically to maximize their self-sufficiency in critical respects and thus to minimize their foreign trade. Only about 7 percent of Japan's exports go to communist countries, and 5 percent of its imports derive from such states; whereas 48 percent of exports and 42 percent of imports are with the developed noncommunist countries, and 45 percent of exports and 53 percent of imports are with noncommunist developing states. This is a pattern of distribution of economic interests that has very little in common with the distribution of potential threats to Japan's national security that presently seems most likely to emanate from communist sources. This makes it difficult to reinforce political arrangements between Japan and the communist states by strong and mutually advantageous economic ties.

The terms of the strategic equation confronting Japan today are particularly difficult. Very crudely put, there are the two real superpowers, the United States and the Soviet Union. The three other components of a dubious construct that has sometimes been called the "pentagon of world power" are the People's Republic of China, the states of the European

Community, and Japan. In theory, detente regulates relations between the two superpowers in such a way as to diminish tensions and preclude hostilities. In practice, the actual relations between the United States and the Soviet Union are often still antagonistic, competitive, and delicately balanced. The same is true to an even more pronounced extent of Sino-Russian relationships. The NATO states of Western Europe normally play a more passive though important role as a factor in maintaining the military balance on the western frontiers of the Warsaw Pact powers. Actual and potential causes of friction abound among this constellation of great powers. Some of the more ominous of these are to be found in Japan's immediate neighborhood, including the unresolved problems of the two Koreas, the two Chinas, and Sino-Russian relations. Other more distant conflicts, such as the Israeli-Arab confrontation with its potentiality for a further oil embargo, are capable of critically affecting the vital interests of Japan. Although unpredictable, the potentialities for serious trouble under these circumstances are so numerous and so plausible historically that no responsible government can afford to ignore them.

The Japanese government looks on such a world with mixed emotions. The country is located in the very midst of what has been called "the cockpit of Asia." It is literally surrounded by the tensions engendered by the two Koreas, the two Chinas, and the Sino-Russian rivalries. Should any of these erupt into action, the Japanese could not help but be deeply concerned and might well consider their own interests to be seriously endangered. At the same time, their own capacity for asserting or defending their national interests is negligible. Except for domestic subversion, they have deliberately chosen to entrust their defense against external threats almost entirely to the United States. While this has so far proven to be both effective and economical, it has also given rise to frustrations, doubts, and anxieties over whether the United States could be relied upon to act firmly, rapidly, and effectively in defense of Japan in a real international crisis involving the threat of war with the Soviet Union or the People's Republic of China over an issue relating to the security of Japan.

The prospect of local wars in, for example, Southeast Asia, although distasteful, is not a matter of vital concern for Japan unless they should also involve serious interference with its lines of communication. Although the war in Vietnam was repugnant to most Japanese, the government found it possible to live with it, to discharge Japan's logistical obligations under the Security Treaty, and even to profit handsomely from the hostilities. It is closer military operations involving Korea or Taiwan—and, in particular, the prospect that these might ramify to include the People's Republic of China, the Soviet Union, or the United States—that really worry the Japanese. The worst nightmare is, of course, nuclear threat or nuclear blackmail directed against Japan by a power such as the Soviet Union or the People's Republic of China that possesses intercontinental ballistic missiles in numbers sufficient to threaten effective retaliation against an American intercession on Japan's behalf. Under these circumstances, if the security of its own cities and populace was directly at stake, would the United States actually come to Japan's rescue? No one can reliably answer a hypothetical question of this sort, but this very fact is bound to cause serious concern to the Japanese government whose most important responsibility is the assurance of the nation's security.

Japan's answer to this strategic dilemma has been to choose the optimistic hypothesis, to run the risks entailed, and to base its national security on the premises that the Security Treaty is reliable, that an armed confrontation involving either the Soviet Union or the People's Republic of China with the United States will not take place, that civil war in Korea will probably be avoided, that the Soviet Union and the People's Republic of China will be able to settle their differences peaceably, and that Japan will be able to conduct its diplomacy in such a way as to avoid exacerbated relations with any of its more dangerous neighbors or its allies. So far this gamble has paid off handsomely. Japan has set for its diplomacy quite modest and predominantly economic goals: a revival of flourishing trading relations, reacceptance by the international community, the building of an image as a responsible and peaceful state, and the achievement of national prosperity. No other major state can even begin to claim for its postwar diplomacy the degree of success achieved by Japan in accomplishing this limited set of objectives. Only in its endeavor to reclaim the southern Kurile Islands from Russia has it failed. Despite this impressive degree of success, it would be a mistake to regard Japan as satisfied with its international circumstances.

The grounds for dissatisfaction and unrest are many and potent, although they may or may not be valid. There is, first, the doubts entertained by many about the continued credibility and effectiveness of the American security guarantee. The arguments vary and overlap. Some conclude simply that in a nuclear showdown the United States' government would never really endanger San Francisco or New York for Tokyo. Others claim that the United States is in the process of withdrawing its military presence from Eastern Asia and that it has publicly proclaimed this intention through the Nixon Doctrine. It would, therefore, be foolish of Japan to rest its security on an American policy that has now undergone fundamental change. Still others argue that the entire American alliance is mistaken, that the United States by design or blunder is apt to become involved in further hostilities in Asia, and that the Security Treaty will then automatically involve Japan in these. Thus, the treaty involves more risks for Japan than it provides security. Practically all of the opposition parties share this view in some measure.

Beyond such military and strategic dissatisfactions, many Japanese are restless on grounds of national status and prestige. They are troubled by the enormity of the gap that separates Japan's status as an economic power from its status as a "world power" in the broadest sense of that term. The Japanese are a very status-minded people. They are rightly proud of their postwar accomplishments and desire recognition abroad as a truly great power. Yet in the councils of the nations, Japan's lack of military power and concomitant "low posture" on practically all of the more controversial and sensitive international political issues combine to deny such status. While few Japanese are prepared to pay the price of a status based on military or political tests, they continue to desire and to seek recognition. It is perhaps sadly typical of our times that it should be denied to them. Distressingly little attention has been paid the fact that Japan, with whatever mixture of motives, has embarked upon an experiment in the conduct of its foreign relations that is utterly unprecedented in the history of great states. It has deliberately denied itself the normal military means of impressing and enforcing its will or policies upon other states and has done this under circumstances in which its tradition, its wealth, and its technological skills would apparently combine to insure both its inclination and its capacity to decide otherwise. Japan is in effect seeking to demonstrate the feasibility of a great state conducting its foreign relations without recourse to either force or the threat of force—a phenomenon so bizarre in the twentieth century as apparently to exceed the comprehension of most observers. Adding to this the fact that the policy has so far paid very handsome domestic dividends— although frequently leaving Japan's allies both puzzled and frustrated—it would seem at least to merit a far greater degree of interest and understanding than it has to date received.

The other ground for Japanese dissatisfaction with their international circumstances is expressed in more positive terms. This is advocacy of alternative diplomatic and strategic arrangements. In some cases the grounds are primarily ideological; Japan simply chose the wrong side after the war, and it should have linked its fortunes with those of the Soviet Union or the People's Republic of China. Only a small minority subscribe to such views, however. More widespread are sentiments that seek some form of neutralist stance for Japan, a posture that would be equidistant from allegiance to the United States, the Soviet Union, and the People's Republic of China. The disruption of Japan's trading lifelines aside, such persons see the only serious hypothetical threats to Japan's security as stemming from the Soviet Union, the People's Republic of China, the United States, or some combination of these powers. They also feel that Japan has no basic differences with any of these states that are not amenable to peaceful settlement. They would argue, therefore, that Japan's ideal security arrangement would be one in which all three of these great powers joined in guaranteeing the neutrality of Japan.

The current and prospective state of the relationships among the United States, the Soviet Union, and the People's Republic of China and Japan's potential importance to all of these states would seem to negate the possibility of any formal agreement in the near future. Despite this, however, there is reason to believe that Japan will gradually strive to improve and expand its relations with the People's Republic of China and the Soviet Union and that this may well involve some reciprocal attenuation of the closeness of its relations with the United States. This would probably not result in the near future either in the abrogation of the Security Treaty at Japan's initiative or in other than friendly and cooperative relations between Japan and the United States—the inevitable short-term disagreements on trade and financial issues aside.

BIBLIOGRAPHY

ALLISON, JOHN M., *Ambassador from the Prairie, or Allison Wonderland.* Tokyo: Tuttle, 1975, 400 pp.

ASAHI NEWSPAPERS, *The Pacific Rivals: A Japanese View of Japanese-American Relations.* Tokyo: Weatherhill, 1972, 431 pp.

BUCK, JAMES H., ed., *The Modern Japanese Military System.* Beverly Hills, Calif.: Sage Publications, 1975, 253 pp.

CLAPP, PRISCILLA, AND MORTON H. HALPERIN, eds., *United States–Japanese Relations in the 1970's.* Cambridge, Mass.: Harvard University Press, 1974, 234 pp.

CLOUGH, RALPH N., *East Asia and U.S. Security.* Washington, D.C.: Brookings, 1975, 248 pp.

CURTIS, GERALD L., ed., *Japanese-American Relations in the 1970's.* Washington, D.C.: Columbia Books, 1970, 203 pp.

DESTLER, I. M., ET AL., *Managing an Alliance: The Politics of U.S.–Japanese Relations.* Washington, D.C.: The Brookings Institution, 1976, 209 pp.

EMMERSON, JOHN K., *Arms, Yen and Power: The Japanese Dilemma.* Tokyo: Tuttle, 1973, 420 pp.

EMMERSON, JOHN K., AND LEONARD A. HUMPHREYS, *Will Japan Rearm? A Study in Attitudes.* Washington, D.C.: American Enterprise Institute, 1973, 165 pp.

GORDON, BERNARD K., AND KENNETH J. ROTHWELL, *The New Political Economy of the Pacific.* Cambridge, Mass.: Ballinger, 1975, 177 pp.

GREENE, FRED, *U.S. Policy and the Security of Asia.* New York: McGraw-Hill, 1968, 429 pp.

HELLMANN, DONALD C., *Japan and East Asia: The New International Order.* New York: Praeger, 1972, 243 pp.

HELLMANN, DONALD C., *Japanese Foreign Policy and Domestic Politics: The Peace Agreement with the Soviet Union.* Berkeley, Calif.: University of California Press, 1969, 202 pp.

IRIYE, AKIRA, ed., *Mutual Images: Essays in American-Japanese Relations.* Cambridge, Mass.: Harvard University Press, 1975, 304 pp.

LANGDON, FRANK C., *Japan's Foreign Policy.* Berkeley, Calif.: University of California Press, 1973, 231 pp.

LEE, CHAE-JIN, *Japan Faces China: Political and Economic Relations in Postwar Japan.* Baltimore, Md.: Johns Hopkins University Press, 1976.

MENDEL, DOUGLAS H., JR., *The Japanese People and Foreign Policy: A Study of Public Opinion in Post-Treaty Japan.* Berkeley, Calif.: University of California Press, 1961, 269 pp.

MORLEY, JAMES W., *Forecast for Japan: Security in the 1970's.* Princeton, N.J.: Princeton University Press, 1972, 249 pp.

MORLEY, JAMES W., ed., *Prologue to the Future.* New York: Lexington Books, 1974, 232 pp.

NISHIHARA, MASASHI, *The Japanese and Sukarno's Indonesia: Tokyo-Jakarta Relations 1951–1966.* Honolulu: University Press of Hawaii, 1976, 244 pp.

OLSON, LAWRENCE, *Japan in Postwar Asia.* New York: Praeger, 1970, 292 pp.

PASSIN, HERBERT, ed., *The United States and Japan.* Englewood Cliffs, N.J.: Prentice-Hall, 1966, 174 pp.

ROSOVSKY, HENRY, ed., *Discord in the Pacific: Challenges to the Japanese-American Alliance.* Washington, D.C.: Columbia Books, 1972, 251 pp.

SCALAPINO, ROBERT A., *Asia and the Road Ahead.* Berkeley, Calif.: University of California Press, 1975, 337 pp.

STEPHAN, JOHN P., *The Kuril Islands: Russo-Japanese Frontiers in the Pacific.* London: Oxford University Press, 1975, 279 pp.

WEINSTEIN, MARTIN E., *Japan's Postwar Defense Policy, 1947–1968.* New York: Columbia University Press, 1971, 160 pp.

WILCOX, WAYNE, ET AL., *Asia and the Inter-national System.* Cambridge, Mass.: Winthrop, 1972, 383 pp.

WU, YUAN-LI, *U.S. Policy and Strategic Interests in the Western Pacific.* New York: Crane, Russak, 1975, 214 pp.

Chapter *13*

THE PROSPECTS FOR
LIBERAL DEMOCRACY
IN JAPAN

As one looks about the world today, it is all too clear that liberal democracy as a form and philosophy of government has become an "endangered species." Of the one hundred fifty or so existing states, it is doubtful that more than about one-seventh of these have meaningful democratic systems of government. Japan is, on historical grounds, probably the most unexpected of these. It alone stands clearly outside of the Western world, and it has yet to be persuasively demonstrated that the democratic tradition—even in imperfect form—is viable in non-Western states. This adds even greater significance and a high degree of theoretical importance to the Japanese experience, already of absorbing interest on purely intrinsic grounds.

The immediate roots of modern Japan are to be found in the Tokugawa Period (1603–1868). Whatever the most accurate description may be, its principal political or social attributes were neither liberal nor democratic. The period was characterized by a rigorously enforced four-class system that segregated the population into samurai, farmers, artisan, and merchant sectors capped by a hereditary emperor, shogun, and nobility; imperial rule in fiction and oligarchical rule in fact; class-based standards of access to public office and power; and a total lack of institutionalized provision for popular participation in government at any level higher than the village. It

In this chapter I have drawn freely upon my lecture entitled "The Prospects for Liberal Democracy in Japan" delivered at the University of Texas on 25 February 1976, to be published in *The Prospects for Liberal Democracy*, William S. Livingston, editor.

was not until the adoption and enforcement of the Meiji Constitution in 1889–90 that the structure and practice of governance in Japan were substantially altered. This was only about ninety years ago. However, the advent in Japan of political institutions and behavior that are both "liberal" and "democratic" falls in the period since 1946–47 when the present Constitution was adopted. Thus, "liberal democracy" in Japan is only about thirty years old.

Japan's "feudal" past is remarkably close in time to Japan's "democratic" present. In less than a century, Japan has undergone a process of political change that elsewhere—to reach a comparable stage of institutional and behavioral development—has normally entailed several centuries of more gradual evolution. In addition, when Japan adopted the formal and behavioral trappings of a democratic polity in 1946–47, it did not do so of its own free choice. American occupation agents literally wrote the present constitution, translated it into rather awkward Japanese, and by a variety of none-too-subtle pressures, enforced its adoption on a distinctly reluctant Japanese government.

Liberal democracy in Japan seems, on the surface at least, to lack native roots; its basic institutions and values have been borrowed importations from culturally and experientially alien sources; its development in Japan has been singularly brief; and its origins were both involuntary and imposed. However, this unqualified characterization of the antecedents of liberal democracy in Japan is incomplete and seriously inadequate for assessing the phenomenon. More than constitutions and formal political institutions must be taken into account. The following considerations are also relevant and important.

There is considerable agreement among students of political development that durably democratic societies have certain functional prerequisites. Fairly widespread literacy is one such quality. By the time of the Restoration of 1868, it is estimated that somewhat more than 40 percent of Japanese boys and about 10 percent of Japanese girls were getting some kind of formal education outside of their homes. These statistics are impressive, even by English and French standards at the time.

A second functional prerequisite is the existence of a professionally trained, rationally structured, and achievement-oriented bureaucracy. This was largely realized in Japan by the beginning of the eighteenth century. However, political institutions that provided a means of popular participation in the national political process through regular elections, that gave to elected representatives some voice in the decision-making process, and that recognized and protected popular civil and political rights did not come into existence until the effectuation of the Meiji Constitution in 1890, and then only on carefully restricted terms. Nevertheless, from these scant and unpromising beginnings important developments sprang. Political parties were organized and gradually succeeded in expanding their role and influence. In the 1920s party cabinets became a normal aspect of what was then called parliamentary government in Japan. In fact, of course, parties never ruled prewar Japan, but they had a secondary role in a complex system of oligarchical rule. Since the 1870s, these relatively populist and liberal elements in the Japanese policy have existed continuously and played a role of appreciable, if not critical, importance. Also, suffrage expanded continuously and rapidly; from an electorate of only four hundred fifty-one thousand in 1890, universal manhood suffrage had been realized by 1925. Thus, the populace gradually became habituated to the apparatus and mechanics, if not the true substance, of a parliamentary political system. The press was also in many respects a politically active and democratic force in prewar Japan. The courts also showed a surprising degree of independence and impartiality considering the overall political context within which they operated.

The prewar historical record of liberal democracy in Japan is, therefore, mixed and indeterminate. The trend until 1932 was definitely democratic, but these elements never gained the ascendancy. In 1932, however, this trend was temporarily reversed for a period of thirteen years. The seven years of the American occupation of Japan (1945–52) deliberately built upon the pre–1932 foundations in an attempt to refashion the Japanese political system along liberal democratic lines. The tempo of occupation-stimulated change was explosive; its scope was so sweeping that it left untouched no significant Japanese political, economic, or social institution. Its models and goals were largely American with some British influence. More than an evangelistic fervor for democracy lay behind this massive American effort. American officials felt that democratization and demilitarization were the most durable and reliable means of assuring that postwar Japan would remain peaceful and friendly toward the interests and policies of the United States.

The combined results of these American efforts are often referred to as "New Japan." This is appropriate since, with the exception of the early years of Meiji, there has been no period in Japanese history that has given rise to more numerous, more basic, or potentially more seminal changes. It is far too easy, however, to overestimate the American role in effecting these changes, especially those in the political sphere. Americans planned them in almost all instances, cajoled or pressured a reluctant Japanese government into adopting them, and supervised and frequently intervened in their implementation. However, these facts must be seen in a larger context. The antecedents of liberal democracy in Japan were in its prewar history. In postwar Japan there were significant elements of an experienced political leadership that had long been relatively democratic in tendency; political parties had only to be reinstituted, not created; and professional politicians, the bureaucracy, and the citizenry were long familiar with the procedures of a parliamentary system of government.

Also the Japanese people, although for the most part not active agents or instigators of the process of democratization, were at this particular point in their history predisposed to favor some form of political change. The country was faced with a completely unprecedented disaster, crushing defeat, unconditional surrender, and a foreign military occupation. Never before had Japan suffered defeat, let alone occupation. No people, except perhaps Americans, were less prepared psychologically or by prior experience to cope with such an ordeal. Circumstances that produce widespread suffering, physical deprivation, and psychic distress naturally lead to questions about why the disaster occurred, who is responsible, and how to get out of the mess and prevent its recurrence. The assignment of blame or, more accurately, of guilt is an important and probably an inescapable part of the process of mass psychic catharsis that is involved, and the all-too-obvious and probable target for blame is the government and, if the circumstances are sufficiently bad, the entire political system. Thus, a desire to change the old institutions emerges in many quarters that normally would be characterized by ignorance and apathy with respect to such issues.

In the early years of postwar Japan, widespread physical and psychic distress produced attitudes favorable to change on a scale sufficient to legitimize the types of innovations that the occupation authorities, with the support and assistance of some Japanese, were pressing upon the Japanese government. Thus, the people, or at least a critical mass of people, in the early years of postwar Japan were amenable to changes in the old institutions and not averse to the refurbishing and reinvigorating of institutions of party governance with which they were already partially familiar. Actually this negative formulation undoubtedly understates the real degree of popular support and positive approval for the democratic innovations that existed in postwar Japan.

Moving beyond the occupation, several more recent developments are also important. People tend to evaluate both particular governments and entire political systems by their fruits, especially those that relate to such basic matters as standards of living, physical well-being, and the provision of national security. It is not irrelevant, therefore, that postwar Japanese governments have for the most part presided over a record of explosive economic growth and mounting general prosperity unprecedented in Japanese experience, and probably in world history as well. At the same time, and however fortuitous the consequences, they have also held office during a period characterized by unbroken peace in Japan's foreign relations during a period when the world in general has been continuously beset by stress and strife. Naturally, both the governments in power and the liberal democratic political system on which these governments are based gain considerable, if less than total, credit and acceptability from this record.

This retrospective assessment of the origins and development of liberal democracy in Japan suggests several conclusions that are relevant to the present and future of liberal democracy in Japan. First, liberal democratic institutions and beliefs are not new in Japan. They have foundations that extend back to at least the late seventeenth and early eighteenth centuries and institutionalized forms that date back to 1890. They have existed continuously since that date and have developed progressively with only occasional setbacks. Second, the fact that the present institutional forms of liberal democracy in Japan are of American, not indigenous, authorship may not be of critical importance. There was a substantial and favorable disposition toward political change in postwar Japan, and many felt that this should be along liberal democratic lines. When after 1952 Japan regained a truly independent and sovereign status, the Japanese government altered materially a number of the occupation's reform programs but has shown no serious disposition to abandon any of the essential institutions or practices of a democratic society. Third, Japan's national experience since the end of the occupation in 1952 has been such as to confirm in the popular mind the impression that this new system of government is on balance effective and productive of important values to an extent that argues for its acceptance, if not for its enthusiastic support.

These findings lead to the further conclusion that the unique cultural and historical circumstances that have attended the advent of liberal democracy in Japan may not prove critical in determining its future. The facts that it is now established, that it has gained general acceptance, that it is producing goods that its citizenry values, and that it benefits from the inertia and the accumulation of supportive interests that accompany any established and functioning system are probably considerations of greater importance for the present and the future than are the adverse cultural and political circumstances of the past. These conclusions, although relevant and important, assert a negative rather than a positive hypothesis about the future of liberal democracy in Japan. They simply argue that, in the light of offsetting factors, peculiarities of past experience will not necessarily have a determining effect on the survival of liberal democracy in Japan. This is not to say that its future is either assured or free from other serious perils. In *The Crisis of Democracy,* Professor Joji Watanuki concludes that "Japanese democracy is not in a serious crisis at the present moment."[1] This is probably true, but there are some grounds for concern.

A most significant factor in facilitating the popular acceptance of a liberal democratic form of government in postwar Japan has been the dramatic expansion of the economy and its products. The story is well known. Beginning in 1952 and accelerating with amazing rapidity after 1960, domestic production, consumption, and prosperity have boomed on a scale unprecedented among major states in recent times. Annual and real increases of 10 percent or more in gross national product became the rule not the exception. Despite sectoral inequities and particular grievances, the populace on the whole benefited spectacularly; among other things, real wages nearly doubled between 1960 and 1972. Under these circumstances, politics was not for most people a subject of urgent concern, while a tendency to assign some measure of credit to the party in power and to the underlying political system was quite widespread. Prosperity bred political passivity, if not positive dedication to the system.

The oil crisis of October 1973 changed these happy economic circumstances at least temporarily. In Japan as elsewhere the ramifying effects of the energy crisis coincided with other factors to produce the worst recession in many years. The economic growth statistics went negative in 1974 by a factor of 1.8 percent. In 1975 the gross national product grew by only an estimated 2.2 percent, a far cry from the norm of 10 percent. Even the official statistics indicated more than a million unemployed—a startling figure for a society long habituated to a job surplus. Many companies strug-

[1]Michel J. Crozier et al., *The Crisis of Democracy* (New York: New York University Press, 1975), p. 152.

gled to retain on their payrolls another three million laborers who were surplus to their needs but whom the practice of lifelong employment obligated them to retain. By 1977 the Japanese economy had not yet overcome all of these difficulties. Predictions were mixed, and even the optimistic were concluding that full recovery implied a 5 or 6 percent annual growth rate rather than the former 10 percent.

Even relative economic deprivation is bound to have political consequences. There is no doubt that popular impatience with what is seen as the government's failure to deal effectively with this prolonged economic crisis has steadily mounted. Some ascribe it to inefficiency, some to corruption, and some to the alleged iniquities and inherent weaknesses of a capitalist system. In any event, the circumstances are adverse to the reputation and the fortunes of the party in power and, by extension, to the political system with which that party is strongly identified. Viewed by themselves and solely as a product of three years of economic adversity, such developments might not be serious in the future. What three years of recession had wrought might be remedied by a few years of prosperity, but there are added factors that must be taken into account—some economic, some political, some psychological.

It seems probable that Japan had reached by 1973, somewhat later than all of its major rivals, the end of a truly remarkable spurt of postwar economic growth. In the most analogous case, that of West Germany, the period of dramatic increases in gross national product had tapered off before the end of the 1960s, and even so, West Germany by no means equalled the Japanese performance. Japan's gross national product increased at an average annual rate of 9.6 percent over the sixteen years from 1953 to 1968, whereas the comparable German rate was 5.8 percent (measured at market prices). For comparison, the other major rates for that period were 5 percent for France, 3.5 percent for the United States, and 3 percent for the United Kingdom. In Japan, however, the average annual increase remained very high, 9.6 percent, through 1972, and it only fell to 6.1 percent in 1973, the year of the oil crisis. For the other major states, comparable points of decline in their average growth rates had usually been reached by 1967.

There are a number of persuasive reasons for assuming that this decline is of more than passing significance for the Japanese economy. For example, ready and relatively cheap access to the fruits of foreign, largely American, research and development has become a thing of the past. In recent years potential foreign licensers, fearing Japanese competition, have become much more hesitant to sell technology to the Japanese. When they do, joint ventures are apt to be required; or the price is higher, and restrictions limiting use to Japanese domestic markets only or to Japan and Southeast Asian markets are apt to be attached. The Japanese are trying to compensate by increases in domestic research and development expenditures, which reached 1.6 percent of the gross national product in 1972. Nevertheless, it will not be easy for Japan to compensate for the disadvantages involved in these new circumstances.

The problem of access to raw materials is, of course, especially crucial for

Japan. Oil is the most acute and dramatic of a series of such problems. More than 99 percent of Japan's oil is imported, and this oil in turn accounts for more than 80 percent of Japan's energy needs. In 1972 Japan was already taking about 10 percent of the world's total available oil supply, and the prime minister was warning that this demand could be expected to triple in five or six years. However, no country in Japan's circumstances at a time of generally increased needs and competition for limited supplies of raw materials could realistically hope to purchase 20 to 30 percent of the world supply of a commodity as critical as oil. Japan is also experiencing less dramatic difficulties of access to adequate supplies of iron ore, copper, lumber, and various other natural resources and foodstuffs. The overall cost of the country's essential imports is escalating at a rate that is increasingly more difficult to compensate for by increasing the volume or prices of exports.

Adverse shifts have also been occurring in the relationship between productivity and wages. During the 1955–65 decade, productivity rose at a faster pace than wages. This facilitated the steady increase in real wage rates that has been so notable in Japan. During the second half of the 1960s, however, wage increases began routinely to surpass productivity increases, and this imbalance was exacerbated by the drastic inflation of 1973–75 that witnessed 20 and 30 percent raises for unionized labor. While Japan's performance is still notably superior to that of the United States, Great Britain, West Germany, France, or Italy, its margin of competitive advantage is steadily eroding. As the productivity of labor began on the average to decline vis-à-vis wage increases, the pressures for shorter working hours have been mounting since the mid-1960s. The six-day week is still normal in Japan, and the actual number of working hours per week in manufacturing industries is two to six hours longer than in the West (4 to 13 percent). The trend is definitely downward, however, and more and more of the larger enterprises are shifting to five- or five-and-a-half-day weeks. Thus, the relationship between productivity and wages, another of the factors in the sustained "economic miracle" of Japan's recent growth, is suffering attrition.

Noteworthy also are the rapidly mounting pressures in almost all quarters in Japan to catch up with the West in terms of social infrastructure. The extent to which Japan falls behind its peers in such items as housing, roads, sewage, and parks has been described. If relatively high rates of performance on indicators such as these are characteristic of modernized societies or partial measures of "the good life," Japan's performance is very poor. The Japanese people have become much more aware of this "lag" in their society, and increasing political pressures are being brought to bear on the government to do something about it.

These few samples of the current state, problems, and prospects of the Japanese economy are simply the other side of the "economic miracle." All major processes of social change have their costs, but sometimes it takes a while to appreciate the size and particulars of the bill. The Japanese people and government, long dazzled by the immediate benefits of growth and unprecedented affluence, are now, as the period of explosive development draws to a close, beginning to contemplate the consequences and costs of the entire process, to assess these in the light of new values and their now far higher levels of expectation, and to ask hard questions and make insistent demands for the future—demands that will be difficult for any government to cope with satisfactorily. It is not different elsewhere in the developed world. Japan has just reached this point at a slightly later date and from quite a different background than have its peers. Now Japan is beginning to share fully in the problems and frustrations as well as in the accomplishments of modern societies. Of particular concern, however, is how the economic developments and problems relate to the future of liberal democracy in Japan. The brief answer is that they constitute acute and serious challenges to the capacity of both the government and the underlying political system to cope with extraordinarily difficult problems under circumstances of growing adversity and complexity. The question is, of course, What are the prospects that government will be able to cope effectively? In answering this question, popular perceptions and attitudes are almost as important as actual governmental responses to the problems.

All of the polling data generally agree that there is strong popular support for the 1947 Constitution and the basic democratic concepts on which it rests. Such positive views are even more strongly held among the younger population—an encouraging sign for the future. Shifting attention from the system of government to the people who govern, a dramatic change of opinion is apparent. National political leaders from the prime minister to parliamentary and party leaders are generally held in low repute. The outcomes of the *Mainichi* newspaper's regular assessments of the degree of popular support for the five men who served as prime minister between 1950 and 1972 is representative. Their overall average was only 37 percent, with a range extending from a brief high of 54 percent to a low of 19 percent. During the same period, the American popular support for the president averaged 57 percent—20 points higher—with a range of 87 to 23 percent. Among the Western democracies, only the premiers of France seem to have enjoyed less popularity. It is also interesting that these views appear to be shared even by Japanese school children. The data show a steady decline in most indexes of school childrens' confidence in or approval of the personnel or performance of the Japanese national government, and this intensifies with advancing grade levels. This is unusual by international standards.

Linked with this predominantly negative assessment of the leading figures in Japanese government—a view based on suspicions of inefficiency, dishonesty, irresponsibility, and corruption in office—is another development that promises problems for the future. This is the increase of popular participation in Japanese politics. In the abstract this is seen in sources such as the National Character Studies of the Institute of Statistical Mathematics conducted regularly every five years since 1953. For example, on five separate occasions between 1953 and 1975, a random and stratified sample of the Japanese people was asked if they agreed or disagreed with the following statement: "Some people say that if we get good political leaders, the best way to improve the country is for the people to leave everything to them, rather than for the people to discuss things among themselves." The extent of disagreement with this antiparticipation question rose steadily from 38 percent in 1953 to 51 percent in 1973. Significantly, among twenty- to twenty-four-year olds it rose from 54 percent to 67 percent. In political action, this trend toward a greater degree of popular participation is evident in the proliferation of "residents' movements" that has been so salient an aspect of the recent Japanese political scene, especially at the level of local and, in particular, municipal politics. This is partly a manifestation of the growing disrepute in which most of the formally organized political parties are held. Residents' movements established on an ad hoc basis for the accomplishment of specific goals represent a way of bypassing the parties. They are a means of representing, aggregating, and pressing for popular interests and causes by a more direct, focused, and participatory way of accomplishing particular ends. Such movements, however—unless they end up by becoming political parties themselves—pose serious problems for government that, in a democratic system at least, requires some means of organizing popular support and consent and of representing public views and interests that is possessed of more than a temporary and highly specific mandate from its constituents.

In the light of these contextual factors, several intermediate conclusions suggest themselves. First, the Japanese government is faced with a series of interrelated economic and social problems that are sufficiently difficult and complex to test severely the utmost capacities of any modern democratic political system. Second, it must act under economic circumstances that are increasingly unfavorable and constraining to the effective functioning of government. Third, the government's hold on popular affection and support is already tenuous and attributable more to inertia and a lack of persuasive alternatives than to positive loyalty. At the same time, however, there seems to be general support for the basic institutions and values of the present democratic political system. The performance of the Japanese government itself must be considered against this rather ominous background. In one sense the task is simplified by the fact that the present Liberal Democratic Party or its immediate progenitors have constantly been in power since 1949. In another sense the task of political prognosis is rendered far more uncertain and difficult by the complete lack of data about the competency or probable performance of any alternative form of party government in Japan. There is nothing to go on but the records established by opposition parties, and these are inadequate.

The most obvious fact about the record of Liberal Democratic Party governance is that it has presided successfully over the reemergence of Japan from an unprecedented and disastrous defeat followed by almost seven years of foreign military occupation. Unless one considers the American occupation a sort of deus ex machina gifted with superhuman vision and skills, the Liberal Democrats, their predecessors, and the governmental apparatus that they directed ultimately had more to do—albeit reluctantly and under duress in some instances—with fashioning the current forms, practices, and performance levels of liberal democracy in Japan than did any other foreign or domestic agency. Beyond this, they have presided over the period of the greatest and most rewarding economic growth in the history of Japan. While not distributed with absolute equity among all sectors of the population, the benefits of this new affluence have been generally and massively felt and have resulted in real and large improvements in the national standards of health and physical well-being, of life expectancy, of diet, of access to education, of remunerative employment, of the physical amenities of life, of justice and personal security, and on the whole, of effective and responsive government. These are most impressive accomplishments by any criterion. While the credit does not belong entirely to the party in power, it is certainly more than a coincidence that these changes occurred and were sustained and expanded solely under its regime.

Nevertheless, the Liberal Democrats have not solved all of Japan's problems and have, in solving some, created others; this seems to be ever more important in the public consciousness. A cruel inflation has beset Japan as well as so many other societies. Although diminishing, its effects are still widely felt and earn the government criticism for not dealing with it sooner and more effectively. The hectic pace of urbanization in Japan has brought with it the full array of urban problems, including overcrowding, poor and expensive housing, traffic congestion, long and exhausting travel to work, increasing prices and costs, pollution, a spreading sense of social malaise, a decay of traditional morality, and widespread psychological stress or unease. The countryside has been stripped of population, and the farms and villages—long the mainstay of traditional Japanese virtues and values—have been left to the elderly and to part-time labor. Thus, the quality of Japanese life has suffered as well as benefited, and the blame is inevitably assigned to the government, both for the incidence of such evils and for an alleged failure to confront them squarely and to "cure" them. Unfortunately, the political style of the Liberal Democratic Party lends added credence to such critics. It has yet, since Yoshida Shigeru, to produce a leader possessed of even modest charisma. It is internally divided into warring factions, conspicuously competing for intraparty position and power and obviously neglecting their public image or responsibilities. It is corrupt in its electoral finances, although the degree of such corruption is scarcely remarkable. Its relations with the leaders of big business are close and, in the popular view, strongly suspect of secret influence and dealings contrary to the public interest. Above all, the party appears to be indecisive, lacking any firm policies or commitments beyond maintaining its hold on power and endlessly delaying and compromising in the hope that pressing problems will somehow solve themselves or simply disappear if given sufficient time. Finally, all of these traits are ceaselessly spotlighted, dramatized, and magnified for one of the world's most literate and attentive audiences—the Japanese public—by an almost uniformly critical press, by an intelligentsia largely committed to hostile political allegiances, and by a group of opposition parties noted for the uncompromising ardor of their public onslaughts on the party in power.

It is an unresolved question as to how long any government, whatever its record of past accomplishments, can withstand cumulating adversities and attacks on such a scale. Electorates are forgetful, demanding, not grateful; and above all, oriented toward the present and future, not the past. This is documented by the recent electoral performance of the Liberal Democratic Party. Prior to the thirty-first general election of 1967, the Liberal Democratic Party or its predecessors had on the average captured 60.8 percent of the popular vote in postwar competition. In 1967 this shrank to 48.8 percent, in 1969 to 47.6 percent, in the general election of 1972 to 46.8 percent, and in 1976 to 41.8 percent. The drop has been gradual, and because of superior campaigning skills and independent support, it has not yet resulted in a proportional loss of power in the lower house of the Diet where the party still controls about 51 percent of the seats. Nevertheless, the implications for the future are ominous for the Liberal Democratic Party. Japan seems to be edging closer to the point at which either the parties will reconstitute themselves along somewhat different lines or a coalition government becomes necessary.

One can only speculate about what this combination of mounting public dissatisfactions, indecisive policy responses, and possible loss of power by the party that has ruled without interruption since 1949 portends for the future of liberal democracy in Japan. The greatest strength of the Liberal Democratic Party is the lack of any generally acceptable or attractive alternative to its continued rule. The opposition parties are hopelessly fragmented, quarrelsome, and lacking individually in the capacity to attract majority support at a general election. In some cases the extraordinarily doctrinaire quality of their commitments and in others very real and deep-seated elements of mutual distrust, rivalry, and real programmatic differences make it highly improbable that the opposition parties could piece together a viable coalition government. Under these circumstances either the Liberal Democrats will retain a tenuous hold on power or, if they lose control of either house of the National Diet, they will probably attempt to form a coalition government in which the Liberal Democrats would continue to play the dominant role but in association with either the Democratic Socialist Party or the Clean Government Party, or both. Alternatively this might give rise to a move to reconstitute major elements of such a coalition, and perhaps some others as well, into a single new majority party.

The advent of either such a coalition or a new party would doubtless assure the continuance in power of individuals and the persistence of policies not very different from those that presently prevail under the Liberal Democrats. Under these circumstances, the groups remaining in opposition would probably adopt two principal strategies. First, at the national level the adverse impact on the remaining opposition parties of the advent of a new ruling coalition that excluded them should not be underestimated. There would be heightened incentives and new pressures inducing them to explore afresh the possibility of coalescing into some more formidable political grouping. Since the principal elements involved would be the Japan Socialist and Communist parties, it is hard to see how this could be on other than Marxist grounds. In such a combination, it also seems probable that the Communist tactics of gradualism, nationalism, and change achieved by peaceful, parliamentary means would prevail over the more doctrinaire and less compromising stands of the dominant left wing in the Japanese Socialist

Party. Under such circumstances, the erstwhile Socialist Party elements could probably look forward to a dwindling role in the councils of a new combined opposition party. Second, the remaining opposition forces, however constituted, would probably explore and develop further the potentialities of a strategy of political struggle at the local as well as at the national level. By April 1975 over 20 percent of Japan's 642 mayoral positions and ten of the forty-seven prefectural governorships were held by "progressive" candidates, that is, those elected with primary support from the Japan Socialist Party or the Communist Party, or both. These regimes, while not without their problems, have proven quite resilient and have gained strong local support for their relative honesty, openness, solicitude for the citizenry and local interests and problems, and their records in office. The resulting situation is very reminiscent of the Italian experience, and the general strategy involved seems to be similar. If a party is debarred, at least temporarily, from making significant progress at the level of national politics, then it shifts a portion of its efforts to the local scene; cultivates a firm base there, especially in the largest metropolitan areas; and strives to disarm popular suspicions and to acquire new followers who may ultimately support the party at the national as well as the local level.

If this is a reasonable scenario for Japan's political future, what does it portend for the fate of liberal democracy in Japan? Unfortunately, it argues for more of the same. The most probable developments are not calculated to provide a fresh infusion of leadership or policy into the current political scene. By themselves, they solve none of the underlying problems. Either an essentially unchanged Liberal Democratic Party clings to power or new elements and viewpoints from other parties in coalition with the Liberal Democratic Party simply multiply the occasions for dissensus and the obstacles to decisive policy formation and action. There seems to be small prospect that the efficacy or the authority of governance at the national level will increase appreciably given both its internal liabilities and the unprecedented complexity and difficulty of the domestic and international problems that confront it. On the other hand, there seems every probability that public demands and dissatisfactions will gradually mount both because of objective circumstances and by reason of careful and effective cultivation by the media, the intelligentsia, and the opposition parties. These are conditions that make probable continuing increases in popular participation in the political process through the expansion of residents' movements. Under such circumstances the possibilities of increasing governmental lag coupled with rising popular participation and demands adversely affecting the interests of liberal democracy are undoubtedly present.

Against such a scenario, however, one can posit arguments that, while powerful, are equally difficult to assess: the patience, discipline, and good sense of the Japanese people; the undoubted talents and truly remarkable record of a system of government that, however lacking in personalized leadership and political flair, has successfully met and coped with all major challenges to date; the changing and basically unpredictable impacts on domestic politics of international developments; or the capacity of the system to respond along innovative and effective lines when confronted with truly serious threats. I am cautiously optimistic about the prospects of liberal democracy in Japan but must in honesty admit that the grounds for such optimism are as much an act of faith as of dispassionate scholarly analysis. But of what country might not the same be said?

BIBLIOGRAPHY

CROZIER, MICHEL J., ET AL., *The Crisis of Democracy*. New York: New York University Press, 1975, 220 pp.

APPENDIXES

APPENDIX 1

COMPARATIVE TABLE OF NATIONAL POPULATIONS, AREAS, AND LIFE EXPECTANCIES

Country or area	LATEST POPULATION, CENSUS OR ESTIMATE[a] Year	Population	Annual rate of increase[a] 1970-73(%)	URBAN-RURAL POPULATION DISTRIBUTION[c](%) Year	Urban	Rural	1974 Area[b] (sq. km.)	Inhabitants per sq. km.[b] (1974)	ARABLE LAND AS PERCENTAGE OF TOTAL AREA[d] Year	Percent	EXPECTATION OF LIFE AT BIRTH (YEARS)[b] Year or period	Male	Female
Northeast Asia													
Japan	1975	111,933,818*	1.4%	1975	76	24	372,393	297	1975	16%	1975	72	77
People's Republic of China	1974	824,961,000	1.7				9,596,961	86	1971	13	1970-75	60	63
Republic of China	1976	16,419,888	2.4	1972	64	36	35,203	466	1972	25	1972	68+	68+
Republic of Korea	1974	33,459,000	1.7	1970	41	59	98,484	340	1973	23	1970	63	67
Democratic People's Republic of Korea	1974	15,439,000	2.7	...	...	...	120,538	128	1960	16	1970-75	59	63
Mongolia	1974	1,403,000	3.0	1973	46	54	1,565,000	1	1973	1	1965-70	58+	58+
Hongkong	1974	4,249,000	1.8	...	...	...	1,045	4,066	1973	11	1970-75	59	62
Macao	1974	266,000	1.8	1970	97	3	16	16,625	1973	12			
Southeast Asia													
Philippine Republic	1973	40,219,000	3.0	1970	32	68	300,000	138	1973	29	1970-75	57	60
Indonesia	1973	124,602,000	—	1974	18	82	1,491,564	86	1971	10	1960	48+	48+
Vietnam	1976	45,327,000	1.9	1973	30[c]	70	332,559	136	1973	19	1970-75	47	50
Laos	1973	3,181,000	2.4	1973	15	85	236,800	14	1971	4	1970-75	39	42
Khmer Republic	1973	7,643,000	—			—	181,035	44	1971	10	1970-75	44	47
Malaysia	1973	11,609,000	3.7	1970	29	71	329,749	35	1970	17	1972	63	68
Singapore	1973	2,185,000	1.7	1973	100	—	581	3,819	1972	1	1970	65	70
Brunei	1973	145,000	3.7	1971	64	36	5,765	25	1971		—	—	—
Thailand	1973	39,787,000*	3.2	1970	13	87	514,000	80	1971	24	1960	54	59
Burma	1973	28,886,000*	2.3		—	—	676,552	45	1970	27	1970-75	49	52
Indian Subcontinent													
India	1973	574,216,000	2.1	1974	21	79	3,280,483	179	1972	49	1951-60	42	41
Pakistan	1973	66,749,000	3.6	1968	27	73	803,943	85	1973	24	1962	54	49
Bangladesh	1974	71,317,000*	—	1973	7	93	143,998	521	1972	62	1970-75	36	36
Nepal	1973	12,020,000	2.3	1971	4	96	140,797	87	1971	14	1970-75	42	45
Bhutan	1973	894,000	2.0		—	—	47,000	24	—	—	1970-75	42	45
Sikkim	1973	206,000	2.0	1974	5	95	7,107	30	1973	1	—	—	—
Sri Lanka	1973	13,249,000	1.9	1971	22	78	65,610	208	1973	17	1967	65	67

Country or area	Year	Population	Annual rate of increase[a] 1970-73(%)	Year	Urban	Rural	1974 Area[b] (sq. km.)	Inhabitants per sq. km.[b] (1974)	Year	Percent	Year or period	Male	Female
Middle East													
Afghanistan	1973	18,294,000	2.3	1973	15	85	647,497	29	1968	12	1970-75	40	41
Iran	1973	31,298,000	3.0	1975	44	56	1,648,000	19	1971	9	1970-75	51	51
Iraq	1973	10,413,000	3.3	1974	63	37	434,021	25	1971	11	1970-75	51	54
Saudi Arabia	1973	8,443,000	2.9		—	—	2,149,690	4	1971	1	1970-75	44	47
Kuwait	1973	883,000	5.8		—	—	17,818	52	1973	0	1970	66	72
Bahrain	1973	227,000	1.8	1972	78	22	622	391	1973	1	—	—	—
United Arab Emirates	1973	208,000	2.7		—	—	83,600	3	1973	0	—	—	—
Qatar	1973	86,000	2.9		—	—	11,000	8	1973	0	—	—	—
Oman	1973	722,000	3.2		—	—	212,457	3	1971	1	—	—	—
Yemen	1970	5,767,000	—		—	—	195,000	33	1969	6	1970-75	44	46
Democratic Republic of Yemen	1973	1,590,000	2.7	1973	33	67	332,968	5	1966	1	1970-75	44	46
Egypt	1973	35,619,000	2.2	1975	45	55	1,001,450	36	1973	3	1961	52	54
Jordan	1973	2,537,000	3.3	1973	43	57	97,740	27	1970	12	1959-63	53	52
Israel	1973	3,183,000	3.0	1973	82	18	20,700	159	1973	16	1973	70	73
Syria	1973	6,890,000	3.3	1974	46	54	185,180	38	1973	30	1970	54	59
Lebanon	1973	3,055,000	3.1	1970	60	40	10,400	268	1973	23	1970-75	61	65
Turkey	1973	37,933,000	2.5	1974	43	57	780,576	49	1973	33	1966	54+	54+
United States and Europe													
United States	1975	213,610,000	0.9	1970	74	26	9,363,123	23	1969	20	1974	68	76
Federal Republic of Germany	1975	61,830,000	0.7	1969	38	62	248,577	250	1973	30	1969-70	69	74
France	1975	52,910,000	0.9	1968	70	30	547,026	96	1972	31	1972	69	76
United Kingdom	1975	55,960,000	0.3	1973	78	22	244,046	229	1973	29	1968-70	68	74
Soviet Union	1975	255,000,000	1.0	1974	60	40	22,402,200	11	1973	10	1971-72	64	74

*Indicates an actual census figure. All other figures are midyear estimates.

+Available data do not distinguish by sex.

a U.S. Department of Commerce, Bureau of the Census, *Statistical Abstract of the United States, 1975*, pp. 836-38.

b United Nations, *Demographic Yearbook*, 1974, pp. 139-48, 110-13, 120-24; and 1975, pp. 153-57 and 167-87.

c Former Republic of Viet Nam only.

d United Nations, Food and Agriculture Organization, *Production Yearbook*, 1974, vol. 1, pp. 3-7.

COMPARATIVE TABLE OF GNP AT MARKET PRICES AND
GNP PER CAPITA FOR 1974

Country or area	Amount (millions of US $)	Per capita (US $)	Global rank order by per capita gross domestic product in 1973[a]	Growth rate of GNP per capita, 1965-73(%)
Northeast Asia				
Japan	425,880	3,880	23	9.6
People's Republic of China	245,840	300	135	4.6
Republic of China	11,370	720	—	7.3
Republic of Korea	15,800	470	112	8.7
Democratic People's Republic of Korea	5,960	390	121	2.7
Mongolia	860	620	88	1.6
Hongkong	6,550	1,540	53	5.8
Southeast Asia				
Philippine Republic	13,030	310	140	2.6
Democratic Republic of Vietnam	3,000	130	170	−0.5
South Vietnam	3,440	170	153	−0.7
Laos	220	70	172	2.5
Khmer Republic	570	70	185	−5.2
Malaysia	7,610	660	92	3.7
Singapore	4,700	2,120	41	9.4
Thailand	12,140	300	143	4.5
Burma	2,710	90	183	0.7
Indian Subcontinent				
India	78,990	130	167	1.5
Pakistan	8,770	130	164	2.5
Bangladesh	7,260	100	173	−1.6
Nepal	1,310	110	176	−0.1
Bhutan	80	70	187	−0.2
Sri Lanka	1,790	130	146	2.0
Middle East				
Afghanistan	1,620	100	184	0.9
Iran	35,120	1,060	68	7.4
Iraq	10,400	970	82	2.9
Saudi Arabia	16,690	2,080	56	10.1
Kuwait	10,830	11,640	1	−0.2
Bahrain	550	2,250	70	−7.8
United Arab Emirates	4,590	13,500	2	16.1
Qatar	1,110	5,830	6	7.9
Oman	930	1,250	95	19.4
Yemen	740	120	162	—
Democratic Republic of Yemen	200	120	171	—
Egypt	10,090	280	141	0.8
Jordan	1,040	400	125	−2.6
Israel	11,150	3,380	30	6.7
Syria	3,480	490	117	3.6
Lebanon	3,300	1,080	74	3.5
Turkey	26,800	690	90	4.4

Country or area	Amount (millions of US $)	Per capita (US $)	Global rank order by per capita gross domestic product in 1973[a]	Growth rate of GNP per capita, 1965–73(%)
United States and Europe				
United States	1,406,610	6,640	3	2.5
Federal Republic of Germany	365,220	5,890	8	4.0
France	272,410	5,190	15	5.0
United Kingdom	188,630	3,360	27	2.3
Soviet Union	580,750	2,300	40	3.5

Source: World Bank Atlas, 1975, pp. 6–7, 27–30.

[a] United Nations Conference on Trade and Development (UNCTAD), *Handbook of International Trade and Development Statistics, 1976*, pp. 654–55. Note that these are global rankings for 1973, not 1974, and that they are couched in terms of gross domestic product on a per capita basis, not gross national product. They precede the economic effects of the quadrupling of the price of oil in late 1973 and 1974 and thus substantially understate the present global rankings of many oil-producing states.

APPENDIX 3

COMPARATIVE TABLE OF INDEXES OF INDUSTRIALIZATION

Country	ORIGINS OF GROSS DOMESTIC PRODUCT AT CURRENT FACTOR COST[a] (% IN 1973)				PRODUCTION AND CONSUMPTION OF ENERGY (1974)[e]		PRODUCTION AND CONSUMPTION OF CRUDE STEEL (1974)[e]	
	Agriculture[b] (%)	Manufacturing[c] (%)	Other Industry[d] (%)	Services (%)	Production of electric energy (in million kilowatt hours)	Consumption per capita (in kilograms of coal equivalent)	Production (in thousands of metric tons)	Consumption (per capita in kilograms)
Northeast Asia								
Japan	6.6	28.6	16.5[f]	48.3	460,705	3,839	117,131	681
People's Republic of China	27.0	45.9	8.1	27.2[h]	—	632	27,000	37
Republic of China	15.5	29.8	7.8	46.6	—	—	—	124
Republic of Korea	28.1	24.3	7.8	39.7	17,892	961	1,935	223
Democratic People's Republic of Korea	18.0[i]	64.0[i]	10.0[i]	8.0[i]	—	2,698	2,900	—
Mongolia	2.5[j]	—	—	—	741	1,046	—	—
Hongkong	—	32.1[j]	5.1[j]	60.3[j]	6,722	1,232	—	156
Southeast Asia								
Philippine Republic	36.4	21.3	6.5	35.8	13,047	309	—	29
Democratic Republic of Vietnam	—	—	—	—	—	90	—	7
South Vietnam	38.0	7.1	2.8	52.1	1,345[m]	210	—	6
Laos	—	—	—	—	255[m]	65	—	1
Khmer Republic	38.3[k]	11.7[k]	8.1[k]	46.6[k]	150[m]	17	—	1
Malaysia	30.5	15.4	12.1	42.0	4,973	556	—	69
Singapore	2.7	26.2	8.9	62.2	3,864[m]	2,060	—	710
Thailand	34.3	17.7	8.6	39.5	7,789	300	—	22
Burma	35.8	10.0	3.9	50.3	758	56	—	1
Indonesia	40.9[j]	9.2[j]	12.3[j]	37.6[j]	3,246[m]	158	—	9
Indian Subcontinent								
India	47.8[k]	13.4[l]	7.5[l]	31.3[l]	75,452	201	6,704	14
Pakistan	35.8	15.5	6.0	42.7	6,400[m]	188	73	6
Bangladesh	56.1	8.3	4.3	31.3	1,221[m]	31	—	1
Nepal	68.4	9.6	1.6	20.3	116	12	—	—
Sri Lanka	33.1	13.6	6.5	46.8	1,050	140	—	4

Middle East

Afghanistan	50.9k	10.8k	3.0k	35.3k	484	67	—	1
Iran	12.1	11.9	47.4	28.6	12,500	1,272	—	93
Iraq	17.6	10.4	36.2	35.8	2,600m	906	—	173
Saudi Arabia	3.0	6.6	72.4	18.0	1,474m	976	—	117
Kuwait	0.3	2.7	69.8	27.1	4,000m	10,094	—	454
Bahrain	1.0j	42.4j	32.3j	24.3j	390j	11,819	—	521
United Arab Emirates	—	—	—	—	—	13,503	—	—
Qatar	—	—	—	—	—	18,423	—	—
Oman	9.8	0.1	71.4	18.7	200	250	—	—
Yemen	67.5	1.9	4.7	25.9	29m	30	—	—
Democratic Republic of Yemen	21.4k	1.8k	8.9k	67.9k	174	360	—	—
Egypt	31.2	21.6	5.2	42.1	8,200	322	270	30
Jordan	14.1	12.1	9.2	64.7	310	388	—	27
Israel	5.8	23.6	13.1	57.5	9,153	2,914	120	338
Syria	17.3	19.3	3.6	59.8	1,366	590	—	76
Lebanon	9.5	14.6	6.2	69.8	1,975	1,073	—	187
Turkey	27.3	23.6	6.5	42.3	13,465	628	1,458	51

United States and Europe

United States	4.4	24.7	8.5	62.4	1,967,289	11,485	132,196	680
Federal Republic of Germany	3.0	46.0	13.7	42.8	311,655	5,689	53,231	679
France	6.1	34.4	13.8	45.7	180,402	4,330	27,023	460
United Kingdom	2.5	30.1	9.8	57.6	273,316	5,464	22,426	412
Soviet Union	20.3	51.3g	10.7	17.7	975,800	5,252	136,229	546

a International Bank For Reconstruction and Development, *World Tables, 1976*, pp. 416-23. Gross domestic product is a measure of the total final output of a country's economy, that is, of all goods and services rendered within its territory by residents and nonresidents. It is calculated before deductions are made for depreciation and other capital consumption allowances. It differs from gross national product in that the latter is a measure of total domestic *and foreign* output claimed by residents of a country and thus includes all income received by residents from abroad (remittances, interest, dividends, etc.) reduced by corresponding payments to abroad.

b Agriculture includes livestock, forestry, fishing, and hunting.

c Manufacturing includes handicrafts.

d Other industries include mining, construction, electricity, gas, and water.

e *UN Statistical Yearbook, 1975*, pp. 378-81, 392-401, 327, 593-94.

f Includes transportation and communications.

g Includes mining, electricity, gas, and water.

h Includes "other industries."

i As of 1965.

j As of 1972.

k As of 1969.

l As of 1971.

m By enterprises generating primarily for public use.

APPENDIX 4

COMPARATIVE TABLE OF EDUCATIONAL ATTAINMENT AND CIRCULATION OF MASS MEDIA

Country	Literacy rate in latest available year[a] (% of pop)	Year	Educational Attainment[b] — First Level[c] Teachers (1,000s)	First Level Students (1,000s)	Second Level[d] Teachers (1,000s)	Second Level Students (1,000s)	Combined primary and secondary enrollment ratio (1972)[g] (%)	Daily Newspapers Year	Number	Total (1,000s)	Circulation per 1,000 pop	Radio Receivers 1973 Number (1,000s)	Per 1,000 pop	TV Receivers 1973 Number (1,000s)	Per 1,000 pop
Northeast Asia															
Japan	98	1971	353	9,595	456	8,865	95	1973	188	58,181	537	70,794[k]	658	24,797	229
People's Republic of China	—	1959	—	90,000	—	9,990	58	—	—	—	—	12,000[j]	16	500	0.6
Republic of China	—	—	—	—	—	—	—	—	—	—	—	—	—	—	—
Republic of Korea	88	1972	106	5,776	65	2,438	66	1972	33	4,400	136	4,115[k]	127	1,182	36
Democratic People's Republic of Korea	—	—	—	—	—	—	—	—	—	—	—	—	—	—	—
Mongolia	95	—	—	—	—	—	81	1970	2	133	103	166[j]	129	3	2
Hongkong	77	1971	23	757	11	290	70	1973	72	—	—	1,000	240	748	180
Macao	79	—	—	—	—	—	50	—	—	—	—	12[k]	37	—	—
Southeast Asia															
Philippine Republic	83	1972	248	7,022	58	1,791	69	1971	18	785	21	1,800	45	450	11
Indonesia	60	1971	415	13,475	164	2,105	44	1973	154	1,110	—	13,169[j]	114	95	0.8
Democratic Republic of Vietnam	65	—	—	—	—	—	—	—	—	—	—	—	—	—	—
South Vietnam	65	1969	43	2,376	—	—	64	1973	28	412	21	1,550	80	500	26
Laos	15	—	—	—	—	—	28	1973	2	—	—	102	32	—	—
Khmer Republic	41	—	—	—	—	—	66	1970	16	70	10	1,110	145	26	3
Malaysia	—	—	—	—	—	—	61	1973	37	1,097	95	462	40	359	31
Singapore	69	1971	12	358	8	160	77	1973	10	—	—	303	139	231	106
Brunei	64	—	—	—	—	—	—	1972	1	—	—	16	110	—	—
Thailand	79	1970	163	5,635	45	627	44	1973	33	—	—	3,009	76	241[k]	7
Burma	60	1969	65	3,328	22	700	41	1973	10	283	—	627	21	—	—

APPENDIX 4 *(continued)*

Indian Subcontinent															
India	34	1967	—	54,326	—	8,987	38	1972	793	8,873	16	14,034	24	163	0.3
Pakistan	16	1971	97	3,888	81	2,266	26	1972	71	—	—	1,033	16	129k	2
Bangladesh	22	—	—	—	—	—	29	1973	22	85	—	—	—	—	—
Nepal	13	—	—	—	—	—	18	1973	26	—	—	100k	9	—	—
Bhutan	—	—	—	—	—	—	6	—	—	—	—	—	—	—	—
Sikkim	16	—	—	—	—	—	—	—	—	—	—	—	—	—	—
Sri Lanka	81	1969	—	2,298	—	356	72	1972	24	—	—	515	39	—	—
Middle East															
Afghanistan	8	1971	15	605	7	162	11	1973	18	90	5	—	—	—	—
Iran	23	1971	103	3,231	45	1,468	46	1972	39	750	24	7,000k	229	1,200	39
Iraq	26	1971	54	1,196	15	325	49	1973	4	226	22	1,250	120	520	50
Saudi Arabia	15	—	—	—	—	—	23	1973	11	96	11	87k	11	18j	2
Kuwait	55	—	—	—	—	—	77	1973	7	75	85	210	238	180	204
Bahrain	—	—	—	—	—	—	—	—	—	—	—	80	352	18	78
United Arab Emirates	21	—	—	—	—	—	—	—	—	—	—	—	—	—	—
Qatar	—	—	—	—	—	—	—	—	—	—	—	—	—	—	—
Oman	—	—	—	—	—	—	—	—	—	—	—	—	—	—	—
Yemen	10	—	—	—	—	—	5	1970	6	56	10	—	—	—	—
Democratic Republic of Yemen	10	—	—	—	—	—	45	1972	3	2	1	525	23	26	17
Egypt	26	1971	99	3,873	58	1,555	45	1971	14	745	22	5,100	143	600	17
Jordan	32	1971	8	299	5	102	61	1973	4	48	19	521	211	80	31
Israel	84	1971	30	500	13	142	81	1972	26	—	—	680k	221	370k	120
Syria	40	1971	28	1,006	7	371	66	1973	6	64	—	2,500k	374	150k	22
Lebanon	86	1971	—	176e	—	—	73	1973	32	280	92	605k	211	321	105
Turkey	51	1971	141	5,099	51	1,430	49	1973	450	—	—	4,033	106	257	7
United States and Europe															
United States	99	1971	1,293f	31,800	1,003	19,810	105h	1973	1,794	62,147	300	368,600	1,752	110,000	523
Federal Republic of Germany	—	1971	258	6,477	275	4,506	89	1973	1,211	18,667	301	20,586	332	18,486	298
France	96	1971	182e	4,854	292	4,524	92	1972	100	11,969	231	17,034k	329	12,332	237
United Kingdom	—	1971	242	5,406	—	3,741	92	1973	109	24,500	438	39,000	697	17,294	309
Soviet Union	100	1971	2,383	39,932	—	9,355	94	1973	658	93,243	373	110,300	442	49,200	197

APPENDIX 4 *(continued)*

a U.N. Conference on Trade and Development, *Handbook of International Trade and Statistics, 1976*, pp. 417–28.

b U.S. Department of Commerce, Bureau of Census, *Statistical Abstract of the United States, 1975*, pp. 842–43; and U.N. Conference on Trade and Development, *Handbook of International Trade and Statistics, 1976*, pp. 417–28.

c Schools providing basic training and education for children within compulsory or customary ages of full-time education. Length of this education may vary from four to nine years. Excludes nursery school and kindergarten.

d Middle, secondary, or high schools providing general instruction more advanced than primary level.

e Public education only.

f Includes preschool education.

g Numbers of pupils enrolled at the first and second levels as a percentage of the estimated school-age population, i.e. 5–19 years of age.

h Includes preprimary education.

i U.N. *Statistical Yearbook, 1975*, pp. 890–94, 899–903.

j In 1970.

k In 1972.

THE CONSTITUTION OF JAPAN (1947)

We, the Japanese people, acting through our duly elected representatives in the National Diet, determined that we shall secure for ourselves and our posterity the fruits of peaceful cooperation with all nations and the blessings of liberty throughout this land, and resolved that never again shall we be visited with the horrors of war through the action of government, do proclaim that sovereign power resides with the people and do firmly establish this Constitution. Government is a sacred trust of the people, the authority for which is derived from the people, the powers of which are exercised by the representatives of the people, and the benefits of which are enjoyed by the people. This is universal principle of mankind upon which this Constitution is founded. We reject and revoke all constitutions, laws, ordinances, and rescripts in conflict herewith.

We, the Japanese people, desire peace for all time and are deeply conscious of the high ideals controlling human relationship, and we have determined to preserve our security and existence, trusting in the justice and faith of the peace-loving peoples of the world. We desire to occupy an honored place in an international society striving for the preservation of peace and the banishment of tyranny and slavery, oppression and intolerance for all time from the earth. We recognize that all peoples of the world have the right to live in peace, free from fear and want.

We believe that no nation is responsible to itself alone, but that laws of political morality are universal; and that obedience to such laws is incumbent upon all nations who would sustain their own sovereignty and justify their sovereign relationship with other nations.

We, the Japanese people, pledge our national honor to accomplish these high ideals and purposes with all our resources.

Chapter I
The Emperor

ARTICLE 1.   The Emperor shall be the symbol of the State and of the unity of the people, deriving his position from the will of the people with whom resides sovereign power.

ARTICLE 2.   The Imperial Throne shall be dynastic and succeeded to in accordance with the Imperial House Law passed by the Diet.

ARTICLE 3.   The advice and approval of the Cabinet shall be required for all acts of the Emperor in matters of state, and the Cabinet shall be responsible therefor.

ARTICLE 4.   The Emperor shall perform only such acts in matters of state as are provided for in this Constitution and he shall not have powers related to government.

The Emperor may delegate the performance of his acts in matters of state as may be provided by law.

ARTICLE 5.   When, in accordance with the Imperial House Law, a Regency is established, the Regent shall perform his acts in matters of state in the Emperor's name. In this case, paragraph one of the preceding article will be applicable.

ARTICLE 6.   The Emperor shall appoint the Prime Minister as designated by the Diet.

The Emperor shall appoint the Chief Judge of the Supreme Court as designated by the Cabinet.

ARTICLE 7.   The Emperor, with the advice and approval of the Cabinet, shall perform the following acts in matters of state on behalf of the people:

Promulgation of amendments of the constitution, laws, cabinet orders and treaties.

Convocation of the Diet.

Dissolution of the House of Representatives.

Proclamation of general election of members of the Diet.

Attestation of the appointment and dismissal of Ministers of State and other officials as provided for by law, and of full powers and credentials of Ambassadors and Ministers.

Attestation of general and special amnesty, commutation of punishment, reprieve, and restoration of rights.

Awarding of honors.

Attestation of instruments of ratification and other diplomatic documents as provided for by law.

Receiving foreign ambassadors and ministers.

Performance of ceremonial functions.

ARTICLE 8.   No property can be given to, or received by, the Imperial House, nor can any gifts be made therefrom, without the authorization of the Diet.

Chapter II
Renunciation of War

ARTICLE 9.   Aspiring sincerely to an international peace based on justice and order, the Japanese people forever renounce war as a sovereign right of the nation and the threat or use of force as means of settling international disputes.

In order to accomplish the aim of the preceding paragraph, land, sea, and air forces, as well as other war potential, will never be maintained. The right of belligerency of the state will not be recognized.

Chapter III
Rights and Duties of the People

ARTICLE 10.   The conditions necessary for being a Japanese national shall be determined by law.

ARTICLE 11. The people shall not be prevented from enjoying any of the fundamental human rights. These fundamental human rights guaranteed to the people by this Constitution shall be conferred upon the people of this and future generations as eternal and inviolate rights.

ARTICLE 12. The freedoms and rights guaranteed to the people by this Constitution shall be maintained by the constant endeavor of the people, who shall refrain from any abuse of these freedoms and rights and shall always be responsible for utilizing them for the public welfare.

ARTICLE 13. All of the people shall be respected as individuals. Their right to life, liberty, and the pursuit of happiness shall, to the extent that it does not interfere with the public welfare, be the supreme consideration in legislation and in other governmental affairs.

ARTICLE 14. All of the people are equal under the law and there shall be no discrimination in political, economic or social relations because of race, creed, sex, social status or family origin.

Peers and peerage shall not be recognized.

No privilege shall accompany any award of honor, decoration or any distinction, nor shall any such award be valid beyond the lifetime of the individual who now holds or hereafter may receive it.

ARTICLE 15. The people have the inalienable right to choose their public officials and to dismiss them.

All public officials are servants of the whole community and not of any group thereof.

Universal adult suffrage is guaranteed with regard to the election of public officials.

In all elections, secrecy of the ballot shall not be violated. A voter shall not be answerable, publicly or privately, for the choice he has made.

ARTICLE 16. Every person shall have the right of peaceful petition for the redress of damage, for the removal of public officials, for the enactment, repeal or amendment of laws, ordinances or regulations and for other matters; nor shall any person be in any way discriminated against for sponsoring such a petition.

ARTICLE 17. Every person may sue for redress as provided for by law from the State or a public entity, in case he has suffered damage through illegal act of any public official.

ARTICLE 18. No person shall be held in bondage of any kind. Involuntary servitude, except as punishment for crime, is prohibited.

ARTICLE 19. Freedom of thought and conscience shall not be violated.

ARTICLE 20. Freedom of religion is guaranteed to all. No religious organization shall receive any privileges from the State, nor exercise any political authority.

No person shall be compelled to take part in any religious act, celebration, rite or practice.

The State and its organs shall refrain from religious education or any other religious activity.

ARTICLE 21. Freedom of assembly and association as well as speech, press and all other forms of expression are guaranteed.

No censorship shall be maintained, nor shall the secrecy of any means or communication be violated.

ARTICLE 22.　Every person shall have freedom to choose and change his residence and to choose his occupation to the extent that it does not interfere with the public welfare.

Freedom of all persons to move to a foreign country and to divest themselves of their nationality shall be inviolate.

ARTICLE 23.　Academic freedom is guaranteed.

ARTICLE 24.　Marriage shall be based only on the mutual consent of both sexes and it shall be maintained through mutual cooperation with the equal rights of husband and wife as a basis.

With regard to choice of spouse, property rights, inheritance, choice of domicile, divorce and other matters pertaining to marriage and the family, laws shall be enacted from the standpoint of individual dignity and the essential equality of the sexes.

ARTICLE 25.　All people shall have the right to maintain the minimum standards of wholesome and cultured living.

In all spheres of life, the State shall use its endeavors for the promotion and extension of social welfare and security, and of public health.

ARTICLE 26.　All people shall have the right to receive an equal education correspondent to their ability, as provided for by law.

All people shall be obligated to have all boys and girls under their protection receive ordinary education as provided for by law. Such compulsory education shall be free.

ARTICLE 27.　All people shall have the right and the obligation to work.

Standards for wages, hours, rest and other working conditions shall be fixed by law.

Children shall not be exploited.

ARTICLE 28.　The right of workers to organize and to bargain and act collectively is guaranteed.

ARTICLE 29.　The right to own or to hold property is inviolable.

Property rights shall be defined by law, in conformity with the public welfare.

Private property may be taken for public use upon just compensation therefor.

ARTICLE 30.　The people shall be liable to taxation as provided by law.

ARTICLE 31.　No person shall be deprived of life or liberty, nor shall any other criminal penalty be imposed, except according to procedure established by law.

ARTICLE 32.　No person shall be denied the right of access to the courts.

ARTICLE 33.　No person shall be apprehended except upon warrant issued by a competent judicial officer which specifies the offense with which the person is charged, unless he is apprehended, the offense being committed.

ARTICLE 34.　No person shall be arrested or detained without being at once informed of the charges against him or without the immediate privilege of counsel; nor shall he be detained without adequate cause; and upon demand of any person such cause must be immediately shown in open court in his presence and the presence of his counsel.

ARTICLE 35.　The right of all persons to be secure in their homes, papers and effects against entries, searches and seizures shall not be impaired except upon warrant issued for adequate cause and particularly describing the place to be searched and things to be seized, or except as provided for by Article 33.

Each search or seizure shall be made upon separate warrant issued by a competent judicial officer.

ARTICLE 36.   The infliction of torture by any public officer and cruel punishment are absolutely forbidden.

ARTICLE 37.   In all criminal cases the accused shall enjoy the right to a speedy and public trial by an impartial tribunal.

He shall be permitted full opportunity to examine all witnesses, and he shall have the right of compulsory process for obtaining witnesses on his behalf at public expense.

At all times the accused shall have the assistance of competent counsel who shall, if the accused is unable to secure the same by his own efforts, be assigned to his use by the State.

ARTICLE 38.   No person shall be compelled to testify against himself.

Confession made under compulsion, torture or threat, or after prolonged arrest or detention shall not be admitted in evidence.

No person shall be convicted or punished in cases where the only proof against him is his own confession.

ARTICLE 39.   No person shall be held criminally liable for an act which was lawful at the time it was committed, or of which he has been acquitted, nor shall he be placed in double jeopardy.

ARTICLE 40.   Any person, in case he is acquitted after he has been arrested or detained, may sue the State for redress as provided by law.

Chapter IV
The Diet

ARTICLE 41.   The Diet shall be the highest organ of state power, and shall be the sole law-making organ of the State.

ARTICLE 42.   The Diet shall consist of two Houses, namely the House of Representatives and the House of Councillors.

ARTICLE 43.   Both Houses shall consist of elected members, representative of all the people.

The number of the members of each House shall be fixed by law.

ARTICLE 44.   The qualifications of members of both Houses and their electors shall be fixed by law. However, there shall no discrimination because of race, creed, sex, social status, family origin, education, property or income.

ARTICLE 45.   The term of office of members of the House of Representatives shall be four years. However, the term shall be terminated before the full term is up in case the House of Representatives is dissolved.

ARTICLE 46.   The term of office of members of the House of Councillors shall be six years, and election for half the members shall take place every three years.

ARTICLE 47.   Electoral districts, method of voting and other matters pertaining to the method of election of members of both Houses shall be fixed by law.

ARTICLE 48.   No person shall be permitted to be a member of both Houses simultaneously.

ARTICLE 49.   Members of both Houses shall receive appropriate annual payment from the national treasury in accordance with law.

ARTICLE 50.   Except in cases provided by law, members of both Houses shall be exempt from apprehension while the Diet is in session, and any members apprehended before the opening of the session shall be freed during the term of the session upon demand of the House.

ARTICLE 51.   Members of both Houses shall not be held liable outside the House for speeches, debates or votes cast inside the House.

ARTICLE 52.   An ordinary session of the Diet shall be convoked once per year.

ARTICLE 53.   The Cabinet may determine to convoke extraordinary sessions of the Diet. When a quarter or more of the total members of either House makes the demand, the Cabinet must determine on such convocation.

ARTICLE 54.   When the House of Representatives is dissolved, there must be a general election of members of the House of Representatives within forty (40) days from the date of dissolution, and the Diet must be convoked within thirty (30) days from the date of the election.

When the House of Representatives is dissolved, the House of Councillors is closed at the same time. However, the Cabinet may in time of national emergency convoke the House of Councillors in emergency session.

Measures taken at such session as mentioned in the proviso of the preceding paragraph shall be provisional and shall become null and void unless agreed to by the House of Representatives within a period of ten (10) days after the opening of the next session of the Diet.

ARTICLE 55.   Each House shall judge disputes related to qualifications of its members. However, in order to deny a seat to any member, it is necessary to pass a resolution by a majority of two-thirds or more of the members present.

ARTICLE 56.   Business cannot be transacted in either House unless one-third or more of total membership is present.

All matters shall be decided, in each House, by a majority of those present, except as elsewhere provided in the Constitution, and in case of a tie, the presiding officer shall decide the issue.

ARTICLE 57.   Deliberation in each House shall be public. However, a secret meeting may be held where a majority of two-thirds or more of those members present passes a resolution therefor.

Each House shall keep a record of proceedings. This record shall be published and given general circulation, excepting such parts of proceedings of secret session as may be deemed to require secrecy.

Upon demand of one-fifth or more of the members present, votes of the members on any matter shall be recorded in the minutes.

ARTICLE 58.   Each House shall select its own president and other officials.

Each House shall establish its rules pertaining to meetings, proceedings and internal discipline, and may punish members for disorderly conduct. However, in order to expel a member, a majority of two-thirds or more of those members present must pass a resolution thereon.

ARTICLE 59.   A bill becomes a law on passage by both Houses, except as otherwise provided by the Constitution.

A bill which is passed by the House of Representatives, and upon which the House of Councillors makes a decision different from that of the House of Representatives, becomes a law when passed a second time by the House of Representatives by a majority of two-thirds or more of the members present.

The provision of the preceding paragraph does not preclude the House of Representatives from calling for the meeting of a joint committee of both Houses provided for by law.

Failure by the House of Councillors to take final action within sixty (60) days after receipt of a bill passed by the House of Representatives, time in recess excepted, may be determined by the House of Representatives to constitute a rejection of the said bill by the House of Councillors.

ARTICLE 60.   The budget must first be submitted to the House of Representatives.

Upon consideration of the budget, when the House of Councillors makes a decision different from that of the House of Representatives, and when no agreement can be reached even through a joint committee of both Houses, provided for by law, or in the case of failure by the House of Councillors to take final action within thirty (30) days, the period of recess excluded, after the receipt of the budget passed by the House of Representatives, the decision of the House of Representatives shall be the decision of the Diet.

ARTICLE 61.   The second paragraph of the preceding article applies also to the Diet approval required for the conclusion of treaties.

ARTICLE 62.   Each House may conduct investigations in relation to government, and may demand the presence and testimony of witnesses, and the production of records.

ARTICLE 63.   The Prime Minister and other Ministers of State may, at any time, appear in either House for the purpose of speaking on bills, regardless of whether they are members of the House or not. They must appear when their presence is required in order to give answers or explanations.

ARTICLE 64.   The Diet shall set up an impeachment court from among the members of both Houses for the purpose of trying those judges against whom removal proceedings have been instituted.

Matters relating to impeachment shall be provided by law.

Chapter V
The Cabinet

ARTICLE 65.   Executive power shall be vested in the Cabinet.

ARTICLE 66.   The Cabinet shall consist of the Prime Minister, who shall be its head, and other Ministers of State, as provided for by law.

The Prime Minister and other Ministers of State must be civilians.

The Cabinet, in the exercise of executive power, shall be collectively responsible to the Diet.

ARTICLE 67. The Prime Minister shall be designated from among the members of the Diet by a resolution of the Diet. This designation shall precede all other business.

If the House of Representatives and the House of Councillors disagree and if no agreement can be reached even through a joint committee of both Houses, provided for by law, or the House of Councillors fails to make designation within ten (10) days, exclusive of the period of recess, after the House of Representatives has made designation, the decision of the House of Representatives shall be the decision of the Diet.

ARTICLE 68. The Prime Minister shall appoint the Ministers of State. However, a majority of their number must be chosen from among the members of the Diet.

The Prime Minister may remove the Ministers of State as he chooses.

ARTICLE 69. If the House of Representatives passes a non-confidence resolution, or rejects a confidence resolution, the Cabinet shall resign en masse, unless the House of Representatives is dissolved within ten (10) days.

ARTICLE 70. When there is a vacancy in the post of Prime Minister, or upon the first convocation of the Diet after a general election of members of the House of Representatives, the Cabinet shall resign en masse.

ARTICLE 71. In the cases mentioned in the two preceding articles, the Cabinet shall continue its function until the time when a new Prime Minister is appointed.

ARTICLE 72. The Prime Minister, representing the Cabinet, submits bills, reports on general national affairs and foreign relations to the Diet and exercises control and supervision over various administrative branches.

ARTICLE 73. The Cabinet, in addition to other general administrative functions, shall perform the following functions:

Administer the law faithfully; conduct affairs of state.

Manage foreign affairs.

Conclude treaties. However, it shall obtain prior or, depending on circumstances, subsequent approval of the Diet.

Administer the civil service, in accordance with standards established by law.

Prepare the budget, and present it to the Diet.

Enact cabinet order to execute the provisions of this Constitution and of the law. However, it cannot include penal provisions in such cabinet orders unless authorized by such law.

Decide on general amnesty, special amnesty, commutation of punishment, reprieve, and restoration of rights.

ARTICLE 74. All laws and cabinet orders shall be signed by the competent Minister of State and countersigned by the Prime Minister.

ARTICLE 75. The Ministers of State, during their tenure of office, shall not be subject to legal action without the consent of the Prime Minister. However, the right to take that action is not impaired hereby.

Chapter VI
Judiciary

ARTICLE 76.   The whole judicial power is vested in a Supreme Court and in such inferior courts as are established by law.

No extraordinary tribunal shall be established, nor shall any organ or agency of the Executive be given final judicial power.

All judges shall be independent in the exercise of their conscience and shall be bound only by this Constitution and the laws.

ARTICLE 77.   The Supreme Court is vested with the rule-making power under which it determines the rules of procedure and of practice, and of matters relating to attorneys, the internal discipline of the courts and the administration of judicial affairs.

Public procurators shall be subject to the rule-making power of the Supreme Court.

The Supreme Court may delegate the power to make rules for inferior courts to such courts.

ARTICLE 78.   Judges shall not be removed except by public impeachment unless judicially declared mentally or physically incompetent to perform official duties. No disciplinary action against judges shall be administered by any executive organ or agency.

ARTICLE 79.   The Supreme Court shall consist of a Chief Judge and such number of judges as may be determined by law; all such judges excepting the Chief Judge shall be appointed by the Cabinet.

The appointment of the judges of the Supreme Court shall be reviewed by the people at the first general election of members of the House of Representatives following their appointment, and shall be reviewed again at the first general election of members of the House of Representatives after a lapse of ten (10) years, and in the same manner thereafter.

In cases mentioned in the foregoing paragraph, when the majority of the voters favors the dismissal of a judge, he shall be dismissed.

Matters pertaining to review shall be prescribed by law.

The judges of the Supreme Court shall be retired upon the attainment of the age as fixed by law.

All such judges shall receive, at regular stated intervals, adequate compensation which shall not be decreased during their terms of office.

ARTICLE 80.   The judges of the inferior courts shall be appointed by the Cabinet from a list of persons nominated by the Supreme Court. All such judges shall hold office for a term of ten (10) years with privilege of reappointment, provided that they shall be retired upon the attainment of the age as fixed by law.

The judges of the inferior courts shall receive, at regular stated intervals, adequate compensation which shall not be decreased during their terms of office.

ARTICLE 81.   The Supreme Court is the court of last resort with power to determine the constitutionality of any law, order, regulation or official act.

ARTICLE 82.   Trials shall be conducted and judgment declared publicly. Where a court unanimously determines publicity to be dangerous to public order or morals, a trial may be conducted privately, but trials of political offenses, offenses involving the press or cases wherein the rights of people as guaranteed in Chapter III of this Constitution are in question shall always be conducted publicly.

Chapter VII
Finance

ARTICLE 83.   The power to administer national finances shall be exercised as the Diet shall determine.

ARTICLE 84.   No new taxes shall be imposed or existing one modified except by law or under such conditions as law may prescribe.

ARTICLE 85.   No money shall be expended, nor shall the State obligate itself, except as authorized by the Diet.

ARTICLE 86.   The Cabinet shall prepare and submit to the Diet for its consideration and decision a budget for each fiscal year.

ARTICLE 87.   In order to provide for unforeseen deficiencies in the budget, a reserve fund may be authorized by the Diet to be expended upon the responsibility of the Cabinet.

The Cabinet must get subsequent approval of the Diet for all payments from the reserve fund.

ARTICLE 88.   All property of the Imperial Household shall belong to the State. All expenses of the Imperial Household shall be appropriated by the Diet in the budget.

ARTICLE 89.   No public money or other property shall be expended or appropriated for the use, benefit or maintenance of any religious institution or association, or for any charitable, educational or benevolent enterprises not under the control of public authority.

ARTICLE 90.   Final accounts of the expenditures and revenues of the State shall be audited annually by a Board of Audit and submitted by the Cabinet to the Diet, together with the statement of audit, during the fiscal year immediately following the period covered.

The organization and competency of the Board of Audit shall be determined by law.

ARTICLE 91.   At regular intervals and at least annually the Cabinet shall report to the Diet and the people on the state of national finances.

Chapter VIII
Local Self-Government

ARTICLE 92.   Regulations concerning organization and operations of local public entities shall be fixed by law in accordance with the principle of local autonomy.

ARTICLE 93.   The local public entities shall establish assemblies as their deliberative organs, in accordance with law.

The chief executive officers of all local public entities, the members of their assemblies, and such other local officials as may be determined by law shall be elected by direct popular vote within their several communities.

ARTICLE 94.   Local public entities shall have the right to manage their property, affairs and administration and to enact their own regulations within law.

ARTICLE 95.   A special law, applicable only to one local public entity, cannot be enacted by the Diet without the consent of the majority of the voters of the local public entity concerned, obtained in accordance with law.

Chapter IX
Amendments

ARTICLE 96.   Amendments to this Constitution shall be initiated by the Diet, through a concurring vote of two-thirds or more of all the members of each House and shall thereupon be submitted to the people for ratification, which shall require the affirmative vote of a majority of all votes cast thereon, at a special referendum or at such election as the Diet shall specify.

Amendments when so ratified shall immediately be promulgated by the Emperor in the name of the people, as an integral part of this Constitution.

Chapter X
Supreme Law

ARTICLE 97.   The fundamental human rights by this Constitution guaranteed to the people of Japan are fruits of the age-old struggle of man to be free; they have survived the many exacting tests for durability and are conferred upon this and future generations in trust, to be held for all time inviolate.

ARTICLE 98.   This Constitution shall be the supreme law of the nation and no law, ordinance, imperial rescript or other act of government, or part thereof, contrary to the provisions hereof shall have legal force or validity.

The treaties concluded by Japan and established laws of nations shall be faithfully observed.

ARTICLE 99.   The Emperor or the Regent as well as Ministers of State, members of the Diet, judges, and all other public officials have the obligation to respect and uphold this Constitution.

Chapter XI
Supplementary Provisions

ARTICLE 100.   This Constitution shall be enforced as from the day when the period of six months will have elapsed counting from the day of its promulgation.

The enactment of laws necessary for the enforcement of this Constitution, the election of members of the House of Councillors and the procedure for the convocation of the Diet and other preparatory procedures necessary for the enforcement of this Constitution may be executed before the day prescribed in the preceding paragraph.

ARTICLE 101. If the House of Councillors is not constituted before the effective date of this Constitution, the House of Representatives shall function as the Diet until such time as the House of Councillors shall be constituted.

ARTICLE 102. The term of office for half the members of the House of Councillors serving in the first term under this Constitution shall be three years. Members falling under this category shall be determined in accordance with law.

ARTICLE 103. The Ministers of State, members of the House of Representatives and judges in office on the effective date of this Constitution, and all other public officials who occupy positions corresponding to such positions as are recognized by this Constitution shall not forfeit their positions automatically on account of the enforcement of this Constitution unless otherwise specified by law. When, however, successors are elected or appointed under the provisions of this Constitution, they shall forfeit their position as a matter of course.

THE TREATY OF MUTUAL COOPERATION AND SECURITY BETWEEN THE UNITED STATES AND JAPAN
(1960 Revision)

The United States of America and Japan,

Desiring to strengthen the bonds of peace and friendship traditionally existing between them, and to uphold the principles of democracy, individual liberty, and the rule of law,

Desiring further to encourage closer economic cooperation between them and to promote conditions of economic stability and well being in their countries,

Reaffirming their faith in the purposes and principles of the Charter of the United Nations, and their desire to live in peace with all peoples and all governments,

Recognizing that they have the inherent right of individual or collective self-defense as affirmed in the Charter of the United Nations,

Considering that they have a common concern in the maintenance of international peace and security in the Far East,

Having resolved to conclude a treaty of mutual cooperation and security,

Therefore agree as follows:

Article I

The Parties undertake, as set forth in the Charter of the United Nations, to settle any international disputes in which they may be involved by peaceful means in such a manner that international peace and security and justice are not endangered and to refrain in their international relations from the threat or use of force against the territorial integrity or political independence of any state, or in any other manner inconsistent with the purposes of the United Nations.

The Parties will endeavor in concert with other peace-loving countries to strengthen the United Nations so that its mission of maintaining international peace and security may be discharged more effectively.

Article II

The Parties will contribute toward the further development of peaceful and friendly international relations by strengthening their free institutions, by bringing about a better understanding of the principles upon which these institutions are founded, and by promoting conditions of stability and well being. They will seek to eliminate conflict in their international economic policies and will encourage economic collaboration between them.

Article III

The Parties, individually and in cooperation with each other, by means of continuous and effective self-help and mutual aid will maintain and develop, subject to their constitutional provisions, their capacities to resist armed attack.

Article IV

The Parties will consult together from time to time regarding the implementation of this Treaty, and, at the request of either Party, whenever the security of Japan or international peace and security in the Far East is threatened.

Article V

Each Party recognizes that an armed attack against either Party in the territories under the administration of Japan would be dangerous to its own peace and safety and declares that it would act to meet the common danger in accordance with its constitutional provisions and processes.

Any such armed attack and all measures taken as a result thereof shall be immediately reported to the Security Council of the United Nations in accordance with the provisions of Article 51 of the Charter. Such measures shall be terminated when the Security Council has taken the measures necessary to restore and maintain international peace and security.

Article VI

For the purpose of contributing to the security of Japan and the maintenance of international peace and security in the Far East, the United States of America is granted the use by its land, air and naval forces of facilities and areas in Japan.

The use of these facilities and areas as well as the status of United States armed forces in Japan shall be governed by a separate agreement, replacing the Administrative Agreement under Article III of the Security Treaty between the United States of America and Japan, signed at Tokyo on February 28, 1952, as amended, and by such other arrangements as may be agreed upon.

Article VII

This Treaty does not affect and shall not be interpreted as affecting in any way the rights and obligations of the Parties under the Charter of the United

Nations or the responsibility of the United Nations for the maintenance of international peace and security.

Article VIII

This Treaty shall be ratified by the United States of America and Japan in accordance with their respective constitutional processes and will enter into force on the date on which the instruments of ratification thereof have been exchanged by them in Tokyo.

Article IX

The Security Treaty between the United States of America and Japan signed at the city of San Francisco on September 8, 1951 shall expire upon the entering into force of this Treaty.

Article X

This Treaty shall remain in force until in the opinion of the Governments of the United States of America and Japan there shall have come into force such United Nations arrangements as will satisfactorily provide for the maintenance of international peace and security in the Japan area.

However, after the Treaty has been in force for ten years, either Party may give notice to the other Party of its intention to terminate the Treaty, in which case the Treaty shall terminate one year after such notice has been given.

In witness whereof the undersigned Plenipotentiaries have signed this Treaty.

Done in duplicate at Washington in the English and Japanese languages, both equally authentic, this 19th day of January, 1960.

For the United States of America:

Christian A. Herter
Douglas MacArthur II

For Japan:

Nobusuke Kishi
Aiichiro Fujiyama

INDEX